Econometric Society Monographs in Pure Theory

Money and value

Econometric Society Publication No. 5

Books in both the Econometric Society Monographs in Pure
Theory and the Econometric Society Monographs in Quanti-
tative Economics are numbered in a single sequence for the
purposes of the Econometric Society.

Econometric Society Monographs in Pure Theory

Edited by
Angus Deaton *University of Bristol*
Daniel McFadden *Massachusetts Institute of Technology*
Hugo Sonnenschein *Princeton University*

The Econometric Society is an international society for the advancement of economic theory in relation to statistics and mathematics. The Econometric Society Monograph Series in Pure Theory is designed to promote the publication of original research contributions of high quality in mathematical economics.

First book in the series
Gerard Debreu *Mathematical economics*: *Twenty papers of Gerard Debreu*

This book is published as part of the joint publishing agreement established in 1977 between the Foundation de la Maison des Sciences de l'Homme and the Press Syndicate of the University of Cambridge. Titles published under this arrangement may appear in any European language or, in the case of volumes of collected essays, in several languages.

New books will appear either as individual titles or in one of the series that the Maison des Sciences de l'Homme and the Cambridge University Press have jointly agreed to publish. All books published jointly by the Maison des Sciences de l'Homme and the Cambridge University Press will be distributed by the Press throughout the world.

Money and value

A reconsideration of
classical and neoclassical monetary theories

JEAN-MICHEL GRANDMONT

Centre d'Etudes Prospectives d'Economie Mathématique
Appliquées à la Planification

CAMBRIDGE UNIVERSITY PRESS

Cambridge
London   New York   New Rochelle
Melbourne   Sydney

EDITIONS DE LA MAISON DES SCIENCES
DE L'HOMME

Paris

Published by the Press Syndicate of the University of Cambridge
The Pitt Building, Trumpington Street, Cambridge CB2 1RP
32 East 57th Street, New York, NY 10022, USA
296 Beaconsfield Parade, Middle Park, Melbourne 3206, Australia
and
Editions de la Maison de l'Homme
54 Boulevard Raspail, 75270 Paris Cedex 06

First published in 1983

Printed in the United States of America

Library of Congress Cataloging in Publication Data
Grandmont, Jean-Michel.
Money and value.
(Econometric Society monographs in pure theory;
no. 5)
Bibliography: p.
Includes index.
1. Money. I. Title. II. Series.
HG221.G735   1983   332.4   82–14763
ISBN 0 521 25141 9

To Paulette and Jean
To Céline and Juliette

Contents

Preface

This book studies the regulating mechanisms at work in a monetary economy with flexible prices and the possibility for monetary authorities to influence economic activity by manipulating the money supply or the interest rates. This work belongs, accordingly, to two different fields, namely, to general equilibrium analysis and monetary theory, and will actually employ the methods of both disciplines. This filiation makes clear how great is my intellectual debt to the economists who have shaped these fields, in particular to Kenneth Arrow, Gerard Debreu, Milton Friedman, Frank Hahn, John Hicks, Werner Hildenbrand, Don Patinkin, and James Tobin, to name only a few.

My interest in the subject arose while I was a graduate student at the University of California at Berkeley from 1968 to 1970. I wish to express my deep gratitude to Gerard Debreu, Avinash Dixit, and Daniel Mac-Fadden, who taught me the techniques of mathematical economics while I was at Berkeley, and especially to Bent Hansen, whose provocative course on macroeconomic and monetary theories from a general equilibrium viewpoint was a great stimulation for me.

I owe a considerable intellectual debt to my friends and colleagues Guy Laroque and Yves Younès, for many of the ideas developed in this book originated in the research work that we did over the past decade, either separately or jointly.

During recent years, I have taught on the subject of this book at the University of Bonn, at the University of Toulouse, at the University of Pennsylvania, at the summer course for Finnish university teachers, organized by the Yrjö Jahnsson Foundation, Helsinki, at the Ecole Nationale de la Statistique et de l'Administration Economique (ENSAE), and at the Ecole Polytechnique in Paris. I wish to thank here many colleagues and students. Their reactions contributed greatly in shaping this monograph.

Different versions of the manuscript, or large parts of it, have been read by Jean-Pascal Benassy, David Cass, Frank Hahn, Werner Hildenbrand, Alan Kirman, Jean-Pierre Laffargue, J. Lenninghaus, Jean-Jacques Laffont, Jacques Melitz, and Karl Shell. Their comments and suggestions were quite helpful and are gratefully acknowledged.

The Centre National de la Recherche Scientifique (CNRS) and the Centre d'Etudes Prospectives d'Economie Mathématique Appliquées à la Planification (CEPREMAP) provided a favorable environment, without which the book could not have been written. The financial support of the Deutsche Forschungsgemeinschaft, the National Science Foundation, and the Yrjö Jahnsson Foundation is also gratefully acknowledged.

Last but not least, I wish to express my gratitude to Josselyne Bitan, who typed with great accuracy and skill the various versions of the manuscript, and who had to bear, most of the time with great patience, the dark moods and "absences" of a companion whose work often failed to be in progress.

Jean-Michel Grandmont

CEPREMAP, Paris
March 1982

Introduction

One of the major theoretical issues that underlies, implicitly or explicitly, quite a few recurrent controversies in macroeconomics is whether a competitive monetary economy has built-in mechanisms that are strong enough to remove excess demands and supplies on all markets, through an automatic adjustment of the price system.

Debate on this issue was most intense after the publication of Keynes's *General Theory* in 1936. Keynes denied, in complete contradiction to the then-prevailing doctrine, that price and wage flexibility would guarantee market clearing. On the contrary, he claimed that a fully competitive economy could well get "trapped" into a severe disequilibrium (unemployment) situation.

Pigou (1943) began the counterattack, which was subsequently developed over the years by Patinkin (1965), Friedman (1956, 1969), and Johnson (1967), among a host of others. The essential argument was that Keynes overlooked an important class of regulating mechanisms, namely, the real balance, or *wealth effects*, which are associated with a general movement of nominal prices and wages and/or with a variation of nominal interest rates. A broad agreement was reached in the 1950s, known as the "neoclassical synthesis": If such wealth effects were properly integrated in the analysis, full price flexibility – by which is meant that the price system reacts infinitely fast to a market imbalance at every moment, e.g., through a Walrasian *tâtonnement* process – was bound to remove all excess demands and supplies, both in the short run and in the long run. Keynes was theoretically mistaken, and the unemployment he talked about was entirely due to his assumption that nominal wages were rigid downward. The assumption was indeed recognized as particularly

1

relevant to the description of actual economies. But the preeminence of the traditional doctrine was reestablished, and in fact reinforced.

Within the confines of this broad consensus on theoretical principles, there has been a widening variety of opinions concerning practical matters. "Keynesians" claim that wealth effects are typically very weak, in fact too weak to be of much empirical relevance over periods that are relatively long (measured in calendar time). For them, market disequilibrium, and, in particular, unemployment, is an admittedly transient but lasting and stubborn phenomenon, which must be cured by discretionary budgetary, fiscal, and monetary stabilization policies (see, e.g., Tobin 1980). "Monetarists" are much more confident of the strength of the regulating mechanisms operating in a "free" market economy. They tend to limit the role of governments to the enforcement of "freedom" and of competition, and to the achievement of fixed target rules such as a constant rate of growth of the money supply (see, e.g., Friedman 1969).

Presumably as the result of a growing dissatisfaction with the recent performances of Keynesian policies, the past decade witnessed a sweeping resurgence of the old buoyant faith in the price mechanism. The "new classical macroeconomists" (Lucas 1975, Barro 1976), who are the modern representatives of this line of thought, claim that markets do clear at every instant – in the Walrasian sense – in actual economies. The conclusions of this school are that there is little scope for systematic governmental policies to dampen economic fluctuations.[1]

Despite these deep divergences about the actual workings of the market's "invisible hand," there is a widespread belief among macroeconomic theorists that if the price system reacts at every instant infinitely fast and costlessly to a market imbalance in a monetary economy, a Walrasian equilibrium in which money has positive value should obtain both in the short run and in the long run.

Another topic much debated in macroeconomics is whether or not money "matters"; or more precisely, whether and how changes of the nominal money supply affect economic variables. One popular thesis, usually associated with "classical" economists like I. Fisher (1963), is that money is a "veil." This involves two distinct but closely related propositions. The first states that there is a *dichotomy* between the real and the money sectors. Real equilibrium magnitudes would then be determined by the real sector. Absolute prices and nominal values would in turn be pinned down by the equilibrium condition for money. The

---

[1]   An excellent discussion of these points can be found in Tobin's Yrjö Jahnsson Lectures (1980) and in Lucas's review (1981). See also Sargent (1979, Chaps. 1, 2, and 16).

second proposition is the *quantity theory*, which states that equilibrium nominal values are proportional to the money stock. After many years of controversy, macroeconomic theorists seem to have agreed that these propositions were correct when applied to stationary states. Changes of the money supply that do not alter the real rate of interest paid on cash balances are indeed thought to be neutral in the long run. Until recently, however, most theorists would have said that changes of the money supply have a potential influence on real economic variables in the short run in flex-price models, whether these changes are brought about by lump-sum taxes or subsidies, through the monetary authorities' credit policy, or through open-market operations. There were indeed sharp differences between (extreme) Keynesians and Monetarists about the relative place of monetary policy among other governmental policies. But the general belief was that money is typically "nonneutral" in the short run.[2] This view has been challenged in recent years, however, by a few "new classical macroeconomists," who claim that deterministic changes of the money supply can have no real effects in a model with flexible prices, even in the short run, if these changes are fully anticipated by private economic units.[3]

The present book attempts to shed some light on these issues, by using the analytical techniques of general equilibrium theory (Arrow and Hahn 1970, Debreu 1959).

The conceptual framework employed throughout this work has a long history in economics, since it originated in Hicks (1946) under the label "temporary competitive equilibrium." The method has been used subsequently by Patinkin (1965) and most neoclassical theorists to study monetary economies. The approach can be described heuristically in a very simple way. Time is divided into infinitely many discrete periods. At each date, economic units make decisions in view of the prices and interest rates that are currently quoted and in light of their expectations of their future environment – which of course includes future prices and interest rates. The resulting (short-run) Walrasian demands and supplies are then confronted. A temporary or *short-run Walrasian equilibrium* is defined as a set of current prices and interest rates that equate aggregate demand and supply on every market at the date under consideration. When the procedure is repeated as time elapses, it yields a sequence of

[2] On these questions, see, e.g., Patinkin (1965), Friedman (1969), and the discussion of Friedman's "Monetary Framework" in the volume edited by R. J. Gordon (1974).
[3] See, e.g., Barro (1974, 1976), S. Fisher (1979), and Lucas (1972, 1975). For a contrary viewpoint, see Tobin (1980).

short-run equilibria. A long-run or *stationary equilibrium* is then a sequence of short-run equilibria where, loosely speaking, all "real" equilibrium variables are constant over time. A *monetary* Walrasian equilibrium involves by definition a positive value for money.

One important feature of the temporary equilibrium method is that the individual agents' short-run learning processes are taken explicitly into account. These learning processes are supposed to obey a few minimal "rationality" requirements, which state essentially that economic units do not make incorrect forecasts when their environment is regular enough (e.g., stationary). But otherwise the method encompasses a wide variety of cases. One may portray, for instance, a trader using simple-minded forecasting rules of thumb, or a trader who has a complex "theory" of the workings of the economy and who employs statistical techniques (e.g., Bayesian or maximum-likelihood procedures) to predict the future. In all cases, a trader's learning process generates a functional relationship – the trader's expectation function – which links at every date his forecast of the economic future to the information he has on the current and past states of the economy at that date. This approach views the traders' learning processes, and their induced expectation functions, as part of the exogenous characteristic data of the model.

Our chief concern in this book will be to analyze the existence and properties of short-run and long-run Walrasian monetary equilibria, in various institutional setups. This will enable us to test the internal consistency of the claim that "full price flexibility leads to market clearing," and to study both the short- and long-term impact of various active monetary policies.

One finding of this inquiry will be that flex-price macroeconomic models that rely mainly on wealth effects as a self-regulating mechanism in the short run, are surely incomplete, and presumably mistaken. More precisely, it will be shown that there are theoretically conceivable and empirically plausible circumstances, which are compatible with the assumptions of that sort of model – which we shall call, to simplify, "neoclassical" – such that there is no short-run Walrasian monetary equilibrium and, in some cases, no short-run Walrasian equilibrium at all.

The reasons underlying such a conclusion are quite intuitive. Neoclassical macroeconomic models postulate that at a given date, a trader's expected prices – discounted by expected interest rates if necessary – are unit elastic with respect to current prices.[4] Movements of the current price level then affect the trader's "real" behavior only through a variation

---

[4]   For a good discussion of neoclassical macroeconomic models, see Sargent (1979, Chap. 1).

of their "real" wealth. But the same assumption implies that the traders' expected "real interest rates" are independent of the price level in the short run. The rigidity of these real interest rates, together with the absence of intertemporal transfers which it involves, will be found to be the cause of the possible inconsistency of short-run neoclassical macroeconomic models.

One corollary of this analysis will be that, to be sure of the existence of a short-run Walrasian monetary equilibrium, one must bring into play a regulating mechanism rather neglected by modern neoclassical theorists, that is, the intertemporal substitution effect. This is the effect on the demand for current goods that is generated by a variation of the traders' expected real interest rates.[5] What is essentially needed to guarantee this outcome in the models that will be considered later is that some, and in some contexts all, traders have price and interest rate expectations that are to a great extent insensitive to a wide variation of current prices and interest rates. The "insensitive" traders act then as a stabilizing flywheel. Such restrictions on the traders' short-run learning processes are, however, somewhat unrealistic. Our conclusion will be, accordingly, that the existence of a monetary equilibrium, in the short run, raises more problems than neoclassical theorists would like to believe.

Our study will have strong implications concerning the monetary authorities' ability to control nominal interest rates and the nominal money supply. It is usually thought that in a closed economy and in the absence of any offsetting actions by private banks and financial intermediaries, a Central Bank can theoretically peg these variables without bound at any moment through its interventions on credit markets or its open-market operations. It will be found that the Bank's control over these variables hinges in the short run on the effectiveness of intertemporal substitution effects and thus, once again, on the hypothetical presence of "insensitive" traders in the economy. The conclusion will be therefore that, owing to the rigidity of the expected real interest rates that may be embodied in the traders' learning processes at any moment, the practical range through which nominal interest rates and the money supply can be manipulated may be quite small in the short run.

Finally, this investigation will confirm the view that money is "neutral" in the long run – apart, of course, from changes in the rate of growth of the money stock engineered through lump-sum taxes or subsidies, since such changes are bound to modify in the long run the real interest rate paid on cash balances. As for the short run, it will be found that, apart

---

[5] Intertemporal substitution effects have been considered by earlier writers such as Hicks (1946) or Lange (1945), but apparently have been forgotten later on.

from the textbook case of a once-and-for-all scalar change of all traders' initial holdings of cash and of assets dominated in money at some date, variations of the money supply generally have "real" effects in the short run.

This book stresses the common-sense observation that short-run learning processes are among the important characteristics of economic agents, and that they accordingly deserve a careful theoretical and empirical study. Paying only lip service to the formation of traders' expectations, as was often done in neoclassical macroeconomic models, may cause theorists to misidentify the short-run regulating mechanisms of a flex-price monetary economy and, in particular, to neglect intertemporal substitution effects which are presumably important. New classical macroeconomic models go somewhat to the other extreme, as many of them use the *rational expectations hypothesis*, i.e., the assumption that at any moment, economic units "correctly" forecast their future environment conditionally on the information they have. By endogenizing expectations, that sort of model indeed incorporates intertemporal substitution effects as a result of the relative variations of current and expected prices, as in the traditional Arrow–Debreu theory of general equilibrium. But our findings show how dangerous the indiscriminate use of the rational expectations hypothesis can be: It seriously underestimates the causes of the "disequilibria" that may exist in a monetary economy with flexible prices, by ignoring a priori the short-run rigidities of expected real interest rates that may result from the traders' learning processes in the world in which we actually live.

The book is organized in the following manner. In the first chapter we look at the simplest framework imaginable: Money is the only asset and its stock is constant over time (*outside money*). The next two chapters extend the analysis to the case where the Government intervenes actively on the supply side of the money market through a banking department, which creates money by granting loans to the private sector. Part of the money stock is then *inside money*. Two important monetary policies – pegging either the interest rate or the money supply – are studied within this framework. Chapter 2 deals with short-run equilibria, and Chapter 3 is devoted to steady states of the model. Finally, Chapter 4 considers another important technique through which a bank can manipulate the money supply, that is, open-market exchanges of long-term for short-term assets.

These four chapters together with the Conclusion are concerned with the statement and discussion of the assumptions and of the results of the models. Most of the results are justified by means of diagrams and through heuristic arguments. Formal proofs, on the other hand, are deferred to the appendixes at the end of the book. Unfortunately, this is likely to necessitate that mathematically oriented readers flip back and forth. But it was felt that this mode of exposition was best suited to making the economic arguments more transparent through relieving them of overly complex technicalities.

The desire to bring out clearly the economics of the argument led us to employ simple assumptions, and not to present direct generalizations when they were available. We chose, in particular, to work with exchange economies rather than to take production explicitly into account. This restriction is not important: Analogous conclusions would be obtained if production activities were included in the models. The other simplifying assumption concerns the formulation of expectations. Portraying a trader who uses statistical techniques like Bayesian procedures to forecast his future environment should lead one to describe expectations as probability distributions. In fact, many research papers from which this monograph evolved actually used such a formulation.[6] We chose to work nonetheless with point expectations in order to ease the exposition. This is again inessential, for most of the results here can be transposed easily to the case of probabilistic expectations by anyone who knows the mathematics involved, without altering the economic argument. Some notes at the end of each chapter will indicate to the interested reader where to find such a generalization when it is already available, and how it could be done when it is not.

[6] For an introduction to temporary equilibrium methods using probabilistic expectations, the reader may consult the survey in Grandmont (1977).

CHAPTER 1

Expectations and the real balance effect

This chapter will examine, with the help of a simple microeconomic model, two propositions that play a significant role in neoclassical monetary theory.

The first proposition is that "money does not matter" – or, more precisely, that if the mere presence of money as a medium of exchange and as an asset is important for the smooth functioning of the economy, the quantity of money is unimportant. This is the *quantity theory* tradition, which claims that a change in the money stock will change all nominal values in the same proportion, but will have no effect on "real" variables. This old tradition still plays an important role in modern thinking. We wish to clarify the exact meaning of this theory and its domain of validity.

The second issue will be the belief, which is shared by many theorists, that a short-run Walrasian equilibrium in which money has positive exchange value usually exists. We shall investigate this question by looking at a simple model involving only outside money. "Money" is then printed money, and can be regarded as a part of private net wealth. In such a context, neoclassical theorists assume that the traders' price expectations are "unit elastic," so that expected prices vary proportionally with current prices. The essential short-run regulating mechanism is then the *real balance effect*. When money prices of goods are low, the purchasing power of the agents' initial money balances is large. This fact should generate, according to this viewpoint, an excess demand on the goods market at sufficiently low prices. Conversely, the purchasing power of the agents' initial cash balances becomes small when money prices are high, so that an excess supply of goods should eventually appear. Thus, by continuity, an equilibrium should exist in between.

It will be shown that this argument is wrong because it neglects the intertemporal character of the choices made by the agents. Explicitly modeling these choices will lead us to conclude that theoretically conceivable and empirically plausible circumstances exist in which the real balance effect is too weak to guarantee the existence of a short-run equilibrium in which money has positive value. As a matter of fact, the existence of such an equilibrium position essentially requires, as we shall see, that the price forecasts of some agent be substantially insensitive to current prices. The relative variations of current and expected prices then generate an *intertemporal substitution effect*, which reinforces the real balance effect, and is strong enough to equilibrate the market.

Such conditions on expectations are quite unlikely to prevail in reality. Indeed, the agents' price expectations are presumably very sensitive to the price levels that they currently observe, especially in periods of significant inflation or deflation. Expected rates of inflation may be biased upward when a significant inflation has been observed in the recent past and downward in the case of a deflation. It will be shown that in such circumstances, a short-run monetary equilibrium may not exist. The conclusion that will emerge, therefore, from our analysis is that the existence of a short-run Walrasian equilibrium in which money has positive value is somewhat more problematic in actual market economies than neoclassical economists used to believe.

In order to focus attention on the essentials, we will conduct the analysis within the framework of a simple model. Paper money will act as the *numéraire* and only store of value. Its stock, which can be viewed as the sum of the government's past deficits, will be assumed to be constant over time (outside money). Output, or equivalently, the stream of the agents' real income will be taken as exogenous. This hypothesis is in fact immaterial; analogous results would be obtained with variable output. In this chapter no attention will be paid to the services that actual money yields in our economies (medium of exchange, liquidity).[1] The main question will be whether an equilibrium exists either in the short run or in the long run in which the agents are willing to hold the outstanding quantity of money, and to investigate the properties of these equilibria (if any) in relation to the money stock.

---

[1] Liquidity services of money will be taken up in Chapter 4. The role of money in transactions will be considered in the "Notes on the Literature" section later in this chapter. See also the Conclusion of this book.

1.1   Classical and neoclassical views on money

We first proceed to a brief overview of the issues with which we shall be concerned. In order to fix the ideas, let us assume that there are l perishable goods, indexed by $h = 1, \ldots, l$, traded in each period at *money prices* $p = (p_1, \ldots, p_l)$, whose equilibrium values are to be determined by the market.[2] Fiat money, on the other hand, is the sole asset, and its stock is constant over time.

Classical economists (e.g., I. Fisher 1963) took the view that in order to find the level of equilibrium prices, one could reason in two steps. Markets for goods (the "real sector") would determine equilibrium *relative prices*, i.e., the ratios p_h/p_k, and quantities of goods exchanged in equilibrium. Then consideration of the money market would determine the level of equilibrium money prices, which would be in fact proportional to the money stock. The view that the real and money markets can be considered separately in this way is called the *classical dichotomy*. The proportionality of the money prices to the money stock is the essence of the quantity theory.

To be more precise, let us consider a specific agent a. In the classical approach, his array of excess demands for goods is written as a function of money prices alone, $z_a(p) = [z_{a1}(p), \ldots, z_{al}(p)]$. Equilibrium of the goods market would require that aggregate excess demand is zero, where the summation sign runs over the set of all agents a:

(1.1.A) $\sum_a z_a(p) = 0$

Classical economists would assume that equation (1.1.A) displays the usual properties of an ordinary Walrasian system, that is, homogeneity of degree zero of excess demand functions; i.e., $z_a(\lambda p) = z_a(p)$ for every p and every positive λ, and what has been called *Say's Law* by Lange (1942) and Patinkin (1965): The value of aggregate excess demand $p \sum_a z_a(p)$ is zero for every price system p.[3] The structure of equations like (1.1.A) was understood to depend significantly on the mere presence of money in the economy. The main point is that these equations were assumed to be independent of the quantity of money, and of its distribution among traders.

One must next consider the money market. Let $m_a^d(p)$ be agent a's demand for (nominal) money when the price system is p. The classical view that only "real" money balances matter can be expressed here by

---

[2]   All prices that are considered in this monograph are positive.
[3]   In what follows, given two vectors x and y with l components, the notation $x\,y$ will stand for $\sum_h x_h\, y_h$.

the assumption that $m_a^d(p)$ is homogenous of degree 1 in p; i.e., $m_a^d(\lambda p) = \lambda m_a^d(p)$ for every p and λ. Then equilibrium of the money market requires that aggregate demand for money be equal to the amount of money M in circulation:

(1.1.B) $\sum_a m_a^d(p) = M$

Writing down a system of equations like (1.1.A) and (1.1.B) seems to formulate in a consistent way classical views about the classical dichotomy and quantity theory. Modern competitive equilibrium theory tells us that (1.1.A) indeed has solution(s) in p under rather general conditions. Due to the homogeneity of degree zero of (1.1.A), such solutions are defined only up to a positive real number. Consideration of the real sector alone leads to the determination of equilibrium relative prices and real quantities exchanged. On the other hand, for any solution $\bar{p}$ of (1.1.A), there exists a unique λ such that $\sum_a m_a^d(\lambda \bar{p}) = M$, provided that aggregate demand for money at prices $\bar{p}$, i.e. $\sum_a m_a^d(\bar{p})$, is positive. Money prices are determined by the money market. Lastly, the homogeneity properties of the system imply that, say, a doubling of the quantity of money M leads to a doubling of equilibrium money prices and nominal money balances, leaving unchanged relative prices and real quantities exchanged.

Whether the system (1.1.A) and (1.1.B) is intended to represent the behavior of an economy with outside money in the short run or in the long run (i.e., along stationary states) has been the object of some debate. In particular, Patinkin (1965) claimed that (1.1.A) and (1.1.B) cannot describe the short-run determination of equilibrium prices. He argued that a change of the prices p that prevail at a given date alters the purchasing power of the money stocks $\bar{m}_a$ that the traders own at the outset of the period, and that it should accordingly influence in particular their short-run demands for goods. This is the *real balance effect*, which is clearly absent from the classical system (1.1.A), (1.1.B). A related criticism made by Patinkin is that agents face a budget constraint. If the system (1.1.A), (1.1.B) applies to the short period, it should therefore satisfy *Walras's Law*

$$\sum_a p z_a(p) + \sum_a m_a^d(p) = \sum_a \bar{m}_a = M$$

for every p. But adding this identity to the system leads to major drawbacks. Together with Say's Law, this identity implies $\sum_a m_a^d(p) = M$ for every p, in which case any solution of (1.1.A) fulfils (1.1.B): The level of money prices becomes indeterminate. Even if one puts aside Say's Law, Walras's Law contradicts the assumed homogeneity properties of the functions $z_a(p)$ and $m_a^d(p)$. For these imply that the left-hand side of the foregoing identity is homogenous of degree 1 in prices, whereas the right-hand side is a constant independent of them.

These arguments led Patinkin to the conclusion that any consistent monetary theory applicable to short-period problems must incorporate real balance effects. Modern neoclassical short-run macroeconomic models are built around the same idea.[4]

In order to make precise the structure of these models in our simple framework, let us consider our economy at a given date, say date 1, which we may call the "current period." Following Friedman (1956) and others, this line of theorizing emphasizes that money should be treated as a particular capital good. According to this viewpoint, the agents' demand functions at date 1 should depend in the present context on their initial money wealth (i.e., on their initial money holdings $\bar{m}_a$), on their current and expected real incomes (which we take here as exogenous), on the current prices of goods p_1, and on the prices that traders forecast for the future. Most theorists of this school postulate that expected prices are given by $(1 + \pi_a)^{t-1}p_1$ for $t = 2, 3, \ldots$, where π_a is the "expected rate of inflation" of trader a. What characterizes neoclassical models, however, is that the traders' expected rates of inflation are taken as exogenous in the short run; that is, they are assumed to be independent of the current price system p_1. A trader's excess demand for current goods and current demand for money can then be written $z_a(p_1,\bar{m}_a)$ and $m_a^d(p_1,\bar{m}_a)$, if one keeps implicit the influence of the exogenously given parameters π_a. A short-run monetary Walrasian equilibrium price system is then a solution of the following system of equations:

(1.1.C) $\sum_a z_a(p_1,\bar{m}_a) = 0$

(1.1.D) $\sum_a m_a^d(p_1,\bar{m}_a) = \sum_a \bar{m}_a$

According to this viewpoint, the foregoing system obeys Walras's Law

$$p_1\sum_a z_a(p_1,\bar{m}_a) + \sum_a m_a^d(p_1,\bar{m}_a) = \sum_a \bar{m}_a$$

for every p_1, as a consequence of the budget restraints that the agents face at date 1. Moreover, neoclassical theorists remark that a doubling of a trader's initial money holding $\bar{m}_a$ and of current prices p_1 – and thus of expected prices – leaves unaltered the "real" opportunities available to him, and thus should not change his "real" behavior if he is free of "money illusion." They postulate accordingly that *the short-run excess*

---

[4] For a good account of neoclassical macroeconomic models, see, e.g., Sargent (1979, Chap. 1).

demand functions for goods $z_a(p_1,\bar{m}_a)$ *are homogenous of degree 0, and the short-run money demand functions* $m_a^d(p_1,\bar{m}_a)$ *are homogenous of degree 1 in* $(p_1,\bar{m}_a)$.

The following propositions, which are immediate consequences of these assumptions, are central to neoclassical monetary theory.

First, the classical dichotomy is invalid in the short run. For Walras's Law implies that any solution of p_1 of (1.1.C) satisfies (1.1.D). Consideration of the real sector alone determines not only relative prices and real variables, but also the level of money prices and all nominal values, in contradiction to what the classicists claimed.

Second, quantity theory must be reformulated in order to be valid in the short run. It is clear that a change of the money stock that alters the distribution of initial money holdings $\bar{m}_a$ among agents has distributional effects and thus is likely to modify relative prices. On the other hand, an equiprotionate change in initial money balances (every $\bar{m}_a$ being changed to $\lambda\bar{m}_a$) will change in the same proportion the equilibrium level of money prices and nominal money balances at the end of the period, but will leave unaltered relative prices and real variables, whenever the functions $z_a(p_1,\bar{m}_a)$ and $m_a^d(p_1,\bar{m}_a)$ are assumed to be homogenous of degree 0 and 1, respectively, with respect to $(p_1,\bar{m}_a)$. Indeed, under these homogeneity assumptions, if p_1 is a solution of (1.1.C) and (1.1.D) when initial money holdings are $\bar{m}_a$, λp_1 must be a solution of the same equations when every initial money stock $\bar{m}_a$ is multiplied by λ.

Finally, the essential short-run regulating mechanism in the neoclassical system (1.1.C), (1.1.D) is the real balance effect. To see this point more precisely, let us ignore the modifications of relatives prices, and consider accordingly the "macroeconomic" case where there is only one good ($l = 1$). In view of the assumed homogeneity properties of the functions z_a and m_a^d, each trader's excess demand for goods and demand for "real money balances" can be written:

$$z_a(p_1,\bar{m}_a) = z_a(1,\bar{m}_a/p_1)$$

and

$$m_a^d(p_1,\bar{m}_a)/p_1 = m_a^d(1,\bar{m}_a/p_1)$$

A variation of p_1 influences the trader's real behavior only through a variation of the initial real balance $\bar{m}_a/p_1$, that is, only through the real balance effect.

The neoclassical argument to assert the existence of a solution to (1.1.C), (1.1.D) then goes as follows. If the good is not inferior, aggregate excess demand in (1.1.C) is a decreasing function of p_1. If the price is low, initial real balances are large, and that should generate an excess demand on the good market. Conversely, if p_1 is large, initial real balances are low, and that should generate an excess supply of the good. By continuity, a unique value of p_1 should exist that achieves equilibrium of the good market, and thus by Walras's Law, of the money market as well. Furthermore, the unique short-run Walrasian monetary equilibrium is stable in any *tâtonnement* process.

That sort of argument is apparently viewed as theoretically valid by many macroeconomists today. As a matter of fact, the controversies have focused mainly on its empirical relevance. Many economists believe that real balance effects are weak, and thus can be neglected in practice. One may note, however, that the foregoing argument is only heuristic, and that it does not provide a consistent proof of the existence of a short-run monetary equilibrium, as Hahn (1965) pointed out some time ago. Moreover, it is based on quite restrictive assumptions on expectations. In particular, it neglects the potential short-run variations of the traders' expected rates of inflation π_a as a function of the current price system p_1, and thus ignores the corresponding intertemporal substitution effects, which seemed important to earlier writers such as Hicks (1946) or Lange (1945).

It has also been argued that, while Patinkin's critique of the classic views was apparently valid for a short period, the classical dichotomy and quantity theory retained their full force when applied to long-run (i.e., stationary) monetary phenomena (Archibald and Lipsey 1958, Samuelson 1968). According to this view, the system of equations (1.1.A), (1.1.B), is not intended to represent the result of an adjustment of prices within a given period nor over time. Rather, the functions $z_a(p)$ and $m_a^d(p)$ appearing in these equations should be interpreted as describing the stationary net trades and money stocks detained by the agents along stationary states, when prices remain constant and equal to p.

This brief review shows that, although a great deal of work has been done, a fully consistent integration of money and value theory in a neoclassical framework is still needed. The primary task of this chapter is to look at this matter. Sections 1.2–1.5 will be devoted to the study of the short-run behavior of the economy. Stationary states will be analyzed in Section 1.6. Finally, the question of the neutrality of changes of the money supply will be taken up in Section 1.7.

1.2   Structure of the model

Consider a simple exchange economy, where time is divided into infinitely many discrete periods. There are l consumption goods available in each period. The simplifying assumption that the agents' real income is fixed is expressed by the fact that each agent owns in each period an exogenously given endowment of consumption goods. The endowments cannot be stored, and must be traded and consumed within the period during which they are available. On the other hand, paper money is the only store of value, and its stock is constant over time. Thus, at any date, the traders (consumers) come to the market with their endowment of goods, and their (nonnegative) cash balances carried over from the past. The short-run competitive equilibrium of the markets at that date will determine Walrasian money prices of the goods $p = (p_1, \ldots, p_l)$, the consumers' net trades in the good markets and the nonnegative money balances they will hold until the next period.

The framework in which we choose to work is that of an overlapping generation model, without bequest (Samuelson 1958). There are accordingly various "types" of consumers. Each type is described by: the number of periods during which agents of this type live, the endowments of consumption goods that these agents own in each period of their lives, and their preferences among consumption streams during their lifetime. An important feature of the model is the fact that there are always "new-born" agents coming into the market at any date. Thus when an agent wishes to get rid of his cash balances at some time in his life, there will be always younger agents living in the same period for whom money may have value for saving purposes.

We will first consider this economy in a given period, which we call period 1, and study its properties in the short run (Sections 1.3–1.5). At this stage, there is no need to be specific about the characteristics of each "type" of agent nor about the demographic structure of the model. We shall make such a specification in Section 1.6, when studying stationary states of this economy. For the moment, what we need to know are the characteristics of every agent a living in the period under examination, i.e.:

(i)   the number n_a of remaining periods for which the agent is going to live, including the current one;

(ii) the agent's preferences, represented by a utility function u_a which depends upon current and future consumption c_t, $t = 1, \ldots, n_a$, where c_t is a vector with l nonnegative components;

(iii) the agent's endowment of consumption goods, e_{at}, in every remaining period of his or her life, $t = 1, \ldots, n_a$, where again, e_{at} is a vector with l components;

(iv) the money stock $\bar{m}_a$ the agent owns at the outset of period 1, which is the result of past saving and consumption decisions.

From this point on we shall make the following traditional assumptions:

(a) *The utility function* u_a *is continuous, increasing, and strictly quasi-concave, for every* a;

(b) *All components of the endowment vector,* e_{at}*, are positive for every* a *and* t;

(c) *Each initial money stock* $\bar{m}_a$ *is nonnegative, and the total money stock* $M = \Sigma_a \bar{m}_a$ *is positive.*

1.3   Short-run demand functions

Consider a typical agent at date 1, the "current period." The agent's problem (dropping the subscript a for convenience) is to choose his current consumption of goods $c_1 \geqq 0$, current money holdings $m_1 \geqq 0$, and to plan future consumptions $(c_2, \ldots, c_n) \geqq 0$ and money holdings $(m_2, \ldots, m_n) \geqq 0$. If current money prices of goods are represented by the vector p_1, and if the agent expects the prices $p_2, \ldots, p_n$ to prevail in the future, this choice will be the solution of the following problem.

(1.3.I)   *Maximize* $u(c_1, \ldots, c_n)$ *with respect to* $(c_1, \ldots, c_n) \geqq 0$ *and* $(m_1, \ldots, m_n) \geqq 0$ *subject to the current and expected budget constraints:*

$$p_1 c_1 + m_1 = p_1 e_1 + \bar{m}$$

$$p_t c_t + m_t = p_t e_t + m_{t-1} \qquad (t = 2, \ldots, n)$$

This decision-making problem has a solution, which is unique, when current and expected prices are positive. This solution gives rise to an excess demand for consumption goods $c_1 - e_1$ and a demand for money m_1 that are actually expressed on the market (plans for the future remain in the mind of the trader). These demands depend upon initial cash holdings $\bar{m}$, on current prices p_1, on the sequence of expected prices p_t, and on current and future endowments of goods $e_1, \ldots, e_n$.

The solution of (1.3.I) displays very simple and straightforward homogeneity properties with respect to the initial money stock and the sequence of current and expected prices. Consider a change of $\bar{m}$ in $\lambda \bar{m}$, of p_1 and p_t in λp_1 and λp_t $(t = 2, \ldots, n)$, and call (1.3.I') this new problem. No "real" change has been made in the constraints faced by the agent. In fact, it can easily be verified that $(c_1, \ldots, c_n)$ and $(m_1, \ldots, m_n)$ are solutions of (1.3.I) if and only if $(c_1, \ldots, c_n)$ and $(\lambda m_1, \ldots, \lambda m_n)$ are solutions of (1.3.I'), a property that we can call the *absence of money illusion.* We have obtained, in particular:

(1.3.1)   *The excess demand for goods* $c_1 - e_1$ *arising from (1.3.I) is homogenous of degree* 0 *in the initial money stock* $\bar{m}$*, current prices* p_1 *and expected prices* $p_2, \ldots, p_n$*. The corresponding money demand* m_1 *is homogenous of degree* 1 *in the same variables.*

In order to complete our specification of a trader's behavior in the short run, it is necessary to describe how price expectations are formed. The agent's expectations are functions of his information on past history and on the current state of the economy. Since past history is fixed in a short-period analysis and cannot be altered by current events, we shall not explicitly mention its influence at the formal level. On the other hand, we shall assume that the only information our agent has on the current state of the economy is described by the current price system p_1, and shall write expected prices p_t as a function $\psi_t(p_1)$ ($t = 2, \ldots, n$). Expected prices are thus independent of the agent's own actions. This formulation is warranted in a competitive framework, where the number of traders is implicitly assumed to be large, since in that case every agent can have only a negligible influence on market prices by varying his own decisions.

Let us call (1.3.II) the problem obtained from (1.3.I) by changing p_t in $\psi_t(p_1)$ for $t = 2, \ldots, n$:

(1.3.II) *Maximize* $u(c_1, \ldots, c_n)$ *with respect to* $(c_1, \ldots, c_n) \geqq 0$ *and* $(m_1, \ldots, m_n) \geqq 0$ *subject to:*

$$p_1 c_1 + m_1 = p_1 e_1 + \bar{m}$$

$$\psi_t(p_1)c_t + m_t = \psi_t(p_1)e_t + m_{t-1} \qquad (t - 2, \ldots, n)$$

The solution to this problem yields an excess demand for goods $c_1 - e_1$ and a demand for money m_1, which are expressed by the agent on the market in response to p_1. They depend upon the initial money stock $\bar{m}$ and upon current prices p_1 (and implicitly, on the trader's information on past history as well as on current and future endowments of goods). We can write them as $z_a(p_1, \bar{m}_a)$ and $m_a^d(p_1, \bar{m}_a)$ respectively, reintroducing finally the agent's subscript a.

We next discuss various properties of short-run demand functions. First, every agent must fulfill his current budget constraint, $p_1 z_a(p_1, \bar{m}_a) + m_a^d(p_1, \bar{m}_a) = \bar{m}_a$. Therefore aggregate excess demands satisfy Walras's Law:

$$p_1 \sum_a z_a(p_1 \bar{m}_a) + \sum_a m_a^d(p_1, \bar{m}_a) = \sum_a \bar{m}_a \quad \text{for every } p_1$$

On the other hand, short-run aggregate excess demand for goods does not in general satisfy Say's Law, $p_1 \sum_a z_a(p_1, \bar{m}_a) = 0$ for every p_1 since at some prices traders can find it profitable to save or dissave by adding to or subtracting from their initial cash balances $\bar{m}_a$.

Second, we must examine if the functions $z_a(p_1, \bar{m}_a)$ and $m_a^d(p_1, \bar{m}_a)$ are homogenous of degree 0 and 1 respectively with respect to current prices p_1 and initial cash balances $\bar{m}_a$, as neoclassical monetarists assume. In view of the absence of money illusion property stated in (1.3.1), the answer is in general no, unless the agents' expected prices $\psi_{at}(p_1)$ are unit elastic with respect to current prices, that is to say, $\psi_{at}(\lambda p_1) = \lambda\psi_{at}(p_1)$ for every p_1 and λ, and for every t. This is in particular the case if one assumes that expected prices are always equal to current ones, as Patinkin did (static expectations), or that every agent's expected rate of inflation π_a depends only in the short run on past history but not on current prices $(\psi_{at}(p_1) = (1 + \pi_a)^{t-1} p_1$ for every $t)$, as neoclassical writers do. Such assumptions appear therefore to be highly specific: strict proportionality of expected prices with respect to current ones is quite unlikely, since expectations depend on the sequence of past prices as well. To sum up:

(1.3.2)   *The functions* $z_a(p_1, \bar{m}_a)$ *and* $m_a^d(p_1, \bar{m}_a)$ *are homogenous of degree 0 and degree 1, respectively, with respect to* p_1 *and* $\bar{m}_a$ *if expected prices are unit elastic with respect to current prices* $(\psi_{at}(\lambda p_1) = \lambda\psi_{at}(p_1)$ *for every* p_1 *and* λ, $t = 2, \ldots, n_a)$.

Finally, this formulation allows us to understand on a more precise basis the consequences of a change in the level of current prices on a trader's excess demand z_a. Let us ignore the complications that arise from the possible modifications of relative current prices and/or of relative expected prices, and look at the macroeconomic case where there is only one good $(l = 1)$. Consider a variation of the current price from p_1 to λp_1, and the induced change of trader a's excess demand for the good:

$$\Delta z_a = z_a(\lambda p_1, \bar{m}_a) - z_a(p_1, \bar{m}_a)$$

We can split Δz_a in two parts:

$$\Delta z_a = \Delta' z_a + \Delta'' z_a$$

where $\Delta' z_a$ stands for the variation of excess demand that would occur when the current price changes from p_1 to λp_1, if the trader's expected prices had moved proportionally to p_1 – that is, from $\psi_{at}(p_1)$ to $\lambda\psi_{at}(p_1)$. The second term $\Delta'' z_a$ represents then the variation of excess demand that results from the change of expected prices from $\lambda\psi_{at}(p_1)$ to their true values $\psi_{at}(\lambda p_1)$, the current price being kept at the level λp_1.

The first term $\Delta' z_a$ represents the real balance effect. In view of the absence of money illusion property stated in (1.3.1), multiplying current and expected prices by λ, $\bar{m}_a$ being fixed, has the same consequence on excess demand for the current good as dividing the initial money balance $\bar{m}_a$ by λ, current and expected prices being kept at their initial level. What happens then is that the purchasing power of the initial money stock has been actually divided by λ. The real balance effect is thus measured by:

$$\Delta' z_a = z_a(p_1, \bar{m}_a/\lambda) - z_a(p_1, \bar{m}_a)$$

When the good is not inferior, an increase of p_1 generates, through the real balance effect, a decrease of the demand for the current good.

The second term,

$$\Delta'' z_a = z_a(\lambda p_1, \bar{m}_a) - z_a(p_1, \bar{m}_a/\lambda)$$

vanishes when $\psi_t(\lambda p_1) = \lambda \psi_t(p_1)$ for every t. This fact is indeed equivalent to (1.3.2) above and justifies the viewpoint of neoclassical macroeconomists, who exclusively consider real balance effects, since they assume explicitly or implicitly that price expectations are unit elastic.

The elasticity of price expectations with respect to current prices, however, differs typically from unity. In that case the second term $\Delta'' z_a$ must be taken into account. We shall call it, following Hicks and Lange, the *intertemporal substitution effect*, since it measures the consequence of the modification of expected prices relative to the current price. But the reader must keep in mind that it involves "income" as well as *stricto sensu* "substitution" effects, as in the traditional Slutsky equation.

Suppose now that the current price goes up from p_1 to λp_1, and that the elasticity of price expectations is greater than one, so that expected prices $\psi_{at}(\lambda p_1)$ are greater than $\lambda \psi_{at}(p_1)$. In that case, the intertemporal substitution effect is likely to favor an increase of current consumption, and thus to counteract the real balance effect. Conversely, when the elasticity of price expectations is less than unity, the intertemporal substitution effect is likely to reinforce the real balance effect.

The following example permits a simple representation of the properties of short-run demand functions. Let us assume that there is only one real good ($l = 1$), and consider a typical consumer who is planning for the current period and the next one only. If current and expected prices are p_1 and p_2, the consumer's current and expected budget constraints are (dropping the subscript a for simplicity):

$$p_1 c_1 + m_1 = p_1 e_1 + \bar{m}$$

$$p_2 c_2 + m_2 = p_2 e_2 + m_1$$

It is convenient to rewrite these constraints by eliminating the variables m_1 and m_2. By adding the two equalities and by taking into account the fact that $m_2 \geqq 0$, one gets the intertemporal budget constraint:

(i) $\qquad p_1 c_1 + p_2 c_2 \leqq p_1 e_1 + p_2 e_2 + \bar{m}$

The fact that m_1 must be nonnegative yields the liquidity constraint:

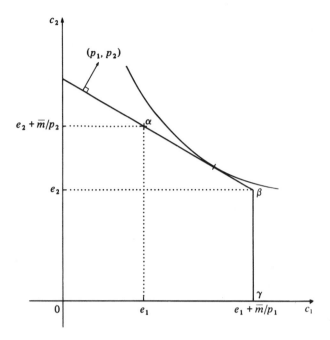

FIGURE 1.1.

(ii) $p_1 c_1 \leqq p_1 e_1 + \bar{m}$

The optimum current and future consumptions of the agent are thus obtained by maximizing the utility function $u(c_1, c_2)$ under the two constraints (i) and (ii). The associated demand for money is then given by $m_1 = \bar{m} + p_1 e_1 - p_1 c_1$, or by $m_1 = p_2 c_2 - p_2 e_2$.

The consumer's opportunity set described by the constraints (i) and (ii), as well as the result of the utility maximization, are pictured in Figure 1.1, in the plane (c_1, c_2). There, the line going through the points α and β represents the intertemporal budget constraint (i), and the vertical line $\beta\gamma$ represents the constraint (ii).

The absence of money illusion property stated in (1.3.1) can easily be verified in Figure 1.1. Consider a change of $\bar{m}$, p_1, p_2 in $\lambda\bar{m}$, λp_1, and λp_2. The change obviously leaves unaltered the coordinates of the points α and β. This means that the opportunity set described by (i) and (ii) is unchanged. The optimum values of c_1 and c_2 are accordingly the same. This is exactly what was stated in (1.3.1).

The decomposition between a real balance effect and an intertemporal substitution effect of the impact of an increase of p_1 on the trader's

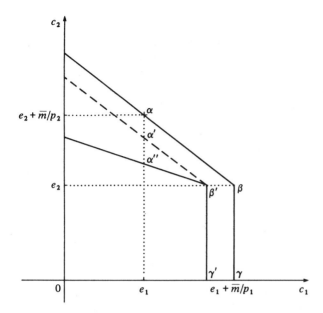

FIGURE 1.2.

behavior is easily visualized by using Figure 1.2. When price expectations are unit elastic, an increase of the current price p_1 causes a horizontal displacement toward the left of the lines $\alpha\beta$ and $\beta\gamma$, which then become $\alpha'\beta'$ and $\beta'\gamma'$, the slopes of these lines being unchanged. This generates a pure income or real balance effect. When price expectations are not unit elastic, there is in addition a rotation of the intertemporal budget line $\alpha'\beta'$ around the point β', downward if the elasticity exceeds 1, upward if the elasticity is less than 1. This rotation generates what we called the intertemporal substitution effect.

1.4 The existence of a short-run Walrasian monetary equilibrium

A short-run Walrasian monetary equilibrium in period 1 obtains when the current price system p_1 achieves equality of supply and demand in the goods and the money markets. By taking into account the demand functions $z_a(p_1, \bar{m}_a)$ and $m_a^d(p_1, \bar{m}_a)$ constructed in Section 1.3, this leads us to define such an equilibrium price system as a solution of a system of equations such as (1.1.C) and (1.1.D):

(1.1.C) $\sum_a z_a(p_1, \bar{m}_a) = 0$

(1.1.D) $\sum_a m_a^d(p_1, \bar{m}_a) = \sum_a \bar{m}_a$

These equations obey Walras's Law, as in the neoclassical system. By contrast, we do not assume here any specific homogeneity properties.[5]

The neoclassical conclusions about the invalidity of the classical dichotomy in the short run apply equally well here, since by Walras's Law any solution of (1.1.C) fulfills (1.1.D): the equilibrium of the real sector determines not only relative prices, but also the level of money prices. But the main question is to find the conditions under which this system of equations has indeed a solution.

In order to study this problem, it is most convenient to look at the simple case in which there is only one good ($l = 1$), so that equations (1.1.C) and (1.1.D) are in fact equivalent. The usual argument to assert the existence of a solution to this system goes as follows:

(i)   If the price p_1 is low enough, there is an excess demand for the good (or equivalently, an excess supply for money);

(ii) If conversely p_1 is large, there is an excess supply of the good (equivalently, an excess demand for money).

Then, by continuity, there would exist a value of p_1 achieving equilibrium on both markets.

Neoclassical macroeconomists focus attention on the real balance effect by restricting price expectations to be unit elastic. Moreover, they usually claim, as we recalled in Section 1.1, that the real balance effect is strong enough in the present context to bring about the above properties of the aggregate excess demand function. We shall see that this argument is wrong, and that there are theoretically conceivable and empirically plausible circumstances in which the real balance effect is too weak to equilibrate the market. What is actually needed is a strong intertemporal substitution effect in order to reinforce it.

In order to see this point more precisely, let us consider the simple example given in Section 1.3, where there is only one good and where every consumer is planning only one period ahead. The choices open to a typical agent were represented in the plane (c_1, c_2) in Figure 1.1, which forms the basis of Figure 1.3.

It is clear from Figure 1.3 that the agent's demand for current consumption c_1 will exceed his endowment e_1 if and only if the slope of the normal to the intertemporal budget line $\alpha\beta$, that is p_2/p_1, exceeds the

---

[5] In view of our discussion of the neoclassical system in Section 1.1, it would seem that the short-run quantity theory no longer holds, and that money is not in general neutral in the short run. The issue is in fact more subtle. We shall go back to it in Section 1.7 below.

marginal rate of substitution u'_2/u'_1 evaluated at the point α.[6] If we assume that a typical trader's utility function can be written $w(c_1) + \delta w(c_2)$, where w is strictly concave and differentiable, and δ is a parameter between 0 and 1, this fact can be expressed by:

$$c_1 - e_1 > 0 \quad \text{if and only if} \quad \frac{p_2}{p_1} > \delta \, \frac{w'(e_2 + \bar{m}/p_2)}{w'(e_1)}$$

It is quite easy by using this simple result to design examples where there is a persistent disequilibrium on the good market for all values of the current price.

Example 1: Persistent excess demand

Assume that a typical trader's expectations are biased upwards, so that the ratio p_2/p_1 is greater than or equal to the marginal rate of substitution at the endowment point (e_1, e_2), that is $p_2/p_1 \geqq \delta \, [w'(e_2)/w'(e_1)]$ for all p_1. Since w' is a decreasing function, the trader's demand for consumption c_1 will then always exceed his endowment e_1. If *all* traders' expectations are biased upward in this way, there will be an aggregate excess demand on the good market at all values of the current price p_1, and no short-run Walrasian equilibrium in which money has positive value can exist.

The phenomenon just described may occur in particular when price expectations are unit elastic with respect to the current price, that is, when the ratio p_2/p_1 is independent of p_1. The real balance effect is then the sole regulating mechanism of the economy, but it is too weak to bring the market into equilibrium. This conclusion can be valid for small expectational "inflationary bias," since the ratio p_2/p_1 need not be very large. In particular, the phenomenon occurs in the case of static expectations ($p_2 = p_1$ for every p_1), if the marginal rate of substitution at the endowment point is less than or equal to 1.

Example 2: Persistent excess supply

A similar story can be told in the case of "deflationary" expectations. Assume that a typical trader's expectations are biased upward, so that various points of the vertical line going through the endowment point in Figure 1.3 is bounded below by some positive number v. If the consumer's expectations are biased downward, so that $p_2/p_1 < v$ for every p_1, the

---

[6] It is assumed for the simplicity of the argument that every agent's money endowment $\bar{m}$ is positive.

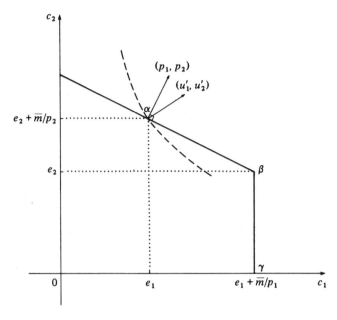

FIGURE 1.3.

agent's demand for current consumption c_1 is less than his endowment e_1 for every p_1. If all traders' price expectations are biased downward in this way, there is an aggregate excess supply on the good market for all values of the current price system p_1, and no short-run Walrasian equilibrium can exist. Again, the phenomenon can occur when price expectations are unit elastic with respect to the current price. The real balance effect, which is then the only regulating mechanism of the economy, is too weak in that case to equilibrate the market.

Many other examples can be designed along these lines. For instance, consider a utility function of the type $c_1^\lambda + \delta c_2^\lambda$, where λ and δ are parameters between 0 and 1. Then straightforward computations show that $c_1 - e_1 > 0$ if and only if $p_1 < f(p_2)$ where:

$$f(p) = (1/\delta e_1^{1-\lambda})p^\lambda(pe_2 + \bar{m})^{1-\lambda}$$

The function f increases from 0 to infinity when p varies from 0 to infinity, and therefore has an inverse. Then an excess demand on the good market will exist at all current prices p_1 if $p_2 > f^{-1}(p_1)$ for every p_1, an excess supply if $p_2 < f^{-1}(p_1)$ for all p_1.

These examples can of course be transposed to the case of several goods. For instance, consider the case where a typical trader's utility function is of the form $w(c_1) + \delta w(c_2)$, where w is strictly concave and δ between 0 and 1. Assume moreover that the trader's real income is constant over time ($e_1 = e_2$) and that he has static expectations ($p_2 = p_1$). It is then straightforward to check that the value of the trader's excess demand for current consumption, $p_1(c_1 - e_1)$, always exceeds $\bar{m}/2$. If all traders satisfy these conditions, the goods markets cannot be brought simultaneously into equilibrium. The reader will easily design other examples along these lines.

The above examples show that *the real balance effect may be too weak,* and that *it must be reinforced by a strong intertemporal substitution effect if one wishes to be able to equilibrate the market.* As we shall see, *this essentially requires in the present model that the expected prices of at least one agent be substantially insensitive to current prices.*

To verify this point, let us return to the simple case where there is only one good and where all traders are planning only one period ahead, and let us assume that there is a particular consumer whose price expectations are "insensitive" to the current price, in the sense that two positive real numbers ϵ and η exist such that $\epsilon \leqq \psi(p_1) \leqq \eta$, for all p_1.

We hope that an excess supply appears on the good market when its price p_1 is large. Let us consider accordingly what happens when p_1 tends to $+\infty$. Money balances being necessarily nonnegative, every agent's excess demand for the good, $c_1 - e_1$ must not exceed his initial real balance $\bar{m}/p_1$, which tends to 0 as p_1 tends to infinity. Intuitively, it suffices that the demand c_1 of our "insensitive" agent eventually becomes less than his endowment e_1 in order that an excess supply appears on the good market at the aggregate level. This is precisely what happens. Indeed, if we look at Figure 1.3 and view it as describing the behavior of the insensitive trader, we see that the point β tends to the endowment point (e_1, e_2) and that the intertemporal budget line tends to be almost vertical. The intertemporal substitution effect favors future consumption against current consumption. The insensitive trader's planned consumption c_2 actually goes to $+\infty$, as well as his current demand for money $m_1 = \psi(p_1) c_2 - \psi(p_1) e_2$. There is eventually an aggregate excess demand for money, and thus, by Walras's Law, an aggregate supply of the good when p_1 tends to $+\infty$.

Let us consider next what happens when the price p_1 goes to 0, and look again at Figure 1.3. For the "insensitive" trader, the point β in the figure goes to the far right, whereas α stays at a finite distance. The insensitive agent's intertemporal budget line becomes almost horizontal as p_1 decreases: the intertemporal substitution effect favors current consumption relative to future consumption. Since $\bar{m}$ is positive, the agent's demand for current consumption actually goes to infinity, and this is sufficient to generate an excess demand on the good market at the aggregate level.

We can therefore conclude that, by continuity, a short-run monetary equilibrium does exist in such a case.[7]

In order to describe a formal result along this line on the existence of a short-run equilibrium, we introduce a few definitions. Let us say that whenever $n_a \geqq 2$, agent a's price expectations are *continuous* if the functions $\psi_{at}(p_1)$ are continuous in p_1, for every t. An agent's price expectations are said to be *bounded* if there are two vectors ϵ and η, with all their components positive, such that $\epsilon \leqq \psi_{at}(p_1) \leqq \eta$ for every current price system p_1 and every t. The last condition, which is of course incompatible with the neoclassical assumption of unit elastic price expectations, ensures the presence of a strong intertemporal substitution effect, which reinforces the real balance effect. It is the key condition for the following existence theorem.[8]

(1.4.1) *Assume (a), (b), and (c) of Section 1.2. Assume moreover that every agent's price expectations are continuous, and that there is at least one agent a, with $n_a \geqq 2$ and $\bar{m}_a > 0$ whose price expectations are bounded. Then, there exists a short-run Walrasian monetary equilibrium.*

The general idea that underlies this result and the arguments that led to it is that one needs a strong intertemporal substitution effect that reinforces the real balance effect in order to be sure of the existence of a short-run monetary equilibrium. This essentially requires that some agent's price forecasts display a substantial degree of insensitivity to large variations of current prices. The insensitive traders are then there to act as a flywheel, and to stabilize the market process. That such conditions can be met in actual market economies is hardly to be expected. Price forecasts are indeed somewhat volatile, and are presumably quite sensitive to the level of current prices. The traders' expected rates of inflation may be biased upward when a significant inflation has been observed in the recent past, and downward in the case of a deflation. The examples we gave show that a short-run equilibrium may not exist

---

[7] What was actually used in this simple example, as the careful reader may have noticed, was that the insensitive trader's expected price is bounded below by $\epsilon > 0$, and that the ratio $\psi(p_1)/p_1$ tends to 0 when p_1 goes to $+\infty$. In the more realistic case where $l \geqq 2$ and $n \geqq 3$, matters are less simple, and one has to resort to the condition of the text.

[8] A formal proof of the theorem is given in Appendix B.

in such circumstances. The general conclusion that emerges from this analysis is accordingly that *the existence of a short-run Walrasian equilibrium, in which money has positive value is somewhat problematic in actual market economies, contrary to what neoclassical economists like to believe.*

1.5   The expected utility of money[9]

It is common practice among monetary theorists to write down a utility function for each agent depending on consumption and "real" balances, on the ground that money, for instance, renders services as a liquid asset and a medium of exchange. Short-run demand functions are then obtained as the result of maximizing such utility functions under the relevant budget constraints. The aim of this section is to describe a method of general applicability that justifies this procedure, provided that the indirect utility of money balances is correctly derived.

Consider again a typical consumer (dropping his subscript a for convenience) who is faced in period 1 by a price system p_1. We are trying to construct an index that would describe his preferences among current consumption $c_1 \geq 0$ and money balances $m_1 \geq 0$. Since m_1 represents a stock, the usefulness of which depends on its purchasing power in the future, such an index will certainly depend upon expected prices, and thus on current prices inasmuch as they determine price expectations. More precisely, consider the maximum level of utility that the consumer can expect to achieve over the remainder of his lifetime if he now chooses c_1 and m_1. This is the result of the following decision problem:

(1.5.III) *Given* $c_1 \geq 0$, $m_1 \geq 0$ *and* p_1, *maximize* $u(c_1, c_2, \ldots, c_n)$ *with respect to* $(c_2, \ldots, c_n) \geq 0$ *and* $(m_2, \ldots, m_n) \geq 0$, subject to the expected budget constraints:

$$\psi_t(p_1)c_t + m_t = \psi_t(p_1)\, e_t + m_{t-1} \qquad (t = 2, \ldots, n)$$

The maximum value of the utility function depends upons c_1, m_1 and on current prices through their influence on price expectations (and implicitly on past history, as well as on future real incomes). Let $v(c_1, m_1, p_1)$ be this maximum. It can be interpreted as the *expected utility* of (c_1, m_1) when the price system p_1 is currently quoted.

This expected utility $v(c_1, m_1, p_1)$ is indeed the index that we were looking for. It is in fact easy to verify:

(1.5.1) *Maximizing* $v(c_1, m_1, p_1)$ *with respect to* $c_1 \geq 0$ *and* $m_1 \geq 0$ *subject to the current budget constraint* $p_1 c_1 + m_1 = p_1 e_1 + \bar{m}$, *yields an excess*

---

[9] This section may be skipped on a first reading without any loss of continuity.

demand $c_1 - e_1$ *and a demand for money* m_1 *which are equal to* $z(p_1, \bar{m})$ *and* $m^d(p_1, \bar{m})$.

In order to prove this proposition, consider the unique solution of problem (1.3.II), $(c_1^*, \ldots, c_n^*)$ and $(m_1^*, \ldots, m_n^*)$. One has by definition, $c_1^* - e_1 = z(p_1, \bar{m})$, $m_1^* = m^d(p_1, \bar{m})$ and $p_1 c_1^* + m_1^* = p_1 e_1 + \bar{m}$. Moreover, the program of future consumptions $(c_2^*, \ldots, c_n^*)$ and of money holdings $(m_2^*, \ldots, m_n^*)$ is the solution of (1.5.III) corresponding to c_1^*, m_1^* and p_1. Therefore, by definition of the expected utility:

$$u(c_1^*, \ldots, c_n^*) = v(c_1^*, m_1^*, p_1)$$

Consider now other values of current consumption and of money holdings, (c_1, m_1), which differ from (c_1^*, m_1^*) and fulfill the current budget constraint, $p_1, c_1 + m_1 = p_1 e_1 + \bar{m}$. Note that this necessarily implies that c_1 is different from c_1^*. One can associate to (c_1, m_1) the solution $(c_2, \ldots, c_n)$, $(m_2, \ldots, m_n)$ of problem (1.5.III). By definition of the expected utility index:

$$u(c_1, \ldots, c_n) = v(c_1, m_1, p_1)$$

Since the program $(c_1, \ldots, c_n)$, $(m_1, \ldots, m_n)$ fulfills the constraints of problem (1.3.II), and since c_1^* differs from c_1, one must have:

$$u(c_1^*, \ldots, c_n^*) > u(c_1, \ldots, c_n)$$

or equivalently:

$$v(c_1^*, m_1^*, p_1) > v(c_1, m_1, p_1)$$

which proves the claim.

The above construction of the expected utility index $v(c_1, m_1, p_1)$ justifies accordingly the "introduction of money balances in the utility function." Current prices enter the utility function too, since they determine price expectations. We can thus discuss precisely the validity of the neoclassical claim, stating that "only real money balances enter the utility function." The natural counterpart of this statement in the present context would be to say that the expected utility index $v(c_1, m_1, p_1)$ is homogenous of degree 0 with respect to money balance m_1 and current price p_1. If we had let expected prices $p_2, \ldots, p_n$ vary independently of the current price system p_1 in problem (1.5.III), we would have obtained an expected utility index v depending upon c_1, m_1 and the sequences $p_2, \ldots, p_n$ of expected prices, which would have been indeed homogenous of degree 0 in the money balance m_1 and expected prices $p_2, \ldots, p_n$. But once the dependence of price expectations upon current prices is recognized, the conclusion is that $v(c_1, m_1, p_1)$ is *not* in general homogenous of degree 0 with respect to (m_1, p_1) unless price expectations are *unit elastic* with

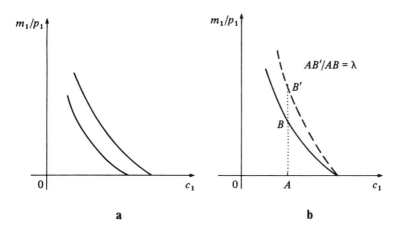

FIGURE 1.4.

respect to current prices. This conclusion is the analog of results (1.3.1) and (1.3.2) on short-run demand functions.

It might be useful to illustrate the concept of an expected utility index by means of an example. Let us consider the case in which there is only one real good ($l = 1$) and in which the typical consumer plans for the current period and the next one only ($n = 2$). If the consumer's money balance is m_1, and if his price forecast is $\psi(p_1)$, he has no freedom of choice in the future, since his consumption c_2 must then equal $e_2 + m_1/\psi(p_1)$. In that case, the expected utility index is:

$$v(c_1,m_1,p_1) = u(c_1,e_2 + m_1/\psi(p_1))$$

Since the expression $m_1/\psi(p_1)$ can be rewritten $(m_1/p_1) [p_1/\psi(p_1)]$, the expected utility index v can be viewed as a function of the current consumption c_1 and the "real balance" m_1/p_1, and of the current price p_1 inasmuch as it determines the ratio $\psi(p_1)/p_1$. Therefore, given p_1, the expected utility index defines a set of indifference curves in the plane $(c_1, m_1/p_1)$ which have the usual shape, as shown in Figure 1.4a.

The reader will easily verify that indifference curves do cut the axis $0c_1$. Indeed, the expression of the marginal rate of substitution between current consumption and current real balances at any point of coordinates $(c_1,0)$ is $[p_1/\psi(p_1)] (u_2'/u_1')$, where the ratio u_2'/u_1' is evaluated at the point (c_1,e_2). This marginal rate of substitution is positive.

It is useful to examine at this stage the effect upon the indifference curves of, say, an increase of the current price from p_1 to p_1'. Consider an indifference curve corresponding to a given level of the expected utility index before the increase of the current price has taken place

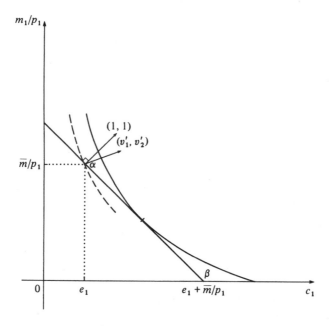

FIGURE 1.5.

(see the plain curve in Figure 1.4b). The new indifference curve associated to the same level of utility is then obtained by applying an affine transformation to the old one, using the axis $0c_1$ and the ratio $\lambda = [\psi(p_1')/p_1']\,[p_1/\psi(p_1)]$ (see the dashed curve in Figure 1.4b). In the neoclassical case, that is, when price expectations are unit elastic, λ is equal to 1, and the indifference curves are unaltered. But when the elasticity of price expectations is greater than unity, for instance, the increase of the current price leads to an "upward affine transformation" of the indifference curves, since then λ is greater than 1. Otherwise the transformation takes place in the other direction.

The result stated in (1.5.1) is obvious in this simple case: given p_1, the trader's optimum consumption c_1 and real balance m_1/p_1 is obtained by maximizing the expected utility index subject to the current budget constraint. This budget constraint can be written:

$$c_1 + (m_1/p_1) = e_1 + (\bar{m}/p_1)$$

and is thus represented in the plane $(c_1, m_1/p_1)$ by a line that is perpendicular to the vector $(1,1)$ and goes through the point $(e_1, \bar{m}/p_1)$. The result of the maximization of the expected utility index is shown in Figure 1.5.

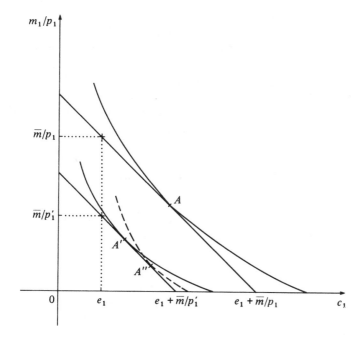

FIGURE 1.6.

It is clear from this diagram that whenever $\bar{m}$ is positive, the trader's optimum consumption c_1 exceeds his endowment e_1 if and only if the marginal rate of substitution between real balances and consumption evaluated at the point $(e_1, \bar{m}/p_1)$ is less than 1. When the utility function u is of the form $w(c_1) + \delta w(c_2)$, where w is strictly concave, differentiable, and where δ is a parameter between 0 and 1, this condition reads:

$$\delta \frac{p_1}{\psi(p_1)} \cdot \frac{w'[e_2 + \bar{m}/\psi(p_1)]}{w'(e_1)} < 1$$

This is of course the same condition that was obtained in the previous section when directly analyzing the trader's intertemporal optimization program.

The relative impacts of the real balance and of the intertemporal substitution effects, which were discussed in Section 1.3, also appear quite clearly on the diagram. Consider an increase of the current price from p_1 to p_1'. The budget line then moves down since it now goes through the point $(e_1, \bar{m}/p_1')$ (Figure 1.6). If price expectations were unit elastic, the indifference curves in the plane $(c_1, m_1/p_1)$ would be unchanged, and the trader's optimum mix of consumption and real balance would move from

A to A', as shown in Figure 1.6. This move corresponds to the real balance effect, which is a pure "income effect," and thus is likely to reduce both the demands for current consumption and for real balances. But when price expectations are not unit elastic, indifference curves are modified as was described above. The point representing the trader's optimum decision moves accordingly from A' to, say, A'' on the new budget line (see Figure 1.6). This move corresponds to the intertemporal substitution effect. When the elasticity of price expectations exceeds 1, there is an upward affine transformation of the indifference curves. The intertemporal substitution effect is thus likely to lead to an increase of current consumption in that case, and thus to counteract the real balance effect.

To conclude, the arguments developed in this section show that "the introduction of money balances in a trader's utility function" is a valid procedure, provided, however, that the utility of money is derived from the trader's intertemporal decision program which lies underneath, as in problem (1.5.III). Once this is done, one can of course choose to work exclusively with the resulting expected utility index, since it embodies all the information that was contained in the trader's intertemporal choice problem.[10] But this analysis points to one of the great dangers of this procedure. For it is greatly tempting to start directly with a utility function that depends upon current consumption, money balance and current prices, and to forget the trader's underlying intertemporal choices. This is in fact what many neoclassical monetarists have done and still do. It is clear that such a neglect renders a precise study of intertemporal substitution effects quite difficult, the importance of which we have stressed at length while studying market equilibrating forces.

1.6   Stationary states

Our goal in this section is to study (monetary) stationary states of the model, that is, sequences of short-run Walrasian monetary equilibria in which the price system is constant over time. Our findings will confirm the view that the classical dichotomy and quantity theory are valid propositions when applied to stationary states. More precisely, we shall show that a stationary equilibrium price system p may be defined as a solution of a system of equations such as the classical system (1.1.A), (1.1.B), displaying the same properties.

[10] In this respect, a useful exercise for the reader would be to transpose the arguments developed in the previous section about the existence, or the nonexistence, of a short-run monetary equilibrium, by using the expected utility index constructed in this section in the plane $(c_1, m_1/p_1)$.

In order to achieve this goal, we need a more detailed specification of the dynamic structure of the model. To fix ideas, we choose to work within the convenient framework of an overlapping generation model without bequest and with a constant population. This is merely a convenience, however, as the conclusions that we shall reach do not depend in an essential way on the specific structure of that sort of model. There are various "types" of agents. Agents of type i are characterized by:

(i)   the number $n_i \geqq 2$ of periods of their lifetimes;
(ii) the profile of their real income during their lives, which is described by the endowment of goods $e_{i\tau}$, a vector with l components, that they own in the τth period of their lives, $\tau = 1, \ldots, n_i$;
(iii) their preferences over consumption streams, which are represented by a utility function $u_i(c_{i1}, \ldots, c_{in_i})$, where $c_{i\tau}$, a vector with l nonnegative components, is their consumption in the τth period of their lives.

It is assumed further that, in each period, a "newborn" agent of each type comes into the market. At the same date, an agent of each type who arrives at the end of his life leaves the market. Thus, in each period, there are n_i agents of type i who participate in market activity, each in a different period of his life. The characteristics of the agents of a given type are supposed to be independent of time, that is, they are independent of the date of their "birth."

In this context, a trader a living in a given period, say period 1, is described by his type i and his "age" τ (which means that he is in the τth period of his life). It is then easy to deduce from the characteristics of his type and a knowledge of his past decisions, the short-run characteristics of this agent, as they were introduced in Section 1.2. Indeed, n_a is then equal to the number of periods he still has to live including the present one, i.e., to $n_i - \tau + 1$. The utility function u_a is obtained from u_i by keeping fixed its $\tau - 1$ first arguments at the level of the trader's past consumptions. The endowment vectors e_{at} are equal to his current and future endowments of goods. Lastly, his money balance $\bar{m}_a$ at the outset of the period is equal to the amount of money he decided to keep at the preceding date. Of course, $\bar{m}_a = 0$ for a "newborn" trader ($\tau = 1$), since by assumption there are no bequests in this model.

In the present section we shall use the following assumptions, which are natural counterparts of the assumptions made in Section 1.2 on the short-run characteristics of every agent.

(a)   *The utility function* u_i *is continuous, increasing, and strictly quasi-concave, for every* i;

(b) The endowment vectors $e_{i\tau}$ have all their components positive, for all i and τ;

(c) The total stock of money M is positive.

The notion of a sequence of short-run equilibria is now intuitively clear. Consider this economy at a given date, say date 1. The economy's past history, in particular past equilibrium prices and the traders' past decisions, are then given. We just saw how these data determine the short-run characteristics of every agent living at date 1. In order to apply the analysis developed in Sections 1.3 and 1.4, all that is needed is to know how price forecasts are formed. This involves the specification of: (i) the information a trader of type i and age τ has in any period about the economy's past history, and (ii) the functional relationship linking his price forecasts for the remaining periods of his life with his information on past history and with current prices. For the purpose of this study, it is not necessary, however, to be precise on these points. It is enough to remark that such a specification implies a relation between expected prices and current prices for every trader, and that the notion of a short-run equilibrium analyzed in the preceding sections applies directly here. Picking up a short-run equilibrium price system at date 1 determines in particular the traders' actions at that date. One can then repeat this procedure at date 2, and so on, and define a sequence of short-run equilibria in this manner.

A *stationary state* in this economy is by definition a sequence of short-run equilibria in which prices remain constant over time. It should be emphasized that, although the analysis carried out in the previous sections casts serious doubts about the existence of a short-run Walrasian equilibrium in general, stationary states are of interest on their own. For they can arise as stationary states of dynamic processes that differ from the one we just described, e.g., from disequilibrium processes in which prices do not clear markets at every date.

It is reasonable to assume that whenever a trader observes at some date that the price system has been the same in the past and in the current period, he believes that the same price system will prevail in the future.[11] This assumption – which implies that traders have "rational" or "correct" expectations along stationary states – permits a very simple derivation of the equations that must be satisfied by stationary equilibrium prices.

[11] This assumption postulates implicitly that a trader's information about the past contains at least past prices. It should be noted that the assumption is a statement on the dependence of expected prices with respect to current *and* past prices. It is therefore compatible with conditions saying that expected prices are to some extent intensive to, or even independent of, current prices, like the conditions used in (1.4.1).

Indeed, along a stationary state in which the price system is p, the consumptions $(c_{i\tau})$ and money holdings $(m_{i\tau})$ of a trader of type i during his lifetime will be solutions of the following program:

(1.6.IV) *Maximize* $u_i(c_1, \ldots, c_{n_i})$ *with respect to* $(c_1, \ldots, c_{n_i}) \geqq 0$ *and* $(m_1, \ldots, m_{n_i}) \geqq 0$, *subject to the budget constraints:*

$pc_\tau + m_\tau = pe_{i\tau} + m_{\tau-1} \qquad (\tau = 1, \ldots, n_i)$
(with the convention $m_0 = 0$*).*

When all components of p are positive, (1.6.IV) has a solution that is unique. We can thus write the excess of consumption over endowments $c_{i\tau} - e_{i\tau}$ and the money stocks $m_{i\tau}$ obtained from (1.6.IV) as functions of p, that is, $z_{i\tau}(p)$ and $m_{i\tau}(p)$, for every τ. We shall note $z_i(p) = \Sigma_\tau z_{i\tau}(p)$ and $m_i(p) = \Sigma_\tau m_{i\tau}(p)$.

Consumers forecast correctly the future along a stationary state. Accordingly, in any period, what a newborn trader plans to do in the future in the τth period of his life is precisely what the agent of the same type and of age τ is actually doing in the same period. Therefore $z_i(p)$ and $m_i(p)$ represent the aggregate excess of consumption over endowment of goods, and the aggregate money stock of all agents of type i in each period along the stationary state. It follows that p is a stationary equilibrium price system if and only if it is a solution of the following equations, which express the fact that all markets clear:

(1.6.A) $\quad \sum_i z_i(p) = 0$

(1.6.B) $\quad \sum_i m_i(p) = M$

where the summation sign runs over all types i of agents.

Before looking at the properties of these equations, a comment is in order. Although the functions appearing in the equations (1.6.A) and (1.6.B) do not depend on the quantity of money, their structure depends crucially on the presence of money in the economy. Indeed, if money did not exist as a store of value, the constraints in (1.6.IV) should read $pc_t = pe_{it}$ for every t, which would lead to an entirely different system of equations. For instance, in the case of a single consumption good, the unique solution would be the autarkic one, $c_{it} = e_{it}$.

We proceed now to show that (1.6.A) and (1.6.B) display all the properties of the classical system that we discussed in Section 1.1. First, examination of (1.6.IV) leads to the immediate conclusion that:

The functions $z_i(p)$ *are homogenous of degree 0, and the functions* $m_i(p)$ *are homogenous of degree 1 in prices.*

As a matter of fact, this is nothing other than the absence of money illusion property (1.3.1), since a newborn agent has no money ($m_0 = 0$). On the other hand, it is easy to verify that:

Walras's Law reduces here to Say's Law, that is, $p\Sigma_i z_i(p) = 0$ *for every* p.

Indeed, if one takes into account that it is never optimal for an agent to keep a positive money balance at the end of his life, summation of the constraints in (1.6.IV) yields $pz_i(p) + m_i(p) = m_i(p)$ for every p and every i, hence, the result.

We have therefore proved that the equations (1.6.A) and (1.6.B) satisfy all the properties of the classical system. The classical dichotomy and quantity theory are thus valid propositions when applied to stationary states in an economy with a constant money stock. The real sector [equation (1.6.A)] determines relative prices and real variables, independently of the quantity of money. The money sector [equation (1.6.B)] in turn determines the level of money prices and of nominal variables, which is proportional to the total money stock.[12]

It remains to be seen whether such a system of equations has a solution under reasonable conditions. Since (1.6.A) looks like an ordinary Walrasian system, one can expect that it has a solution under standard assumptions. As a matter of fact:[13]

(1.6.1) *Assume (a) and (b) of the present section. Then (1.6.A) has a solution* p, *which has all its components positive and is defined up to a positive real number.*

Given any solution $\bar{p}$ of (1.6.A), the level of money prices must be determined by looking at the money market equation (1.6.B). Since the functions $m_i(p)$ are homogenous of degree 1 in prices, this is done by solving in λ the equation $\Sigma_i m_i(\lambda \bar{p}) = M$, or equivalently, $\lambda \Sigma_i m_i(\bar{p}) = M$. This equation has a positive solution, which is then unique, if and only if $\Sigma_i m_i(\bar{p})$ is positive, or equivalently, if and only if there is a type i of traders such that $m_i(\bar{p}) > 0$.

---

[12] It should be intuitively clear to the reader that these conclusions do not depend on the specific structure of the model that we consider. The homogeneity properties of the functions that appear in the market clearing equations (1.6.A), (1.6.B) should hold in any model in which the traders are free of money illusion. On the other hand, the identities, $pz_i(p) + m_i(p) = m_i(p)$ for every p, which give rise to Say's Law, reflect the budget constraints that a trader or a group of traders face in any period, and the fact that money balances are constant along a stationary state. These properties should hold in any well-specified economy with a constant money stock.

[13] A formal proof of this statement is given in Appendix B.

The existence of a stationary equilibrium will therefore be guaranteed if there is a type i of agents who have enough incentives to save when the price system is stationary. Intuitively, this will be the case if they experience a fall in income during their lifetimes, and if their preferences for present consumption are not too strong.

In order to make precise this intuition, let us assume that there is a type i of consumers that satisfies the following two assumptions:

(d) *The utility function* u_i *is of the form* $\Sigma_\tau \delta_i^{\tau-1} w_i(c_{i\tau})$, *where* w_i *is strictly concave and* $0 < \delta_i \leqq 1$;

(e) *There are* τ *and* τ' *with* $\tau < \tau'$ *such that* $e_{i\tau} \geqq e_{i\tau'}$, *with strict inequality for some component.*

Our goal is to show that under these assumptions, the system (1.6.A), (1.6.B) has a solution if the parameter δ_i is close to 1. We shall show in the first place that the result is true when there is no preference for present consumption, that is, when $\delta_i = 1$. Then by continuity, the result is still true when δ_i is close to 1.

It is first clear that *under assumptions (d) and (e)*, $m_i(p)$ *is positive for every stationary price system* p *when* δ_i *is equal to* 1. The proof of this claim is quite simple. Let us suppose on the contrary that there exists a p such that $m_i(p) = 0$. This would mean that the solution of problem (1.6.IV) associated with this specific p, say (c_τ^*, m_τ^*), is such that $m_\tau^* = 0$ for every τ. This implies of course $pc_\tau^* = pe_{i\tau}$ for every τ. But this is impossible, since $pe_{i\tau} > pe_{i\tau'}$. As a matter of fact, the consumption program obtained by replacing c_τ^* and $c_{\tau'}^*$ by

$$c_\tau = c_{\tau'} = \tfrac{1}{2}(c_\tau^* + c_{\tau'}^*)$$

is certainly feasible: The agent can achieve it by saving $m_\tau = p(e_{i\tau} - c_\tau) > 0$ at age τ, by keeping this amount of money until age τ', and by spending it at that time. Given the specific form of the utility function and the fact that $\delta_i = 1$, this new program yields a higher level of utility, since by strict concavity of w_i:

$$w_i(c_\tau) + w_i(c_{\tau'}) > w_i(c_\tau^*) + w_i(c_{\tau'}^*)$$

Hence a contradiction, which proves the claim.

The result we just proved implies that if there is a type i of agents that satisfies (d) and (e), then $\Sigma_i m_i(\bar{p})$ is positive for every solution $\bar{p}$ of (1.6.A) when δ_i is equal to 1. In that case, the system (1.6.A), (1.6.B) indeed has a solution. It is intuitively clear that by continuity, (1.6.A), (1.6.B) still has a solution if δ_i is close to unity. This heuristic argument accordingly justifies the following proposition:[14]

---

[14] A rigorous proof of this proposition is given in Appendix B.

(1.6.2)   *Assume (a), (b), and (c) of the present section. Assume moreover that there is a type* i *of consumers that satisfies (d) and (e). Then the system* (1.6.A), (1.6.B) *has a solution if* δ_i *is close enough to 1.*

Remark. In this section, it was explicitly specified that a stationary equilibrium is one in which money has positive value. Under our assumptions on utility functions and endowments, it can be shown using standard methods of equilibrium theory that a stationary equilibrium exists in which money has zero value. In the case of a single good it corresponds to the autarkic state, where every consumer consumes his own endowment in every period of his life.

1.7   The neutrality of money

We will end this chapter with a few remarks about the "neutrality" of money in the simple model under consideration. More precisely, we wish to look at the impact on equilibrium real and nominal magnitudes, both in the short run and in the long run, of a change of the money stock M that is implemented by the Government through lump-sum transfers – the textbook favorite: "money rain."

We already gave an answer in the preceding section, which concerned stationary equilibria. A once-and-for-all change of the money stock M leaves unaltered the set of "real" quantities that are exchanged along stationary equilibria, and generates a proportional variation of stationary equilibrium money prices and of nominal cash holdings. In this sense, money is "neutral in the long run."

The study of the short-run effects of a change of the money supply requires a little more care. Let us consider accordingly our simple economy at date 1, as we did in Sections 1.2–1.5, and let us assume that the Government implements at that date a *once-and-for-all* change of the outstanding stock of money from M to $\lambda_1 M$, where λ_1 is an arbitrary positive real number, by making a lump-sum subsidy to, or by levying a lump-sum tax on, each trader living at that date. Let $\Delta \bar{m}_a$ be the resulting variation of trader a's initial money holding $\bar{m}_a$.

It is first clear that if the money creation – or destruction – does not respect the initial distribution of cash balances, that is, if the $\Delta \bar{m}_a$ values are not proportional to the $\bar{m}_a$ values, the change of the money supply generates a "distribution effect" among traders and thus is likely to modify short-run equilibrium "real" variables.[15] The only hope, therefore,

---

[15] Such "distribution effects" are partly responsible for the lack of neutrality of money in some monetary models. For instance, if one considers an overlapping generation model without bequests, and if money is injected into the economy

to get neutrality is to consider the Ricardian experiment of a scalar change of the traders' initial money balances, that is:

$$\bar{m}_a + \Delta\bar{m}_a = \lambda_1\bar{m}_a \qquad \text{for all } a$$

What is the impact of this change on Walrasian equilibrium prices at date 1? The answer given by neoclassical theorists is that a new short-run equilibrium price system p_1 is a solution of the equations (1.4.C), (1.4.D), where each trader's initial money holding $\bar{m}_a$ is changed in $\lambda_1\bar{m}_a$, that is:

$$(1.7.C) \quad \sum_a z_a(p_1,\lambda_1\bar{m}_a) = 0$$

$$(1.7.D) \quad \sum_a m_a^d(p_1,\lambda_1\bar{m}_a) = \sum_a \lambda_1\bar{m}_a$$

As we recalled in Section 1.1, the neoclassical argument would then be that the functions z_a and m_a^d that appear in this system are homogenous of degree 0 and 1 respectively, in regard to current prices and initial money holdings, and therefore that changing the money supply in this way has no "real" effects. We have seen, however, that the neoclassical homogeneity postulates are based on extremely specific assumptions – the unit elasticity of price expectations – and that they have to be abandoned anyway if one wishes to get a consistent short-run theory, since in that case intertemporal substitution effects have to be taken into account. Hence, if one follows this approach, it would seem that money is not in general neutral in the short run.

That kind of reasoning is wrong because it neglects the information that is generated by the Government's policy itself, and its influence on the traders' expectations.

Let us assume that the once-and-for-all scalar change of initial money holdings is *publicly* announced by the Government. The parameter λ_1 is then observed by all traders, in addition to the current price system p_1. It must therefore be an argument of each trader's price expectations, which will be denoted accordingly $\psi_{at}(p_1,\lambda_1)$, for $t = 1, \ldots, n_a$. The problem that typical traders must solve at date 1 is then to maximize their utility function under their current and expected budget constraints (we drop the trader's index a for convenience):

$$p_1 c_1 + m_1 = p_1 e_1 + \lambda_1\bar{m}$$

$$\psi_t(p_1,\lambda_1)c_t + m_t = \psi_t(p_1,\lambda_1)e_t + m_{t-1}$$

by giving it partly to the "young" traders – i.e., to those who just came into the market, and who accordingly have no money initially – this injection is bound to be nonneutral, since it does not respect the initial distribution of money holdings.

for $t = 2, \ldots, n$. This is in fact (1.3.II), which is reformulated so as to take into account the information embodied in the Government's policy.

A trader's excess demand for current goods and his current demand for money depend now on the current price system p_1, on his initial money holding $\bar{m}$, and on the parameter λ_1. If we note them $z_a(p_1, \bar{m}_a, \lambda_1)$ and $m_a^d(p_1, \bar{m}_a, \lambda_1)$, the equations defining the short-run equilibrium price vectors that are associated with the policy parameter λ_1 are given by:

$$(1.7.\text{C}') \quad \sum_a z_a(p_1, \bar{m}_a, \lambda_1) = 0$$

$$(1.7.\text{D}') \quad \sum_a m_a^d(p_1, \bar{m}_a, \lambda_1) = \sum_a \lambda_1 \bar{m}_a$$

It becomes easy to see, once the problem has been properly reformulated in these terms, that a publicly announced once-and-for-all scalar change of all traders' initial money holdings is neutral – provided that the economic agents believe this neutrality proposition to be true. Let us assume that *the functions* $\psi_{at}(p_1, \lambda_1)$ *are homogenous of degree 1 with respect to* (p_1, λ_1). In other words, the traders think that moving from a situation in which $\lambda_1 = 1$ and in which the current price system is p_1, to a situation in which λ_1 differs from unity and current prices are $\lambda_1 p_1$, will generate a proportional variation of equilibrium prices in the future.[16] Under this assumption, in view of the absence of money illusion property stated in (1.1.3), the functions z_a and m_a^d appearing in the system (1.7.C'), (1.7.D'), considered as functions of p_1 and λ_1, are homogenous of degree 0 and 1 respectively, in regard to these variables. Then if p_1 is a solution of (1.7.C'), (1.7.D') when $\lambda_1 = 1$, $\lambda_1 p_1$ is a solution of the same system for every value of λ_1. Moreover, real equilibrium quantities are independent of, whereas nominal money balances are proportional to, the parameter λ_1.[17]

---

[16] This assumption relates expected prices to p_1 and λ_1. It is therefore compatible with price expectations that are not unit elastic with respect to current prices p_1 alone, λ_1 being fixed. The assumption is in particular compatible with the kind of conditions which were used in (1.4.1) to ensure the presence of a strong stabilizing intertemporal substitution effect for a given λ_1.

[17] It is not difficult – but a little tedious – to show that short-run equilibrium prices will be multiplied by λ_1 not only at date 1, as we just showed, but at all subsequent dates too, if the agents form their expectations according to the above principle at date 1 and at all later dates. This is left as an exercise to the reader (Hint: Make an argument by induction. A trader's expected prices at date 2 are functions of p_1, λ_1 and p_2, and will be assumed to be homogenous of degree 1 with respect to these variables). In this sense, the postulated homogeneity properties of price expectations with respect to λ_1 and observed prices are "rational" or more precisely, self-fulfilling.

Such a publicly announced one-shot money injection – or destruction – is then neutral. It goes without saying that this result has been obtained by following a route quite different from the neoclassical approach. For we relied on certain homogeneity properties of the functions z_a and m_a^d with respect to current prices p_1 and the Government's policy parameter λ_1, and not with respect to current prices and initial money holdings, as neoclassical theorists do.

The result shows that *the only sources of the nonneutrality of a once-and-for-all scalar change of all traders' initial money holdings are either that economic units do not believe in the neutrality of such a change, or that they are not fully informed about the Government's policy.*

In order to illustrate the latter point, it is most convenient to look at the simple case in which the traders know that the Government is implementing at date 1 a scalar change of their money balances $\bar{m}_a$, but in which the size of this policy, i.e., the parameter λ_1, is not publicly announced. In such a case, of course, all agents who initially own a positive cash balance observe immediately the value of λ_1, since they receive the lump-sum transfer $\Delta \bar{m}_a = (\lambda_1 - 1)\bar{m}_a$. But the traders who have no money at the outset of the period and who accordingly receive nothing, are in a much worse position – this will be the case in particular for the "young" or "newborn" traders in an overlapping generation model without bequests. These traders will have to guess both the value of λ_1 and the real characteristics of the economy at date 1 through the observation of the sole price system p_1. It may be the case that these traders cannot make such an inference because the price system does not convey enough information. Money will then be nonneutral. That kind of "informational" nonneutrality, however, seems to be based on very specific assumptions. It requires the presence in the economy of traders who are not informed of the size of the change of the money supply, whereas that kind of information could be made public quite easily. And perhaps more importantly, *the uninformed traders must initially have no money at all, because otherwise they would immediately observe the size of the Government's policy λ_1.*[18]

Remark (Preannounced changes of the money supply). It should be emphasized that the neutrality proposition that we have established concerns exclusively a publicly announced once-and-for-all scalar variation of the

---

[18] This is one of the basic sources of the nonneutrality of money in Lucas's influential paper (1972), as I understand it, which enabled him to establish the existence of a "Phillips' curve," i.e., of a positive correlation between equilibrium prices and output, in a Walrasian equilibrium setting.

traders' initial money balances in the current period, i.e., at date 1. By contrast, a scalar change of current money holdings will have generally "real" effects if the traders expect, or if the Government announces at date 1 that a variation of the money supply of a given size ΔM_θ will take place too, through lump-sum transfers, at a prespecified date θ in the future. Similarly, the announcement by the Government at date 1 that it will make a once-and-for-all change of the money supply at a given date θ in the future, through lump-sum transfers, will not generally be neutral. It is perhaps useful to spend some time discussing this issue more precisely, for it has been somewhat controversial recently. Moreover, it has important policy implications. For instance, it has been argued that deterministic variations of the timing of taxes have no effect on the equilibrium of the real sector whenever they are expected by private economic units or preannounced by the Government.[19] That sort of argument has been employed to revive under the "new classical macroeconomics" banner, an old proposition which some attribute to Ricardo, namely, that it is equivalent to finance a government's deficit by printing money, by levying taxes, or by issuing bonds, whenever the agents anticipate that interest payments on bonds will have to be covered by taxation later on. In all cases, it is argued, the induced variations of the money stock will be offset by a correlative movement of prices, and the equilibrium of the real sector will be unaltered.[20]

We are going to see that this viewpoint is wrong, and that expected or preannounced modifications of the time profile of the money stock through lump-sum transfers produce generally real effects if one takes into account the various *liquidity constraints* that the agents face.[21]

Let us consider our simple economy at date 1, and let us assume that the Government announces that it makes the outstanding money stock to move from M to $\lambda_1 M$ at that date by making lump-sum transfers to the traders living in the current period. Let us assume furthermore that the Government announces too that it will add to the existing money stock the quantity $\Delta M_t = \lambda_t M$ in every period t in the future, again through lump-sum transfers. The λ_t are arbitrary real numbers for $t \geqq 2$, with the only restriction, of course, that the stock of money at t, i.e., $\Sigma_1^t \lambda_\tau M$, is positive for all t. A once-and-for-all variation of the current money stock corresponds to $\lambda_1 \neq 1$, and $\lambda_t = 0$ for all $t \geqq 2$.

The only way to avoid distribution effects among the traders a who are living in the current period, as it will become clear shortly, is to

---

[19]   See, e.g., Sargent and Wallace (1975).
[20]   See Barro (1974).
[21]   For similar arguments, see Tobin (1980, Chap. 3).

make the transfers $\Delta \bar{m}_{at}$ that they receive in their lifetimes proportional to their initial money holdings $\bar{m}_a$.[22] So we shall assume $\bar{m}_a + \Delta \bar{m}_{a1} = \lambda_1 \bar{m}_a$ and $\Delta \bar{m}_{at} = \lambda_t \bar{m}_a$, for all a and t. The Government's policy is then fully described by the array $\lambda = (\lambda_1, \lambda_2, \ldots)$. Each trader's price expectations at date 1 are now functions of the current price system p_1 and of the "policy parameter" λ. They will be denoted $\psi_{at}(p_1, \lambda)$.

A typical trader's decision problem at date 1 is then to maximize his lifetime utility function under the current and expected budget constraints (we will drop the index a momentarily for convenience):

$$p_1 c_1 + m_1 = p_1 e_1 + \lambda_1 \bar{m}$$

$$p_t c_t + m_t = p_t e_t + m_{t-1} + \lambda_t \bar{m} \qquad t = 2, \ldots, n$$

where the expected prices p_t stand for $\psi_t(p_1, \lambda)$.

The trader's resulting excess demands for current goods and his demand for money at date 1 are then functions of the current prices p_1, of his initial money balance $\bar{m}$, and of the policy parameter $\lambda = (\lambda_1, \lambda_2, \ldots)$. If we note them, for each trader, $z_a(p_1, \bar{m}_a, \lambda)$ and $m_a^d(p_1, \bar{m}_a, \lambda)$, the equilibrium price vectors that are associated at date 1 with the policy parameter λ are given by the equations[23]:

$$(1.7.C'') \quad \sum_a a_a(p_1, \bar{m}_a, \lambda) = 0$$

$$(1.7.D'') \quad \sum_a m_a^d(p_1, \bar{m}_a, \lambda) = \sum_a \lambda_1 \bar{m}_a$$

Examination of a typical trader's decision problem shows that the functions z_a and m_a^d above are homogenous of degree 0 and 1 respectively, in regard to (p_1, λ), whenever the traders' expectation functions $\psi_{at}(p_1, \lambda)$ are themselves homogenous of degree 1 with respect to these variables. Scaling up or down all the λ_t values then generates a proportional variation of equilibrium prices p_1 in the system $(1.7.C'')$, $(1.7.D'')$, and leaves

---

[22] Hence, promising to make a lump-sum transfer $\Delta \bar{m}_{at} \neq 0$ to a trader who initially owns no money will yield a distribution effect if we start, say, from a situation where there are no changes of the money supply. That kind of nonneutrality will occur in particular in an overlapping generation model without bequests whenever the preannounced changes of the money supply ΔM_t, for $t \geq 2$, are implemented by giving money to or by levying taxes from the traders who are "young" or just "newborn" at date 1.

[23] The short-run analysis that was developed in Sections 1.2–1.5 applies, strictly speaking, only to the case where $\lambda_t = 0$ for $t \geq 2$. The reader will easily verify, however, that all the arguments presented there are still valid for an arbitrary λ, provided that the sums $\Sigma_1^t \lambda_\tau$ are positive. In fact, the existence theorem stated in $(1.4.1)$ still applies in such a case, as the mathematically oriented reader will check without difficulty by looking at its proof in Appendix B.

unaltered all real equilibrium magnitudes at date 1. It can be shown, by recurrence, that the same neutrality proposition holds at later dates t too, whenever the traders' price expectations are homogenous of degree 1 with respect to λ and the prices $(p_1, \ldots, p_t)$ that are observed from the date of the announcement of the policy, up to the date t. *A publicly announced scalar variation of all the λ_t values is therefore neutral whenever the traders believe in its neutrality.* This result includes as a particular case the neutrality of a once-and-for-all scalar variation of current money holdings $\bar{m}_a$, which we established previously, since then $\lambda_t = 0$ for all $t \geqq 2$.

It is easily seen that, by contrast, a variation of the λ_t values that modifies the time profile of the money stock, i.e., one that alters some of the ratios λ_{t+1}/λ_t, will generally change the equilibrium of the real sector at date 1.

In order to see this point, it is most convenient to consider again the decision problem of a typical trader. By adding the t first budget constraints, one gets a liquidity constraint that expresses the fact that the money balance m_t cannot be negative:

$$\Sigma_1^t p_\tau(c_\tau - e_\tau) \leqq (\Sigma_1^t \lambda_\tau)\bar{m}$$

The trader's optimum consumption program is then obtained by maximizing his utility function under all these liquidity constraints for $t = 1, \ldots, n$.

Assume now that we start from an initial equilibrium situation at date 1, which corresponds to a given policy parameter λ, and that the λ_t values are changed in an arbitrary way. If one looks at a typical trader's liquidity constraint for $t = n$, i.e., at his lifetime intertemporal budget constraint, one sees that current and expected prices have to move proportionally to $\Sigma_1^n \lambda_\tau$, if $\bar{m}$ is positive, in order to keep the agent's consumption program unchanged. Suppose now that the trader's liquidity constraint for $t = \theta < n$ was initially binding. Then current and expected prices, up to date θ, have to move proportionally to $\Sigma_1^\theta \lambda_\tau$ too in order to avoid a variation of the trader's consumption program. These two requirements are not generally compatible, unless the λ_t values are all changed in the same proportion. In particular, if the initial situation corresponds to $\lambda_1 = 1$, $\lambda_t = 0$ for $t \geqq 2$, and if the policy move is to vary a single λ_t at a given date $\theta < t \leqq n$, such a preannounced change of the money supply will modify the traders' equilibrium consumptions at date 1.

Even if one ignores the possibility that the traders' liquidity constraints for $t < n$ may be initially binding, it remains that in order to keep the equilibrium of the real sector invariant at date 1, current and expected prices must move in proportion to $\Sigma_1^n \lambda_\tau$, for each trader. Again, this will be generally impossible to achieve unless the λ_t values move altogether proportionally, since the (lifetime) planning horizons n_a of the traders who are living at date 1 are typically different.

The conclusion of this brief qualitative analysis is that *preannounced deterministic variations of the money supply that alter the time profile of the money stock through lump-sum transfers may have real effects.* The conclusion should not be surprising after all, for such variations modify the rate of growth of the money supply at some date. This is a "real" change, and one should expect it to generate real effects if money has any meaningful role to play in the economy, by inducing at least momentarily a change of the rate of inflation (this is sometimes referred to in the literature as the "inflation tax"). The foregoing analysis shows that *the basic channel through which such deterministic changes of the rate of growth of the money supply influence the real sector in a Walrasian equilibrium setting, are the various "liquidity constraints" that the agents face.*[24]

Notes on the literature

Part of the analysis presented in this chapter is based on an earlier paper by Grandmont (1974), and on its extensions to overlapping generation models by Grandmont and Laroque (1973), and by Grandmont and Hildenbrand (1974).

The analysis was restricted here to point expectations and certain endowments in order to simplify the exposition. It can be generalized to the case in which price forecasts take the form of probability distributions, as in Grandmont (1974), and in which exogenous random shocks alter the traders' endowments, as in Grandmont and Hildenbrand (1974). The conditions used in these papers to get existence of a short-run equilibrium, when they are specialized to the case of point expectations, yield the assumptions stated in (1.4.1). These papers considered the simple case of all agents making plans at most one period ahead. They can be extended, without changing the economics of the arguments, to the case in which traders are planning for more than two periods and are uncertain about future prices and endowments. The only cost is to introduce more technical complexities. A short-run analysis of the same sort of model, which includes production, can be found in Sondermann (1974).

Hool (1976) studied the existence of a short-run monetary equilibrium in a model where traders are planning only one period ahead ($n_a = 2$ for

[24] For a further study of the effects of changes of the money supply by means of lump-sum transfers, the reader may consult the collective volume edited by Kareken and Wallace (1980) and the references contained there, and Hahn (1982).

all a) and in which money plays a role as a medium of exchange, by employing the methods described in this chapter. Hool shows that the assumptions of (1.4.1) can be weakened in that case, and that a short-run Walrasian monetary equilibrium does exist whenever there is a trader who owns initially a positive money balance, whose expected prices are bounced below by a positive vector ϵ for all current prices p_1, and such that the ratios of expected prices to current prices eventually become less than the trader's marginal rates of substitution between future and current consumption at the trader's endowment point when current prices p_1 go to infinity. These are precisely the sort of conditions used in our heuristic discussion of the short-run regulating mechanisms in Section 1.4 for the case of a single good (see in particular footnote 7, above). Hool's assumptions rule out unit elastic price expectations – contrary to what the author mistakenly claims – and are there to ensure the presence of a stabilizing and strong intertemporal substitution effect.

Grandmont and Younès (1972, 1973) used the methods of this chapter to analyze a model of outside money in a certain environment where the traders may face liquidity constraints on their transactions, within each period, that are due to the role of money as a medium of exchange, and where they have an infinite planning horizon. The authors study in addition, within that framework, Friedman's theory of the "optimum quantity theory of money" (1969, Chapter 1). They show in particular that deterministic changes of the rate of growth of the money supply, through lump-sum transfers, do affect real equilibrium magnitudes whenever the liquidity constraints that the agents face on their transactions within each period are binding (this effect is known in the literature as the "shoe-leather effect"). On this point, the reader may also consult Niehans (1978). For an extension of the model to the case of uncertainty, see Lucas (1980).

Suggested reading

Archibald, G. C. and R. G. Lipsey, "Monetary and Value Theory: A Critique of Lange and Patinkin," *Review of Economic Studies 26* (1958), 1–22.

Barro, R. J., "Are Government Bonds Net Wealth?", *Journal of Political Economy 82* (1974), 1095–1117.

Friedman, M., *The Optimum Quantity of Money*, Aldine, Chicago, 1969, Chaps. 1 and 5.

Grandmont, J. M., "On the Short Run Equilibrium in a Monetary Economy," in J. Dreze (ed.), *Allocation Under Uncertainty, Equilibrium and Optimality*, Macmillan, New York, 1974.

Grandmont, J. M. and Y. Younès, "On the Role of Money and the Existence of a Monetary Equilibrium," *Review of Economic Studies 39* (1972), 355–72.

"On the Efficiency of a Monetary Equilibrium," *Review of Economic Studies 40* (1973), 149–65.

Hahn, F. H., *Money and Inflation*, Blackwell Publisher, Oxford, 1982.

Hicks, J. R., *Value and Capital*, 2nd ed., Oxford University Press, London, 1946, Chaps. 9, 20, and additional note B.

Lange, O., *Price Flexibility and Employment*, Cowles Commission, 1945, Chaps. 1–5.

Patinkin, D., *Money Interest, and Prices*, 2nd ed., Harper & Row, New York, 1965, Chaps 2, 3, and 8.

Samuelson, P. A., "What Classical and Neoclassical Monetary Theory Really Was," *Canadian Journal of Economics 1* (1968), 1–15.

Tobin, J., *Asset Accumulation and Economic Activity*, Yrjö Jahnsson Lectures, Blackwell Publisher, Oxford, 1980, Chap. 3.

CHAPTER 2

Money and credit in the short run

The previous chapter examined an economy in which consumers were constrained to hold nonnegative money balances. The only ways for the Government to alter the money stock were either to engage in fiscal policy by making positive or negative money transfers to the private sector – that type of policy was briefly considered at the end of the chapter – or to trade on the consumption goods markets. That sort of money is often called *outside money* in the literature.

We will now introduce to the model the possibility for consumers to borrow against future income by selling *short-term* bonds to a governmental agency, called the "Bank." Since there is money creation whenever the Bank grants loans by buying bonds from the consumers, the money stock can then vary over time according to the needs of the economy, through the extension of credit.

A useful distinction between "inside" and "outside" money is often developed in credit money economies of this type.[1] The part of the money stock that is "backed" by the Bank's claims on the private sector – that is, that has been issued by the Bank when purchasing consumers' bonds – is called *inside money*. Outside money is not backed by private debts.

Our primary concern in the present chapter will be the study of the economic forces that may bring the markets of such an economy into equilibrium in the short run. The analysis will take into account the fact that the Bank may try to influence economic activity through a deliberate monetary policy on the bond market. Two specific policies will be considered: the case in which the Bank pegs the interest rate that is charged

---

[1] The distinction has been introduced by Gurley and Shaw (1960).

on loans at some given level; and the case in which the Bank seeks to control the money supply, that is, the amount of money that it creates when buying bonds from the private sector.

Neoclassical theorists were faced with serious difficulties when attempting to deal with this problem. There are, according to this viewpoint, two main equilibrating mechanisms in such an economy.

The first, the real balance effect, is generated by a change of the current money prices of goods, the interest rate being given. It is defined in such a context as the consequences upon a trader's demand for goods that results from the change of the "real value" of the trader's initial money stock or debt. According to the neoclassical school, it is this mechanism that is supposed to bring the economy into equilibrium when the Bank pegs the interest rate at a given level.

The real balance effect works in opposite directions for a creditor, who initially holds a positive money balance, and for a debtor, who holds a negative one. Its consequences upon aggregate demand are therefore ambiguous. Neoclassical theorists nevertheless claimed that the real balance effect was an operational regulating mechanism as long as outside money was positive, and that the Bank could then peg the interest rate at any level, i.e., that it had full control over this variable in the short run. The empirical relevance of this claim has been seriously disputed, however, on the ground that a great part of the money stock usually has a direct or indirect counterpart in private debts, so that one would need quite large variations of money prices to make the real balance effect operational.

The other equilibrating mechanism considered by neoclassical theorists is generated by a variation of the nominal interest rate, the current money prices of goods being fixed. This variation is assumed to induce a *substitution* between current and future goods by modifying every trader's optimum consumption savings ratio. According to the neoclassical viewpoint, this mechanism together with the real balance effect enables the Bank to exercise a control in the short run over the money supply by manipulating the nominal interest rate. The empirical relevance of this conclusion has also been seriously disputed, as many economists believe that a modification of the nominal rate of interest has little effect in the short run upon aggregate demand in actual economies.

These issues have generated important disputes among theorists, which do not yet appear to have been resolved. The purpose of the present chapter is to take a fresh look at the problem, by using the methods that were developed in the first chapter. Here again, our main finding will be that neoclassical monetary models may be inconsistent, owing to the short-run rigidities of the traders' expected "real interest rates" which that sort of model involves. As a matter of fact, the situation in a credit money economy will be found to be much worse than in the pure outside money case studied in Chapter 1, in the sense that the range of circumstances under which a short-run monetary equilibrium does not exist is much more important. At the root of the phenomenon is the fact that, when borrowing is allowed, even a small group of traders can "destabilize" the whole market if their expected real interest rates are very low. For they may be led then to borrow a lot from the Bank, and by spending the money borrowed on current goods, to generate an excess demand on the corresponding markets at all current prices and nominal interest rates. In that case, a short-run equilibrium in which money has positive value cannot exist, no matter which policy the Bank chooses to implement. The conclusion that will emerge from our analysis therefore will be that *the market's "invisible hand" is even more likely to go astray in a credit money economy than in the pure outside money case of the previous chapter.*

The second issue we shall be concerned with is the possibility of the Bank influencing the money supply, or, more generally, economic activity in the short run. Our conclusion will be that even in the favorable case in which there is a short-run monetary equilibrium for each nominal interest rate – that is, in which the Bank can fully control this variable – the Bank may have little influence on the money supply or on equilibrium prices of goods. Such a circumstance will occur whenever a rise of the nomimal interest rate is offset, partially or completely, by a correlative increase of the traders' expected rates of inflation, so that their expected real interest rates are left more or less invariant. Such a case is thus not unlikely to be observed in actual economies. *The ability of monetary policy to influence in the short run, by means of a variation of the nominal interest rate, the amount of money created when granting loans to the private sector, accordingly appears somewhat dubious.*

A corollary of the analysis will be that, if one wishes to ensure that the Bank can manipulate without bound either the nominal interest rate or the money supply through the extension of credit – in the sense that a short-run monetary equilibrium corresponding to each Bank's policy does exist – one has to appeal here again to a short-run regulating mechanism neglected by neoclassical theorists, namely to the variations of the traders' expected real interest rates and their associated intertemporal substitution effects. This will require, in the same spirit as in Chapter 1, that the traders' expectations display some insensitiveness to the changes of currently observed prices and nominal interest rates. But the conditions needed for a credit money economy will be found to be much more restrictive than for an outside money economy. In particular, *all traders' expectations will have to be insensitive to large increases of current prices*, whereas only one "insensitive trader" was needed in the preceding chapter. It goes without saying that such conditions on anticipations are hardly to be expected to prevail in actual economies.

The other issue with which we shall be concerned is the neutrality of money in the present context. We shall show, using the methods of the previous chapter, that a publicly announced scalar change of all traders' initial money balances and debts, and of the amount of money created by the Bank through its credit operations, is neutral in the short run whenever the traders believe in its neutrality. Monetary policy, however, usually does not work that way, since the banking institutions' interventions on credit markets aim at changing the amount of money created through loans to the private sector *without altering the traders' initial money balances and debts*. Our analysis, as we said, will cast some doubt upon the Bank's ability to significantly manipulate the money supply in such a way. But it will be shown that any change of the money creation engineered solely through the Bank's credit operations does produce short-run real effects – whenever such a change can actually be implemented.

The chapter is organized as follows. Section 2.1 describes the institutional setup of the model, and Section 2.2 gives a brief account of the neoclassical views about the short-run determination of prices and of the nominal interest rate in our framework. The consumers' short-run demand and supply functions are derived in Section 2.3 from an explicit intertemporal decision-making problem. Section 2.4 explores the case where the Bank pegs the nominal rate of interest at some arbitrary level, and Section 2.5, the case in which the Bank attempts to control the money supply. Finally, the neutrality of monetary policy in this context is examined in Section 2.6.

2.1   Structure of the model

The real part of the model is the same as in the preceding chapter. There are accordingly l nonstorable consumption goods available in each period, whose (positive) equilibrium money prices $p = (p_1, \ldots, p_l)$ are to be determined by the market at every date.

The monetary part of the model differs somewhat, since a government agency is introduced that performs some of the usual functions of a bank. Money takes the form of bank deposits, which may or may not bear interest. Consumers have thus the opportunity to save at each date by keeping a positive money balance at their bank account. The other roles of the Bank are to grant short-term loans to consumers and to receive repayments in money of their past debts. Consumers can thus borrow against future income by selling short-term bonds to the Bank, a unit of bond being a promise made by the issuer to pay back one unit of money one period later. At each date, the money price s of these bonds determines the nominal borrowing interest rate r by the relation $s = 1/(1 + r)$. The Bank is supposed to follow a "competitive" policy, i.e., to maintain equality in every period between the interest rate paid on deposits and the borrowing rate. Since the money price of bonds must be finite, the interest rate must exceed -1 in every period. In this highly stylized model, in which money takes *only* the form of bank deposits on which a negative interest rate can be paid, this is in fact the only constraint that restricts the rate of interest.[2]

It is assumed, for the sake of simplicity, that the Government intervenes in no other way than through its Banking Department, as described above. In particular, there are no government purchases or sales of goods, and no transfer payments such as taxes or subsidies.

The transactions patterns in such an economy can be described as follows. In any period, consumers exchange among themselves their exogenously given endowments of goods. Payments of the purchases are made by transferring the corresponding amounts of money from the buyers' accounts to the sellers' accounts within the Bank. On the other hand, those consumers who wish to borrow sell short-term bonds to the Bank, and receive money in exchange. The monetary counterparts of these transactions, together with the reimbursements made by the consumers who are initially debtors, determine the consumers' money holdings at the end of the period.

Our main concern in this chapter will be the study, in this framework, of the short-run determination of equilibrium prices and of the interest rate at some date, say date 1, or the "current period." The Bank may try to influence the equilibrium position by varying the interest rate or its money supply. Our study will be carried out, therefore, subject to the short-run policy that the Bank wishes to implement on the credit market.

---

[2] If there were an additional sort of money, namely, paper money, on which the interest rate is by definition 0 as is the case in actual economies, an additional constraint would appear, since the interest rate should then be nonnegative under the assumption of full convertibility of the two sorts of money. Indeed, if the interest rate were negative, the consumers could make unlimited profits by borrowing from the Bank and keeping the proceeds in the form of paper money. If the interest rate paid on deposits is positive the consumers' money holdings will take only the form of bank deposits. If the interest rate is zero, paper money and deposits are perfect substitutes. The model studied in this chapter therefore applies directly to such a specification, with the only additional restriction that the interest rate cannot be negative.

Two specific policies will be considered: one in which the Bank seeks to peg the nominal interest rate, and another in which the Bank tries to control the amount of money it creates when granting loans to consumers.

In order to proceed to such a study, one must specify the short-run characteristics of every consumer a living at the date under consideration. The consumers' short-run "real" characteristics are, as in Section 1.2 of Chapter 1, the length n_a of their remaining lifetimes, their preferences u_a among consumption streams, and their endowments of goods e_{at}, for $t = 1, \ldots, n_a$.

The following two assumptions are made throughout this chapter. They are the same as assumptions (a) and (b) of Section 1.2.

(a) *The utility function* u_a *is continuous, increasing, and strictly quasi-concave, for every* a;

(b) *All components of the endowment vectors,* e_{at}, *are positive for every* a *and* t.

The other characteristics of a consumer are his money stock $\bar{m}_a \geqq 0$ at the beginning of the period, which is supposed to include any interest payment, and the amount of the money he initially owes to the Bank, $\bar{b}_a \geqq 0$, which is equal to the number of bonds he supplied at the preceding date. One can assume without loss of generality that either $\bar{m}_a = 0$ or $\bar{b}_a = 0$, and summarize this information by looking at the consumer's "initial net credit position" $\bar{\mu}_a = \bar{m}_a - \bar{b}_a$, which is positive in the case of a creditor, and negative otherwise. The *initial aggregate money stock M* is then, by definition, equal to $\Sigma_a \bar{m}_a$, while the *initial value of outside money* is described by the economy's "aggregate net credit position," that is, $\Sigma_a \bar{\mu}_a$. No specific assumptions will be made about the traders' initial money holdings or debts. They can be, in particular, all equal to zero.

2.2   Neoclassical views on inside and outside money

It will be useful to begin the analysis with a brief summary of the neoclassical views about the short-run determination of equilibrium prices and of the interest rate in the present context.

Since the traders' endowments of goods are taken here as exogenous, to simplify, their decisions at date 1 can be viewed as functions of their initial net credit position $\bar{\mu}_a$, of the current prices of goods p_1 and the nominal rate r_1, and of their anticipations of future prices and interest rates. An assumption commonly made in neoclassical macroeconomic models[3] is that the traders expect prices to grow at the rate π_a and nominal

---

[3] See, e.g., Sargent (1979, Chap. 1).

interest rates to remain at their current level r_1 in the future. Moreover, according to this approach, a trader's short-run decisions are assumed to depend only on $\bar{\mu}_a$, on p_1, and on his "expected real interest rate" ρ_a – which is given by $1 + \rho_a = (1 + r_1)/(1 + \pi_a)$.

According to this viewpoint, a variation of current prices p_1, the nominal interest rate r_1 being fixed, does not alter a trader's expected rate of inflation π_a – or, equivalently, his expected real interest rate ρ_a: expected prices are assumed to move proportionally to current prices. The influence of the nominal rate r_1 on the traders' expected real interest rates is less clear in that class of models, for they do not always make precise the necessary distinction between nominal and real rates. In some specifications, the parameters π_a apparently are taken to be exogenous in the short run. A change of r_1 then indeed has an influence on the consumers' expected real interest rates. In other cases, the parameters ρ_a are apparently assumed to be exogenous, and thus unaffected by a variation of the nominal rate r_1.

Following the neoclassical approach, therefore, the decisions taken at date 1 by a typical consumer a, in the simple context under consideration, can be considered as functions of his initial net credit position $\bar{\mu}_a$, of the current money prices of goods p_1, and of the current nominal rate r_1, the last variable being included in order to capture its possible influence on the trader's expected real interest rate ρ_a. Accordingly, a typical trader's vector of excess demands for goods will be written $z_a(p_1, r_1, \bar{\mu}_a)$ and his demand for money and his supply of bonds will be denoted $m_a^d(p_1, r_1, \bar{\mu}_a)$ and $b_a^s(p_1, r_1, \bar{\mu}_a)$ respectively. On the other hand, the amount of money the consumer gives back to the Bank in reimbursement of his initial debt, if any, will be denoted $R_a(p_1, r_1, \bar{\mu}_a)$. It is equal to $\bar{b}_a$ whenever the consumer succeeds in reimbursing the totality of his debt. Otherwise it may be less – for instance, when the trader is bankrupt.

Neoclassical theorists usually assume that these functions display a few simple properties. First, every consumer faces a budget constraint, which states that the value of his excess demand for goods plus his final money holding should be financed either out of his initial money holding $\bar{m}_a$ (net of any reimbursement to the Bank) or from the proceeds of the sale of bonds. Formally,

$$p_1 z_a(\cdot) + m_a^d(\cdot) = \bar{m}_a - R_a(\cdot) + b_a^s(\cdot)/(1 + r_1)$$

for every p_1 and r_1, where the symbol $(\cdot)$ stands for $(p_1, r_1, \bar{\mu}_a)$. As we shall see, these identities imply that the economic system should satisfy Walras's Law.

Second, neoclassical theorists assume that *the excess demand functions* z_a *are homogenous of degree 0 in* $(p_1, \bar{\mu}_a)$, *and that the functions* m_a^d, b_a^s

and R_a *are homogenous of degree 1 in the same variables.* The traditional argument to justify these assumptions in neoclassical macroeconomic models is that a scalar change of current prices p_1 generates a proportional variation of expected prices, leaving current and expected nominal interest rates unchanged. Thus if the initial net credit position $\bar{\mu}_a$ moves proportionally to current prices, the trader's "real" opportunities, hence his "real" behavior, must not change.

In order to formulate the conditions that describe the equilibrium of all markets at date 1, it is convenient to introduce the following notation for the aggregate demand and supply functions:

$$Z(p_1, r_1) = \sum_a z_a(p_1, r_1, \bar{\mu}_a) \qquad M^d(p_1, r_1) = \sum_a m_a^d(p_1, r_1, \bar{\mu}_a)$$

$$B^s(p_1, r_1) = \sum_a b_a^s(p_1, r_1, \bar{\mu}_a) \qquad R(p_1, r_1) = \sum_a R_a(p_1, r_1, \bar{\mu}_a)$$

where the influence of the trader's initial net credit positions $\bar{\mu}_a$ is kept implicit, for notional simplicity.

Equilibrium of the goods markets requires that aggregate excess demands for goods should be zero:

(2.2.C) $\quad Z(p_1, r_1) = 0$

The Bank's net money supply is equal to the amount of money created through the bonds purchases, say ΔM, minus the money paid back to the Bank in reimbursement of past debts, i.e., $R(p_1, r_1)$. The equilibrium condition for money, then, is that the aggregate demand for money must be equal to the initial aggregate money stock M, plus the Bank's net money supply. If we momentarily take the creation of money ΔM as a given parameter, this yields:

(2.2.D) $\quad M^d(p_1, r_1) = M + \Delta M - R(p_1, r_1)$

With this notation, the Bank's demand for bonds is given by $(1 + r_1)\Delta M$. Equilibrium of the bond market then requires that this expression should be equal to the consumers' aggregate bond supply:

(2.2.E) $\quad (1 + r_1)\Delta M = B^s(p_1, r_1)$

These equations make clear how the money stock adapts itself to the needs of the economy through the variations of the amount of credit distributed. They also have interesting implications concerning the evolution of outside money over time. If one eliminates the money creation ΔM between (2.2.D) and (2.2.E), one gets:

(2.2.D$_1$) $\quad M^d(p_1, r_1) = M + B^s(p_1, r_1)/(1 + r_1) - R(p_1, r_1)$

Note that the expression $M^d(p_1, r_1) - B^s(p_1, r_1)/(1 + r_1)$ represents the value of outside money at the end of the period, before any interest payment. Equation (2.2.D$_1$) implies that this expression must be equal, in equilibrium, to $M - R(p_1,r_1)$, or equivalently, to the sum of the initial value of outside money, $\Sigma_a \bar{\mu}_a$, and of the extent of bankruptcy, i.e., $\Sigma_a \bar{b}_a - R(p_1,r_1)$. Outside money increases within the period by the extent of bankruptcy, which can be interpreted as the Bank's "deficit" in the period under consideration. If on the other hand one considers the value of outside money at the beginning of the next date, which includes interest payments and is thus equal to $(1 + r_1)M^d(p_1,r_1) - B^s(p_1,r_1)$, one sees that outside money must grow from date 1 to date 2, at a rate equal to the short-term interest rate r_1.

It is useful to see, as an incidental remark, how equation (2.2.D$_1$) is modified when we allow the Government to be active on the goods markets and/or to levy taxes and pay subsidies to consumers – for instance, through a separate treasury department. The value of this new department's deficit (the money value of its net purchases of goods, minus net tax receipts) then has to be covered by an issue of money $\Delta\mu$, which must appear on the right-hand side of (2.2.D$_1$) as part of the Government's net supply of money. The increase of outside money from the beginning to the end of the market process at date 1 is then equal to the sum of the extent of bankruptcy and of $\Delta\mu$, that is, to the "deficit" of the Government as a whole. If one considers the additional effects of the interest rates on the growth of outside money, one can say generally, therefore, that outside money at any point of time is equal to the cumulative sum of the past global deficits of the Government, each deficit being compounded by the interest rates that prevailed between the period of its appearance and the date under consideration.[4]

Since consumers face a budget constraint, the system (2.2.C), (2.2.D), (2.2.E) should satisfy Walras's Law, which states that the sum of the value of excess demand over all markets is identically equal to zero:

$$p_1 Z(p_1,r_1) + [M^d(p_1, r_1) - M - \Delta M + R(p_1,r_1)]$$
$$+ [\Delta M - B^s(p_1, r_1)/(1 + r_1)] = 0$$

for every p_1 and r_1. This identity implies as usual that one of the equations may be "eliminated" when studying the equilibrium of the system. There are, therefore, at most $(l + 1)$ independent equations to determine the $(l + 2)$ unknown parameters of the system, namely, p_1, r_1 and ΔM.

---

[4] A *negative* value of initial outside money at date 1 is thus conceivable. This would mean that the Government ran an overall surplus prior to that date, e.g., by levying taxes from consumers. In such a case, the assumption that the Government does not intervene on the goods markets and that it is inactive on the fiscal side, applies, strictly speaking, only to the current period and those following.

The Bank can thus hope a priori to be able to influence the equilibrium position of the economy at date 1 by choosing a short-run monetary policy on the credit market, that is, by specifying how its money creation ΔM varies with current economic observables, e.g., the current prices system p_1 and the current rate of interest r_1. There are evidently infinitely many ways to do this. Two particular and important policies will be considered in this chapter. In the first case, the Bank will peg the interest rate at an arbitrary level r_1, and let its money supply adapt itself so as to equilibrate the credit market. In the other case, the Bank will fix its money creation ΔM at given level, and leave the interest rate r_1 free to vary.

Pegging the interest rate

Let us first consider the case in which the Bank fixes the nominal interest rate at an arbitrary level r_1. Since the Bank pegs the interest rate, its credit supply is assumed to be infinitely elastic: all the bonds supplied by consumers are automatically bought by the Bank. The money creation ΔM is then endogenous, and is in fact defined by the bond-market equation (2.2.E) as a function of the current prices of goods p_1. Replacing ΔM by this expression in (2.2.D) shows that the short-run equilibrium prices associated with this policy are given by the equations (2.2.C) and (2.2.D$_1$), where the rate of interest r_1 is fixed.

Equations (2.2.C) and (2.2.D$_1$) explain, according to neoclassical theorists, the short-run determination of equilibrium prices when the Bank pegs the rate of interest. Their postulates imply that these equations should display the following properties.

As we have seen, the system satisfies Walras's Law, which reads here:

$$p_1 Z(p_1, r_1) + M^d(p_1, r_1) = M + B^s(p_1, r_1)/(1 + r_1) - R(p_1, r_1)$$

for every p_1. By now a familiar argument, this identity implies that the classical dichotomy between the real and the money sectors is invalid in the short run, since any solution of (2.2.C) satisfies (2.2.D$_1$) as well.

The homogeneity properties of short-run demand and supplies assumed by neoclassical theorists, imply that multiplying all initial net credit positions $\bar{\mu}_a$ by a positive number λ is neutral, in the sense that it multiplies by the same factor the level of equilibrium money prices, but leaves unaltered equilibrium relative prices and real quantities. This is the old quantity theory, reformulated in the present context so as to apply to the short period.

More importantly, these homogeneity postulates imply that the main short-run regulating mechanism, when the Bank pegs the rate of interest, is the real balance effect. To see this point, it is most convenient to ignore the complications arising from modifications of relative prices, or alternatively to consider the simple macroeconomic case in which there is only one good ($l - 1$). Equations (2.2.C) and (2.2.D$_1$) are then equivalent, and one can focus the attention on the good market alone.

In that case, each trader's excess demand for the good can be written $z_a(1, r_1, \bar{\mu}_a/p_1)$. The interest rate being fixed, movements of the current price p_1 affect the trader's desired consumption only through their influence on his initial real balance $\bar{\mu}_a/p_1$. An increase of p_1 is thus likely to yield a decrease of the trader's desired consumption in the case of a creditor, since $\bar{\mu}_a$ is then positive. It has the opposite consequence in the case of a debtor, i.e., when $\bar{\mu}_a$ is negative. Variations of p_1 have no influence when $\bar{\mu}_a = 0$.

The consequence upon aggregate consumption of current price variations through the real balance effect are thus ambiguous, since it depends on the relative magnitudes of the creditors' and the debtors' marginal propensities to consume out of real wealth (the derivatives of the functions z_a with respect to $\bar{\mu}_a/p_1$) and on the sizes and the distribution among traders of their initial net monetary wealths $\bar{\mu}_a$.

Most theorists, however, following the tradition set up by Pigou, Patinkin, and others, have deliberately ignored such distributional effects, and have focused their attention on the response of aggregate demand to changes in the community's aggregate real net wealth as the main equilibrating mechanism of a credit money economy. In our context, this viewpoint amounts to saying that aggregate excess demand in (2.2.C) behaves qualitatively, when the interest rate is given, as if it depended solely on the real value of outside money, $\Sigma_a \bar{\mu}_a/p_1$. Many theorists (Hicks, Patinkin, Johnson) accordingly were led to the apparently natural conclusion that the real balance effect is an operational equilibrating mechanism in the case where outside money is positive. Indeed, according to this line of thought, aggregate excess demand in (2.2.C) is inversely related to p_1 if the good is not inferior. Moreover, the community's real net wealth $\Sigma_a \bar{\mu}_a/p_1$ is large when p_1 is low, which should lead to an aggregate excess demand on the good market. Conversely, aggregate real net wealth is low for large prices, in which case an excess supply for the good should appear. By continuity, an equilibrium should exist in between, and moreover, such an equilibrium position should be stable in any *tâtonnement* process in which prices respond positively to excess demand. The proposition that the levels of money prices are indeterminate in a "pure" inside money economy, i.e., when outside money $\Sigma_a \bar{\mu}_a$ is zero, which seems to be an immediate consequence of this sort of analysis, dates back at least to Wicksell and appears in much of the literature.[5]

The theoretical and empirical relevance of the real balance effect in a credit money economy has been and remains on the front lines of the battle between Keynesian and neoclassical economists. Part of Keynes's theoretical work can be (and has been) regarded as an attack on the widespread belief that built-in stabilizers exist in a competitive monetary economy with flexible prices, which would automatically eliminate excess supplies or demands without any government intervention. The traditional neoclassical answer, first stated by Pigou and developed by Patinkin and others, has been that the real balance effect as described above indeed provides such an automatic stabilizer.

This claim appears to be acknowledged as a valid theoretical proposition by many theorists today. Its empirical relevance, however, has been seriously disputed by Keynesian economists on the basis that outside money is usually a small part of the money stock, so that one would need large price variations in order to make the real effect operational. Many contemporary theorists believe that the real balance effect is usually so weak in practice that it can be neglected.

A few dissenting voices question the theoretical validity of the neo-classical position as well, by remarking that the elimination of distribution effects involved in the "cancelling out" of private money holdings and debts may be quite misleading. As early as in the 1930s, Irving Fisher insisted on the increasing burden that a price decline imposed upon debtors, and concluded that deflation was likely to weaken aggregate demand. Quite recently, James Tobin developed the same kind of arguments, on the grounds that the largest part of private monetary assets has a direct or indirect counterpart in private debts, and that the marginal propensities to consume out of wealth are probably greater for debtors than for creditors.[6] In such circumstances, a price increase is likely to yield an increase of aggregate demand, and conversely. The real balance effect in that

---

[5] A few theorists (e.g., Pesek and Saving) claimed that the whole money stock (here $M = \Sigma_a \bar{m}_a$), or at least a positive fraction of it, should be counted as part of the economy's private net wealth, on the basis that money renders services of social value by facilitating exchanges. For these economists, the real balance effect is an operational regulating mechanism (as long as the money stock is positive), independently of the value of outside money. This position, however, does not seem to have been generally accepted by the profession – see, e.g., Patinkin (1972, Chap. 9) or Crouch (1972, pp. 135 or 378) – although one can find some traces of it even in recent writings or textbooks.

[6] See J. Tobin (1980, Chap. 1, especially pp. 9–11) and the references to I. Fisher therein.

case appears to be an automatic destabilizer, in contradiction to what neoclassical theorists claim.

Controlling the money supply

The preceding discussion concerned the case of the Bank pegging the interest rate at some arbitrary level r_1. We will now consider what neoclassical theory has to say about the case of the Bank seeking to control the money supply by fixing a priori the amount it creates by granting loans to consumers at an arbitrary level $\Delta M > 0$. The interest rate r_1 is then free to vary, together with the money prices of goods p_1, in order to equilibrate the markets at date 1.

The equations that determine the equilibrium values of p_1 and r_1 are thus given by the market-clearing conditions (2.2.C), (2.2.D), and (2.2.E), where the Bank's money creation $\Delta M > 0$ is fixed exogenously.

As we have seen, this system of equations satisfies Walras's Law: the sum across all markets of the money values of excess demands is zero for all p_1 and r_1. As a consequence, if equilibrium of all markets but one is achieved, the remaining market is in equilibrium as well. On the other hand, the homogeneity properties of short-run demands and supplies that neoclassical theorists assume, imply that an equiproportionate change of all initial net credit positions $\bar{\mu}_a$ *and of the money supply* ΔM multiplies all equilibrium money prices by the same factor, but leaves equilibrium "real" quantities such as relative prices, and the nominal interest rate, unchanged. This is quantity theory once again, reformulated so as to apply to the short run in the present context.[7]

An important issue is to know whether the foregoing system of equations has a solution for a given ΔM, for it conditions the Bank's ability to control the money supply. In our framework, where the banking sector is wholly in the hands of the Government, neoclassical monetary theory gives an affirmative answer to this question, since many economists of this school claim that monetary authorities can always control the quantity of their own liabilities.[8]

In order to uncover the regulating mechanisms that such a claim presupposes, it is convenient to proceed in two steps by first considering the real, and then the money, sectors of the model.

Let us first "solve" for p_1 the equilibrium condition (2.2.C) for the goods markets, given the interest rate r_1. One can then in such a way

---

[7] By contrast, a change of the money supply ΔM *alone*, the $\bar{\mu}_a$ values being fixed, would have "real" effects, according to this line of thought.

[8] See, e.g., Friedman (1969, Chap. 5). There has been some dispute concerning a central bank's ability to control the money supply by manipulating the quantity

associate to every r_1 the amount of money the consumers wish to borrow from the Bank at the corresponding solution of (2.2.C), i.e., $B^s(p_1,r_1)/1 + r_1$).[9] Equilibrium of bond market will be achieved if one succeeds in finding a value of r_1^* such that this expression is equal to the Bank's money supply ΔM. By Walras's Law, the interest rate r_1^*, together with the corresponding solution p_1^* of (2.2.C), will then bring the whole system into equilibrium.

This way of looking at the problem makes clear that the existence of a solution to (2.2.C), (2.2.D), and (2.2.E) depends, according to the neoclassical viewpoint, on the presence and the intensity of two regulating mechanisms. Solving (2.2.C) in p_1 for a given r_1 is in fact equivalent to finding the equilibrium prices of goods that would arise if the Bank chose to peg the interest rate at this level. We have seen that, at this stage, the essential regulating mechanism, for neoclassical theorists, is the real balance effect generated by a change of the current prices of goods. The other mechanism comes into play in the second phase of the procedure, when the nominal interest rate is made to vary. What is needed here is that a change of the *nominal* rate r_1 causes a significant modification of the traders' expected *real* interest rates, in the same direction, so as to generate a sizeable substitution between current and future consumption, by altering the consumers' desired consumption savings ratio. In that case, large nominal interest rates would be associated with large real rates and should thus discourage borrowers. The amount of money the consumers would like to borrow at such interest rates would then be lower than the Bank's money supply ΔM. Symmetrically, a low nominal interest rate would reduce the real cost of credit, and would incite consumers to borrow a lot. By continuity, one could then, by varying the nominal interest rate, equate the amount of money the consumers wish to borrow from the Bank with the given money supply ΔM, and thus bring the whole system into equilibrium. As the argument does not depend upon the value taken by ΔM, the Bank would then in fact have, according to this viewpoint, full control over the money supply.

The neoclassical argument rests essentially in the present context, therefore, upon the presence and intensity of the real balance effect, which is generated by a variation of the current prices of goods; and upon the intertemporal substitution effect, which is caused by a change

of its own liabilities (sometimes called "base money"), or reserve requirements, in the presence of commercial banks. This dispute is not relevant here, since there is no private banking sector in the model.

[9] We ignore in this heuristic discussion the complications arising from the possible existence of multiple solutions of (2.2.C) for a given value of the interest rate.

of the nominal interest rate. We gave already a brief account of the
controversies concerning the theoretical and empirical relevance of the
real balance effect. The impact of a variation of the nominal interest rate
upon the demand for credit has also generated numerous controversies.
A significant number of economists doubt that changing the nominal rate
has an important influence upon expected real interest rates, and thus on
the desired amount of borrowing in the short run. For these economists,
the ability of monetary authorities to control the money supply through
a variation of the nominal cost of credit is rather limited.

This brief (and somewhat oversimplified) review shows that the literature
on the subject is a little confusing, as one is faced by a number of
conflicting theoretical statements concerning the mechanisms at work in
a credit money economy. Although a great deal of work has been done,
a precise integration of money and value theory in an economy involving
inside and outside money is still badly needed. The goal of the remainder
of this chapter is to make progress in that direction.

2.3   Short-run demand and supply functions

The purpose of the present section is to derive precisely the behavior of
consumers in the short run from an explicit analysis of the intertemporal
choices they have to make. Let us go back to the simple institutional
framework described in Section 2.1, and consider a typical consumer
(we drop his index a for convenience), who observes in the current period
a price system p_1 and an interest rate equal to r_1, and who expects the
price system p_t and the interest rates r_t to prevail in the future, for $t =
2, \ldots , n$.

This trader must choose his current consumption $c_1 \geqq 0$, his money
balance $m_1 \geqq 0$, his supply of short-term bonds $b_1 \geqq 0$, and the amount
of money $R_1 \geqq 0$ that he gives back to the Bank in reimbursement of his
initial debt $\bar{b}$, if any. The consumer also has to plan the same quantities
c_t, m_t, b_t, and R_t for every future period $t = 2, \ldots , n$. The trader's
choices must satisfy the current and expected budget constraints:

$$p_1 c_1 + m_1 - b_1/(1+r_1) = p_1 e_1 + \bar{m} - R_1$$

and

$$p_t c_t + m_t - b_t/(1+r_t) = p_t e_t + m_{t-1}(1+r_{t-1}) - R_t$$

for every $t = 2, \ldots , n$

The borrowing and the lending rates being equal at every date, the
consumer cares in fact only for his net credit position at the Bank in

every period, which is equal to $\mu_t = m_t - b_t/(1+r_t)$ before interest payment. One can therefore specify, without any loss of generality, that the trader is either a creditor or a debtor but not both at each date; or equivalently, that either m_t or b_t is equal to zero for every t. Moreover, it will be assumed that a consumer is never allowed to borrow in the last period of his life. This constraint will be expressed by the condition $b_n = 0$, or equivalently, $\mu_n \geqq 0$.

In order to focus on the essentials, we shall adopt here a set of assumptions concerning a consumer's behavior toward bankruptcy that is as simple as possible.[10] The underlying idea is that there are heavy extra economic penalties associated with bankruptcy, which, for simplicity, will be left unspecified. Accordingly, it will be assumed that in order to avoid these penalties, a consumer never plans to be bankrupt in the future,[11] and that he seeks to reimburse in the current period as much as possible of his initial debt.

The first condition means that for every future date $t = 2, \ldots, n$, the planned reimbursement R_t is equal to the debt b_{t-1}. The current reimbursement R_1 is then easy to determine. The maximum amount of money that the consumer can borrow in the current period – i.e., the maximum value of $b_1/(1+r_1)$ – while avoiding the prospect of defaulting in the future, is equal to the sum of the trader's discounted expected incomes, i.e., to $\Sigma_2^n \beta_t p_t e_t$, where the discount factors β_t are equal to $1/[(1+r_1) \ldots (1+r_{t-1})]$. The maximum amount of cash that is potentially available to the consumer at date 1 is thus given by $\bar{m} + \Sigma_1^n \beta_t p_t e_t$, where by convention $\beta_1 = 1$. When this expression is greater than or equal to the consumer's initial debt $\bar{b}$, his reimbursement to the Bank R_1 is equal to $\bar{b}$. Otherwise, the trader is bankrupt, and R_1 is equal to $\bar{m} + \Sigma_1^n \beta_t p_t e_t$.

These conditions completely specify the constraints under which the consumer is making his choices. By using the net credit positions before interest payment $\mu_t = m_t - b_t/(1+r_t)$, the consumer's decision problem can thus be formulated as:

(2.3.I)   *Maximize* $u(c_1, \ldots, c_n)$ *with respect to* $(c_1, \ldots, c_n) \geqq 0$ *and* $(\mu_1, \ldots, \mu_n)$, *with* $\mu_n \geqq 0$, *subject to the budget constraints:*

$$p_1 c_1 + \mu_1 = p_1 e_1 + \bar{m} - R_1.$$

for $t = 2, \ldots, n$, *where the reimbursement* R_1 *is equal to the minimum of* $\bar{b}$ *and of* $\bar{m} + \Sigma_1^n \beta_t p_t e_t$

[10] The issue of bankruptcy is a complex one, which would necessitate a study on its own. To go deeper into this question would lead us too far from our main argument.

[11] This does not preclude, of course, the possibility that the consumer actually will be bankrupt in the future if his expectations are falsified.

The consumer's choices that arise from (2.3.I) can in fact be obtained very simply by using the following procedure. Let us add the trader's budget constraints, the constraint of period t being multiplied by the discount factor β_t. Taking into account the condition $\mu_n \geqq 0$, this yields:

$$\Sigma_1^n \beta_t p_t c_t \leqq \bar{m} + \Sigma_1^n \beta_t p_t e_t - R_1$$

or equivalently:

$$(*) \quad \Sigma_1^n \beta_t p_t c_t \leqq \mathrm{Max}(\bar{\mu} + \Sigma_1^n \beta_t p_t e_t, 0)$$

Maximizing the utility function u under the intertemporal budget constraint (*) determines the trader's optimal current and future consumptions $c_1, \ldots, c_n$. The corresponding demand for money m_1 and the amount of money borrowed $b_1/(1 + r_1)$ are then deduced from the current budget constraint:

$$\mu_1 = m_1 - b_1/(1 + r_1) = \bar{m} - R_1 - p_1(c_1 - e_1)$$

together with the condition that either m_1 or b_1 is equal to zero. The optimum values of m_t and $b_t/(1 + r_t)$ are finally obtained recursively from the future budget constraints.

The procedure makes clear that (2.3.I) has a solution, which is then unique, if and only if current and expected prices are positive and current and expected interest rates exceed -1. More significantly, *the consumer's current excess demands for goods* $c_1 - e_1$, *his demand for money* m_1, *the amount of money borrowed* $b_1/(1 + r_1)$, *and the reimbursement* R_1, *which arise from (2.3.I), depend only upon the initial net credit position* $\bar{\mu}$, *on current prices* p_1, *and on the discounted expected prices* $\beta_2 p_2, \ldots, \beta_n p_n$.

This statement is the analog of an assumption often made in the macroeconomic literature, namely, that a consumer's behavior depends only on current prices and on his expected real rate of interest. In order to see this point, let us specialize the model to the case in which there is only one good, and in which a consumer expects a constant rate of inflation π as well as a constant rate of interest r_1 for the future ($p_t = (1 + \pi)^{t-1} p_1$, and $r_t = r_1$ for $t = 2, \ldots, n$). Discounted expected prices are then equal to $p_1/(1 + \rho)^{t-1}$, where the expected real interest rate ρ is given by $1 + \rho = (1 + r_1)/(1 + \pi)$. A consumer's short-run behavior in such a case indeed depends only on $\bar{\mu}$, on p_1, and on ρ, as announced.

The homogeneity of degree 1 of the intertemporal budget constraint (*) with respect to $\bar{\mu}$, to current and expected discounted prices, immediately yields the following absence of money illusion property:

(2.3.1) (Absence of money illusion) *The excess demands for goods* $c_1 - e_1$ *resulting from (2.3.I) are homogenous of degree 0 with respect to* $\bar{\mu}$, *and to current and expected discounted prices, p_1, $\beta_2 p_2$, . . . , $\beta_n p_n$. The associated demand for money m_1, the amount of money borrowed $b_1/(1 + r_1)$, and the reimbursement R_1 are homogenous of degree 1 in the same variables.*

In order to completely specify how a consumer's current decisions depend upon his environment, one must describe how his expectations, in fact his *discounted expected prices* $\beta_2 p_2$, . . . , $\beta_n p_n$, depend upon his information about the current state of the economy (the influence of his knowledge of past history is kept implicit, as in Chapter 1, Section 1.3). By assumption, this information consists only of the current price system p_1, and of the current interest rate r_1. Expected discounted prices will thus be written as functions of p_1 and r_1, which will take the specific form $\psi_t^*(p_1,r_1)/(1 + r_1)$ for $t = 2, . . . , n$, in order to isolate the "direct" effect of the current interest rate r_1 upon discounting.[12]

When expected discounted prices $\beta_t p_t$ are replaced in (2.3.I) by their expressions as functions of p_1 and r_1, one gets a current excess demand for goods, a demand for money, a bond supply, and a reimbursement of the initial debt that depend on $\bar{\mu}$, p_1, and r_1 only. They will be denoted respectively $z_a(p_1,r_1,\bar{\mu}_a)$, $m_a^d(p_1,r_1,\bar{\mu}_a)$, $b_a^s(p_1,r_1,\bar{\mu}_a)$, and $R_a(p_1,r_1,\bar{\mu}_a)$, finally reintroducing the index a of the consumer.

These functions are linked by the consumers' current budget constraints, which imply:

$$p_1 z_a(\cdot) + m_a^d(\cdot) = \bar{m}_a + b_a^s(\cdot)/(1+r_1) - R_a(\cdot)$$

for every p_1 and r_1, where the symbol $(\cdot)$ stands for $(p_1,r_1,\bar{\mu}_a)$. These identities will be the basis for Walras's Law.

It is interesting to see in what circumstances short-run demands and supplies display the homogeneity properties assumed in neoclassical theory, namely, the homogeneity of degree 0 of the excess demands for goods $z_a(\cdot)$ with respect to current prices p_1 and initial money wealth $\bar{\mu}_a$, and the homogeneity of degree 1 of the functions $m_a^d(\cdot)$, $b_a^s(\cdot)$, and $R_a(\cdot)$ with respect to the same variables.

In view of the absence of money illusion stated in (2.3.1), these homogeneity properties are valid if, and in general only if, expected discounted prices $\psi_{at}^*(p_1,r_1)/(1 + r_1)$ are unit elastic with respect to current prices, or more precisely, if $\psi_{at}^*(\lambda p_1,r_1) = \lambda \psi_{at}^*(p_1,r_1)$ for every p_1, λ, and t. This would be the case in particular if undiscounted expected prices were proportional to, and expected interest rates independent of, current prices p_1. It is clear, however, that this hypothesis is too specific

---

[12] $\psi_t^*(p_1,r_1)$ accordingly represents the price system the trader expects to prevail in period t, discounted back to date 2, by using the expected interest rates.

and thus unacceptable, since expectations depend not only on current prices but also on the sequence of past prices and interest rates.

It remains to discuss how changes of the current price system p_1 and of the current interest rate r_1 influence a typical consumer's demands and supplies, in particular his excess demands for goods $z_a(p_1,r_1,\bar{\mu}_a)$. To do this, we shall ignore the possible modifications of relative prices within each period, and work accordingly with the case of only one good $(l=1)$.

Consider first, say, an increase of the current price from p_1 to λp_1, with $\lambda > 1$, the interest rate r_1 (and the initial money balance $\bar{\mu}_a$) being fixed, and let us look at the induced change of the trader's excess demand for the good

$$z_a(\lambda p_1,r_1,\bar{\mu}_a) - z_a(p_1,r_1,\bar{\mu}_a)$$

This change can be broken down into two parts, as in Chapter 1, Section 1.3. The first – the real balance effect – measures the variation of the current excess demand that would occur in (2.3.I) if expected discounted prices moved proportionally to p_1 – i.e., from $\psi_{at}^*(p_1,r_1)/(1+r_1)$ to $\lambda\psi_{at}^*(p_1,r_1)/(1+r_1)$ – so as to maintain the trader's expected real interest rate constant. In view of the absence of money illusion property stated in (2.3.1), the current excess demand would vary by the same amount if $\bar{\mu}_a$ was divided by λ, and if the current price, the nominal rate, and expected prices were kept at their initial levels p_1,r_1, and $\psi_{at}^*(p_1,r_1)$. The real balance effect is thus measured by:

$$z_a(p_1,r_1,\bar{\mu}_a/\lambda) - z_a(p_1,r_1,\bar{\mu}_a)$$

If the good is not inferior, the real balance effect induces a decrease of the consumer's excess demand for the good in the case of a creditor, i.e., when $\bar{\mu}_a$ is positive. It works in the opposite direction in the case of a debtor. It has no influence upon current consumption when $\bar{\mu}_a = 0$.

The second part – in our terminology, the intertemporal substitution effect – describes the additional variation of the current excess demand that results from the modification of the trader's expected real interest rate. Or more precisely, this is the variation that results from the change of expected discounted prices from $\lambda\psi_{at}^*(p_1,r_1)/(1+r_1)$ to their true value $\psi_{at}^*(\lambda p_1,r_1)/(1+r_1)$, the current price, the nominal rate, and the initial balance being fixed at the levels $\lambda p_1,r_1$, and $\bar{\mu}_a$. The intertemporal substitution effect is measured by:

$$z_a(\lambda p_1,r_1,\bar{\mu}_a) - z_a(p_1,r_1,\bar{\mu}_a/\lambda)^{[13]}$$

[13] Here as in Chapter 1, the reader is reminded that the intertemporal substitution effect involves income or wealth effects, as well as *stricto sensu* substitution

If, for instance, expected discounted prices rise proportionally more than the current price, the consumer's expected real interest rate goes down, and the intertemporal substitution effect is likely to yield an increase of current consumption. In such circumstances, the intertemporal substitution effect counteracts the real balance effect in the case of a creditor i.e., when $\bar{\mu}_a$ is positive, and reinforces it in the case of a debtor. The important point to note at this stage is that contrary to the real balance effect, the intertemporal substitution effect works a priori in the same direction for a creditor or a debtor.

Consider next an increase of the nominal interest rate r_1, the current price p_1 (and the initial money balance $\bar{\mu}_a$) being fixed. Here too one may split the consequence of this move on the current excess demand z_a into real balance and intertemporal substitution effects. The real balance effect is defined, in the same spirit as before, as the change of the current excess demand that would obtain if expected discounted prices $\psi_{at}^*(p_1,r_1)/(1+r_1)$ moved proportionally to the current price p_1 so as to keep constant the trader's expected real interest rate; or in other words, since p_1 is invariant here, if the forecasts $\psi_{at}^*(p_1,r_1)$ moved proportionally to $(1+r_1)$. The intertemporal substitution effect is then defined as the additional variation of the current excess demand that is caused by the modification of the trader's expected real interest rate, i.e., of his expected discounted prices $\psi_{at}^*(p_1,r_1)/(1+r_1)$.

Since a trader's behavior depends only on his initial balance $\bar{\mu}_a$, and on current and expected discounted prices, the real balance effect associated with a variation of the nominal interest rate vanishes in this context.[14] A change of r_1 has an impact on current excess demand only through the intertemporal substitution effect. If, for instance, the forecasts $\psi_{at}^*(p_1,r_1)$ rise proportionally more than $(1+r_1)$, the trader's expected real interest rate goes down. The intertemporal substitution effect is then likely to favor an increase of current consumption.

We proceed now to the description of an example that permits a graphical illustration of the arguments of this section, and that will be used repeatedly in later parts of this chapter. Consider the simple macroeconomic case of only one good ($l=1$) and of a typical consumer planning only one

effects, like in the Slutsky equation. In particular, a modification of a trader's expected real interest rate obviously changes the present discounted value of his lifetime wealth.

[14] This is of course due to the fact that only short-term assets are taken into account in the particular model under consideration. A variation of the nominal short-term interest rate does not alter the value of a trader's initial money balance $\bar{\mu}_a$. The situation will be different in Chapter 4, where assets of a longer maturity will be considered.

period ahead ($n = 2$). If the current price and interest rate are p_1 and r_1, and if the consumer expects the price $p_2 = \psi^*(p_1, r_1)$ to prevail in the future, his optimum current and future consumptions are obtained, as we have seen, by maximizing the trader's utility function under the intertemporal budget constraint:

$$p_1 c_1 + [p_2/(1 + r_1)]c_2 \leqq \operatorname{Max}\{\bar{\mu} + p_1 e_1 + [p_2/(1 + r_1)]e_2, 0\}$$

The consumer's demand for money and bond supply are deduced in turn from the current budget constraint.

This maximization problem is easily represented in the plane (c_1, c_2). The intertemporal budget constraint is described by a line perpendicular to the vector of discounted prices $[p_1, p_2/(1 + r_1)]$. The slope of this vector is:

$$p_2/[(1 + r_1)p_1] = 1/(1 + \rho)$$

where ρ is by definition the consumer's expected real interest rate. The budget line passes through the points α and β of coordinates $(e_1, e_2 + [(1 + r_1)\bar{\mu}]/p_2)$ and $[e_1 + (\bar{\mu}/p_1), e_2]$ in the case of a creditor, i.e., when $\bar{\mu} \geqq 0$, and in the case of a debtor ($\bar{\mu} < 0$) who is not bankrupt, i.e., such that $\bar{\mu} + p_1 e_1 + p_2/(1 + r_1)e_2 \geqq 0$ (Figure 2.1). The budget line goes through the origin otherwise.

If on this figure the optimum consumption program falls to the right of the point β, the trader is borrowing from the Bank in the current period. One may notice an important difference from the outside money case of the first chapter – apart from the fact that initial money balances $\bar{\mu}$ are here positive or negative, and that the slope of the budget line is now determined by the nominal interest rate r_1 as well as by the ratio p_2/p_1. In Chapter 1 a trader had to face a liquidity constraint in the current period, which would here take the form $c_1 \leqq e_1 + \bar{\mu}/p_1$, and would be represented by the vertical line $\beta\gamma$. This constraint is no longer relevant in the present context, where a trader is allowed to borrow from the Bank without any limitation (compare with Figure 1.1).

The respective roles of the real balance and of the intertemporal substitution effects appear quite clearly on the figure. Consider first an increase of the current price p_1, the interest rate r_1 and $\bar{\mu}$ being unchanged. If the increase of p_1 generates a proportional increase of the expected price p_2, the trader's expected real interest rate ρ is invariant. There is a horizontal displacement of the point β toward the left in the case of a creditor, and toward the right in the case of a debtor, but the slope of the intertemporal budget line is unchanged. The consequence on the optimum consumption pattern is then the real balance effect. But if the increase of the current price p_1 causes a change of the expected price p_2 that is not proportional

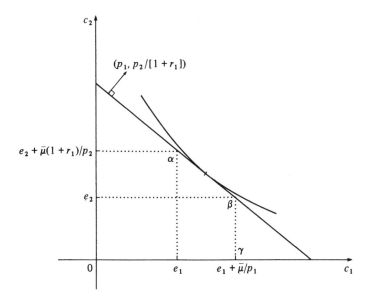

FIGURE 2.1.

to the variation of p_1, there is in addition a rotation of the budget line, since the expected real interest rate ρ is modified. This rotation generates the intertemporal substitution effect. It may weaken, or reinforce, the real balance effect.

Let us next consider the consequence of a variation of the nominal rate r_1, the current price p_1 and $\bar{\mu}_a$ being fixed. If the expected price p_2 moves proportionally to $(1 + r_1)$, the trader's expected real interest rate ρ is unchanged. The variation of the optimum consumption program is then entirely due to the real balance effect. But it vanishes here since the intertemporal budget line is in fact invariant. If the variation of r_1 causes a modification of the expected real interest rate ρ, then there is a rotation of the budget line around β, which generates the intertemporal substitution effect.

We will conclude this section by introducing a notation for aggregate demand and supply functions that will be useful in the next section. Specifically, we shall denote:

$$Z(p_1, r_1) = \sum_a z_a(p_1, r_1, \bar{\mu}_a) \qquad M^d(p_1, r_1) = \sum_a m_a^d(p_1, r_1, \bar{\mu}_a)$$

$$B^s(p_1, r_1) = \sum_a b_a^s(p_1, r_1, \bar{\mu}_a) \qquad R(p_1, r_1) = \sum_a R_a(p_1, r_1, \bar{\mu}_a)$$

where the influence of the traders' initial balances $\bar{\mu}_a$ is kept implicit, in order to ease the exposition.

Remark. It is possible to construct for every consumer, as in Chapter 1, Section 1.5, an expected utility index v, depending upon his current consumption c_1, on his current net credit position $\mu_1 = m_1 - b_1/(1+r_1)$, and on p_1 and r_1 – which, when it is maximized under the current budget constraint, yields the consumer's short-run demand and supply functions. Such an expected utility index is defined as the maximum level of utility the consumer can expect to achieve over his lifetime, when c_1 and μ_1 are given. The study of the properties of this expected utility index is left as an exercise to the reader.

2.4   Pegging the interest rate

The aim of this section is to study the short-run regulating mechanisms that may bring the economy into equilibrium at date 1, when the Bank pegs the interest rate at some given value r_1.

It is quite easy to write down the equations that the corresponding equilibrium prices of goods p_1 must satisfy by using the notation introduced at the end of the previous section. Equilibrium of the goods markets requires:

(2.4.C) $Z(p_1,r_1) = 0$

On the other hand, the interest rate being pegged at r_1, the Bank's credit supply is assumed to be infinitely elastic. All the bonds supplied by the consumers are then automatically bought by the Bank: the bond market is in equilibrium at all current prices p_1. This determines endogenously the Bank's money creation through loans, which is equal to $B^s(p_1,r_1)/(1+r_1)$. The equilibrium condition for the money market then states that the aggregate demand for money must be equal to the initial money stock M, plus the Bank's net money supply:

(2.4.D$_1$) $M^d(p_1,r_1) = M + B^s(p_1,r_1)/(1+r_1) - R(p_1,r_1)$

Short-run equilibrium price systems p_1 are thus determined by the equations (2.4.C) and (2.4.D$_1$), where r_1 is given exogenously. In view of the trader's budget constraints, the system satisfies Walras's Law, that is:

$$p_1Z(p_1,r_1) + M^d(p_1,r_1) = M + B^s(p_1,r_1)/(1+r_1) - R(p_1,r_1)$$

for every p_1. Walras's Law has the familiar implication that if all markets but one are brought into equilibrium, the remaining one is also in equilibrium. In particular, solving the equation for the real sector alone – equation (2.4.C) – determines not only equilibrium relative prices, but the equilibrium levels of money prices as well. The classical dichotomy is invalid in the short run.

The foregoing system of equations thus has the same formal structure as the neoclassical system described by (2.2.C) and (2.2.D$_1$). It differs from the neoclassical system in one important respect, however, since we have not assumed any homogeneity properties of the traders' short-run demand and supply functions.[15] A change of current prices p_1 will therefore influence aggregate demand for goods, essentially through two effects: the real balance effect, which is generated by an equiproportionate variation of current and expected prices; and the intertemporal substitution effect, which is due to the relative variations of current and expected prices, i.e., to the modification of the consumers' expected real interest rates.

Neoclassical theorists, we recall, considered exclusively the real balance effect, and regarded it as an operational regulating mechanism as long as the value of outside money $\sum_a \bar{\mu}_a$ was positive. As we said, this claim appears to be accepted as a valid theoretical proposition by many theorists today, and debate concerning it has mainly focused on its empirical relevance.

As we are going to see, the neoclassical viewpoint is in fact wrong at the theoretical level. This will be shown by means of a series of examples that are compatible with the assumptions of neoclassical models, and in which there is no short-run Walrasian monetary equilibrium corresponding to the given r_1. The examples will involve, as in Chapter 1, short-run rigidities of the traders' expected real interest rates, and will be constructed by using similar methods. But a credit money economy will be found much more vulnerable than the outside money case of Chapter 1, in the sense that the range of circumstances under which a short-run monetary equilibrium does not exist is much more important. At the root of the phenomenon is the fact that, when unlimited borrowing is allowed, even a *small group* of consumers can destabilize the whole market if they forecast a large rate of inflation. For they may then be led to borrow a lot from the Bank, and by spending the money borrowed on current goods, to generate an excess demand on the corresponding markets at all current prices.

In order to present these examples, it is most convenient to consider the simple macroeconomic case in which there is only one good ($l = 1$), and in which every consumer makes plans for the current period and the next one only ($n = 2$). A typical consumer's utility function $u(c_1, c_2)$ will be written as $w(c_1) + \delta w(c_2)$, where $0 < \delta \leq 1$, and where w is differ-

---

[15] As a consequence, it would seem that a scalar change of the traders' initial balances $\bar{\mu}_a$ should produce "real effects" under our assumptions. We shall show in Section 2.6 below that such a change is still neutral if it is publicly announced by the Government and if one takes into account the influence of this announcement on the consumers' expectations.

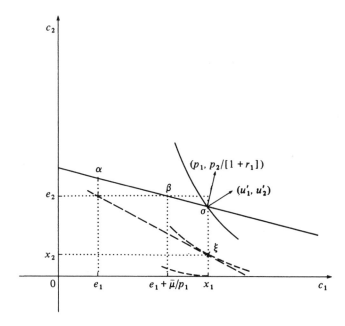

FIGURE 2.2.

entiable, increasing, and strictly concave. It will be assumed furthermore, in order to simplify the exposition, that $w'(0) = +\infty$.

Example 1: Persistent excess demand

We will first give an example in which there is an aggregate excess demand on the good market at all current prices p_1.

Let x_1 be the total amount of the good available in the current period, i.e., the sum of all consumers' current endowments. Consider a consumer, and let e_1 and e_2 be his endowments of good in the current period and the next one. The purpose of the example is to show that this single consumer's demand for consumption c_1 will exceed x_1 for every value of p_1, if he forecasts a large enough rate of inflation. In such a case, there will be an aggregate excess demand on the good market at all current prices, and there will be no monetary equilibrium corresponding to r_1.

Let us first proceed to a preliminary analysis of this consumer's choices in the plane (c_1, c_2) (Figure 2.2). It is clear that the consumer's marginal rate of substitution u_2'/u_1' decreases from $+\infty$ to a positive value when one moves vertically from the point of coordinates $(x_1, 0)$ to the point

(x_1, e_2). Thus there is a unique point ξ on the segment joining these two points, such that the tangent at the indifference curve at ξ goes through the endowment point (e_1, e_2). If (x_1, x_2) denotes the coordinates of ξ, the marginal rate of substitution u_2'/u_1' at ξ is given by $\lambda = (x_1 - e_1)/(e_2 - x_2)$.

Let us assume now that our consumer is not a debtor ($\bar{\mu} \geqq 0$), and that the ratio of his expected discounted price $p_2/(1 + r_1)$ to the current one p_1 exceeds λ. It is then clear from Figure 2.2 that the consumer's intertemporal budget line of equation

$$p_1 c_1 + [p_2/(1+r_1)]c_2 = \bar{\mu} + p_1 e_1 + [p_2/(1+r_1)]e_2$$

intersects the vertical line going through $(x_1, 0)$ at a point σ that is above ξ, and where the marginal rate of substitution is thus less than λ. Since $p_2/[(1+r_1)p_1]$ exceeds λ, the trader's current optimum consumption c_1 must be greater than x_1.

If this single consumer's expectations are biased upward so that $p_2/[(1+r_1)p_1] > \lambda$ for all p_1, there will be an aggregate excess demand on the good market at all current prices, and no monetary equilibrium can exist.

It should be noted that the example is valid independently of the value of outside money $\Sigma_a \bar{\mu}_a$. The disequilibrium phenomenon it describes can occur in particular when all traders' expected discounted prices $p_2/(1 + r_1)$ are proportional to p_1. The real balance effect, which is then the sole regulating mechanism of the economy, is too weak to equilibrate the market, contrary to what neoclassical theorists claim.[16]

The above example describes an extreme case in which a single creditor's demand for consumption exceeds the total amount of good currently available x_1. It can be adapted, of course, to less extreme situations. Consider, for instance, a group of q creditors. Replacing x_1 by x_1/q in the foregoing argument shows that a single creditor's demand for consumption will exceed x_1/q if the ratio of his forecast $p_2/(1 + r_1)$ to the current price p_1 is greater than some appropriate value. If the price expectations of all creditors of this group are biased upward in this way, there will be an aggregate excess demand on the good market at all prices p_1.

[16] One may remark that in this example, the consumer necessarily borrows from the Bank when p_1 is large, since then the point β is to the left of ξ. This explains why the inexistence phenomenon that we just described could not occur in the outside money case of the preceding chapter, where money balances had to be nonnegative (see Section 1.4). As a matter of fact, in the model studied in Chapter 1, no proper subgroup of the set of agents could have generated a persistent excess demand on the good market, as the reader can easily verify.

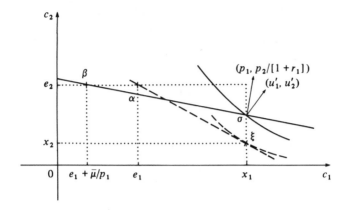

FIGURE 2.3.

The example can also be adapted to the case of a debtor, i.e., when $\bar{\mu} < 0$, as shown in Figure 2.3. Let us assume that the debtor's price expectations are such that the intertemporal budget line of equation

$$p_1 c_1 + [p_2/(1+r_1)]c_2 = \bar{\mu} + p_1 e_1 + [p_2/(1+r_1)]e_2$$

intersects the vertical line going through the point $(x_1,0)$ at a point σ that is above ξ. By using the coordinates (x_1,x_2) of ξ, this means:

$$p_1 x_1 + [p_2/(1+r_1)]x_2 \lessgtr \bar{\mu} + p_1 e_1 + [p_2/(1+r_1)]e_2$$

Since $\lambda = (x_1 - e_1)/(e_2 - x_2)$, this inequality yields the following condition concerning the consumer's expectations:

$$p_2/(1+r_1) \gtrless \lambda p_1 - \bar{\mu}/(e_2 - x_2)$$

Since $\bar{\mu}$ is negative, the ratio $p_2/[(1+r_1)p_1]$ exceeds λ, which is itself greater than or equal to the marginal rate of substitution at σ. The debtor's optimum current consumption is then larger than x_1. If this single debtor's expectations are biased upward in this way for all p_1, an aggregate excess demand appears on the good market at all current prices, and no monetary equilibrium exists.[17]

Example 2: Persistent excess supply

We wish to show that if all traders' price expectations are biased downward for all p_1, there may be an excess supply on the good market at all current prices.

[17] In contrast to the preceding case of a creditor, the example for a debtor is not compatible with the neoclassical assumption of unit elastic price expectations, since $p_2/(1 + r_1)$ must exceed $-\bar{\mu}/(e_2 - x_2)$, which is positive.

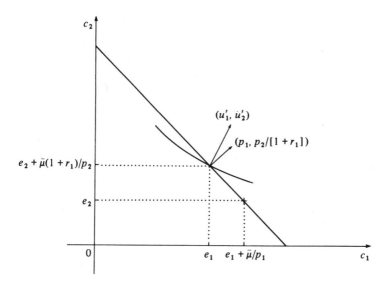

FIGURE 2.4.

The example will in fact be very similar to the case of a persistent excess supply, which was described in Section 1.4 for an outside money economy. Let us again consider a typical consumer, with $\bar{\mu}$ positive or negative, and assume that the marginal rate of substitution u'_2/u'_1 is bounded below by some value $v > 0$ when one moves up the vertical line going through the point $(e_1,0)$ (Figure 2.4). We claim that if $p_2/(1+r_1)p_1]$ is less than v, the trader's optimum current consumption c_1 must be less than e_1.

This is obviously the case if the consumer is bankrupt, since then $c_1 = 0$. In all other cases, the equation of the intertemporal budget line is:

$$p_1 c_1 + [p_2/(1+r_1)]c_2 = \bar{\mu} + p_1 e_1 + [p_2/(1+r_1)] e_2$$

If $\bar{\mu} + [p_2/(1+r_1)]e_2$ is negative, current consumption c_1 must be less than e_1. If this expression is nonnegative, the marginal rate of substitution at the point α exceeds v, and thus the ratio $p_2/[(1+r_1)p_1]$. Again, the trader's optimum current consumption c_1 is less than his endowment e_1.

If *all* consumers have expectations that are biased downward in this way for all p_1, there will be an aggregate excess supply on the good market at all current prices, and no equilibrium corresponding to the given interest rate r_1 can exist.

The disequilibrium phenomenon described in this example is here again independent of the value of outside money $\Sigma_a \bar{\mu}_a$, and it can occur in particular when the ratios $p_2/[(1 + r_1)p_1]$ are independent of p_1, i.e., when price expectations are unit elastic with respect to current prices. It therefore contradicts again the neoclassical position, which claims that the real balance effect is an operational regulating mechanism when outside money is positive.

Remark. The example shows that a persistent excess supply appears on the good market if all consumers are debtors, and if the expression $\bar{\mu} + [p_2/(1 + r_1)]e_2$ is negative for all p_1 and every consumer. This case should be taken of course only as an oddity, since it is unreasonable to assume all consumers to be debtors.

The first class of examples teaches us that, the interest rate r_1 being fixed, even a *small* group of consumers can destabilize the entire market by generating an excess demand for goods at all current prices p_1, if they forecast a large rate of inflation. Expectations of this sort are likely to obtain whenever consumers have observed a significant inflation in the past. *A credit money economy therefore appears to be greatly vulnerable in inflationary situations, since then a short-run Walrasian monetary equilibrium is likely not to exist.*

The second example shows that a *short-run equilibrium corresponding to a given interest rate* r_1 *may not exist when deflation has been observed in the past, since consumers' price expectations are then likely to be biased downward.* A credit money economy seems, however, to be somewhat less vulnerable in a deflationary situation than in the case of inflation, since *all* consumers' price expectations have to be biased downward in order that a persistent excess supply appears on the good market.

These examples have been developed in the case of a given interest rate. The circumstances they describe may obtain of course for every interest rate. For instance, the argument of the first example shows that if a single creditor's price expectations are such that $p_2/(1 + r_1)p_1$ exceeds λ for all p_1 and r_1, an aggregate excess demand appears on the good market at all current prices and interest rates. In a such a case, there can be no values of p_1 and r_1 that achieve equilibrium of the real sector. No short-run monetary equibrium exists, no matter which interest rate is chosen by the Bank. The argument of the second example can be adapted in the same way.

To sum up, these examples teach us that *contrary to what most neoclassical theorists used to believe, the market's "invisible hand" is likely to go astray in a credit money economy with flexible prices, especially in inflationary situations, and that a short-run monetary equilibrium may not exist no matter which value of the interest rate is chosen by the Bank.*

Insensitive expectations

In the foregoing examples, the inexistence of a short-run monetary equilibrium clearly originates with the fact that the traders' expected real interest rates display some rigidities during the price adjustment process at date 1. These examples therefore show that in order to be sure of the existence of such an equilibrium for a given nominal rate r_1, we have to rely upon the intertemporal substitution effect as the main regulating mechanism of the market, by introducing a greater flexibility of expected prices relative to current prices.

This will require, as in Section 1.4, that the traders' price expectations display some insensitiveness to changes of current prices p_1. But in view of the examples given above, the conditions that are needed in the present context will have to be much more restrictive than in the outside money case of the previous chapter.

If we wish an aggregate excess supply to appear on the goods markets when current prices p_1 are large, we need a condition on expectations that prevents the phenomena described in the first example from occurring. Such a condition is that *for all consumers, expected prices are bounded above when current prices increase indefinitely*. Then the intertemporal substitution effect is bound to favor more and more future consumption relative to current consumption, for each consumer, leading eventually to the appearance of an aggregate excess supply in the current markets for goods.

On the other hand, in order to be sure that an excess demand appears on the goods markets when current prices are low, expected prices must behave in such a way that the phenomena described in the second example are excluded. Such a condition on expectations is that *there is at least one consumer, who is not a debtor, for whom expected prices are bounded away from zero when current prices go to zero*. For this particular consumer, the intertemporal substitution effect then favors more and more current consumption relative to future consumption. His desired current consumption must actually tend to infinity, leading eventually to the appearance of an aggregate excess demand on the goods markets.[18] Intuitively, when these conditions on the consumers' expectations are satisfied, one must be able, by moving from low to high current prices p_1, the interest rate r_1 being fixed, to find by continuity a value of p_1 that

---

[18] We need such a condition for a consumer who is not a debtor in order to avoid the phenomenon described in the "Remark" at the end of Example 2. It is quite easy to illustrate these statements as in Section 1.4, by means of a graphical analysis in the plane (c_1, c_2), in the simple case in which there is only one good and in which every consumer makes plans for the current and next periods only. This is left as an exercise to the reader.

brings the good markets – and therefore the whole system – into equilibrium.

We will now present a formal result on the existence of a short-run equilibrium associated with a given interest rate r_1, which makes use of the conditions on expectations that we just described heuristically. Let us say that whenever $n_a \geq 2$, consumer a's price expectations are *continuous in current prices* if, given r_1, the functions $\psi_{at}^*(p_1, r_1)$ are continuous with respect to p_1, for every t. We shall say that a consumer's price expectations are *bounded above* if a vector $\eta(r_1)$ exists, with all its components positive, which may depend upon the interest rate, such that $\psi_{at}^*(p_1, r_1) \leq \eta(r_1)$ for every t and p_1. They are *bounded away from zero* if there is a vector $\epsilon(r_1)$ with all its components positive, which again may depend upon r_1, such that $\epsilon(r_1) \leq \psi_{at}^*(p_1, r_1)$ for every p_1 and t. These boundedness conditions guarantee the presence of a strong stabilizing intertemporal substitution effect when current prices vary. Needless to say, they are incompatible with the neoclassical postulate of unit-elastic price expectations. These boundedness conditions are the key for the following existence result.[19]

(2.4.1)   *Let the interest rate* r_1 *be fixed. Assume* (a) *and* (b) *of Section 2.1, and that every consumer's price expectations are continuous with respect to current prices. Assume moreover that every consumer's price expectations are bounded above, and that there is at least one consumer a with* $n_a \geq 2$ *and* $\bar{\mu}_a \geq 0$ *whose price expectations are bounded away from zero.*

   Then given r_1, *the system of equations* (2.4.C), (2.4.D₁) *has a solution.*

It should be noted that the result does not rest at all on any assumption about the value or the sign of outside money, $\Sigma_a \bar{\mu}_a$. In particular, the result presented is valid even in the case in which all consumers are initially neither creditors nor debtors, i.e., when $\bar{\mu}_a = 0$ for every a. In such a case, if there is only one good, the sole adjustment mechanism in the economy is the intertemporal substitution effect.

The fact that the existence of a short-run monetary equilibrium is guaranteed, under the assumptions of (2.4.1), without any reference to the sign and the size of outside money, is intuitively understandable, since the intertemporal substitution effect generated by the relative variations of current and expected prices works a priori in the same direction for all consumers, whether they are initially creditors or debtors.

The conditions ensuring the presence of a stabilizing substitution effect, for a given interest rate, are evidently quite strong, since they require essentially *all* consumers' price expectations to be eventually insensitive

[19]   A formal proof of the result is given in Appendix C.

to large increases of current prices, and *some* consumers' expectations not to be affected by large decreses of p_1. These assumptions are indeed much more restrictive than in the outside money case of the first chapter, since there only one "insensitive" trader was needed [see (1.4.1)]. Such inelasticity conditions cannot be expected to be met in practice, since price forecasts are likely to depend much, in general, upon the prices that are currently observed. This qualitative conclusion confirms our earlier finding that a short-run Walrasian monetary equilibrium might not exist in actual credit money economies.

2.5   Controlling the money supply

In the preceding section we studied the case in which the Bank tried to peg the interest rate at date 1. The purpose of the present section is to examine what happens when the Bank leaves the interest rate free to vary, and seeks to control the money supply.

Assume accordingly that the Bank fixes the amount of money it creates at date 1 by granting loans to consumers, at some given value, say $\Delta M > 0$. The equations that the equilibrium values of p_1 and r_1 must satisfy are then easy to describe with the help of the consumers' aggregate short-run demand and supply functions.

The equilibrium conditions for the goods markets read as before:

(2.5.C) $Z(p_1, r_1) = 0$

where, in contrast to the previous section, the interest rate is now free to vary. Next, the equation for money states that the aggregate demand for money should be equal, in equilibrium, to the initial money stock M, augmented by the Bank's net money supply, which is described in this case by $\Delta M - R(p_1, r_1)$. This yields:

(2.5.D) $M^d(p_1, r_1) = M + \Delta M - R(p_1, r_1)$.

The Bank's demand for bonds is given by $(1 + r_1)\Delta M$. Equilibrium of the bond market then requires:

(2.5.E) $(1 + r_1)\Delta M = B^s(p_1, r_1)$

Since each consumer satisfies a budget constraint, this system of equations satisfies Walras's Law, which states that the sum across all markets of the money values of aggregate excess demands must be identically equal to zero:

$$p_1 Z(p_1, r_1) + [M^d(p_1, r_1) - M - \Delta M + R(p_1, r_1)]$$
$$+ [\Delta M - B^s(p_1, r_1)/(1 + r_1)] = 0$$

for every p_1 and r_1. The system thus has the same formal structure as the neoclassical system described in Section 2.2. There is again an important difference, since the neoclassical homogeneity postulates are not assumed here, as we wish to stress the importance of the intertemporal substitution effects associated with the relative variations of current and expected prices in the short-run regulating process of the economy.[20]

In order to study the existence of a solution (p_1^*, r_1^*) to the foregoing system of equations, it will be convenient to adopt the following point of view. Let us first solve the goods markets equations (2.5.C) for p_1, given an arbitrary r_1. One can then associate to each such pair (p_1, r_1), whenever it exists, the amount of money, say $\Delta M(p_1, r_1)$, that the Bank should create through credit in order to bring the bond market into equilibrium, i.e.:

$$\Delta M(p_1, r_1) = B^s(p_1, r_1)/(1 + r_1)$$

Since (p_1, r_1) satisfies (2.5.C), this money creation must achieve equilibrium of the money market as well, by virtue of Walras's Law. Thus $\Delta M(p_1, r_1)$ is given equivalently by:

$$\Delta M(p_1, r_1) = M^d(p_1, r_1) - M + R(p_1, r_1)$$

This way of proceeding amounts to looking at a short-run equilibrium price system p_1 that would arise if the bank chose to peg the nominal rate at the level r_1, and at the Bank's corresponding equilibrium money creation $\Delta M(p_1, r_1)$ – assuming, as we did in the previous section, that the Bank's credit supply is then infinitely elastic.

Solving the system (2.5.C), (2.5.D), (2.5.E) for a given $\Delta M > 0$ is equivalent to finding a pair (p_1^*, r_1^*) that satisfies (2.5.C) and such that $\Delta M(p_1^*, r_1^*) = \Delta M$.

Our program should now be clear. If we wish to study the Bank's ability to manipulate the money supply, we have to analyze how $\Delta M(p_1, r_1)$ varies when the pair (p_1, r_1) moves subject to (2.5.C). Specifically, we look for conditions that guarantee that $\Delta M(p_1, r_1)$ approaches 0 when r_1 increases indefinitely, and that $\Delta M(p_1, r_1)$ tends to $+\infty$ when r_1 goes to -1, the price system p_1 moving at the same time so as to maintain the equilibrium of the goods markets.

If we achieve this goal, we shall be able to conclude that the Bank has full control of the money supply at date 1 by manipulating the nominal interest rate r_1. Intuitively, if the Bank decides to peg its money creation at the level $\Delta M > 0$, it should then be possible, by continuity, to find a

---

[20] As before, the neoclassical propositions about the validity of quantity theory in the short run would accordingly seem no longer correct. This is not true, as will be shown in Section 2.6.

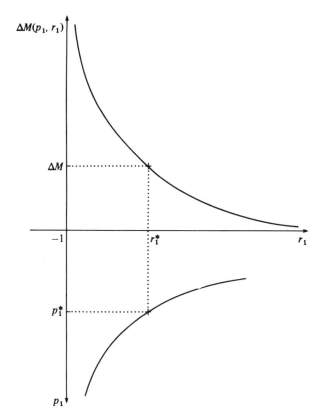

FIGURE 2.5.

pair (p_1^*, r_1^*) satisfying (2.5.C) and $\Delta M(p_1^*, r_1^*) = \Delta M$, by moving from low to large values of the nominal rate r_1.[21] In fact, the above system (2.5.C), (2.5.D), (2.5.E) would then have a solution for every positive ΔM.

The "qualitative" picture we are aiming at is represented in Figure 2.5. The top of the diagram describes the desired variation of $\Delta M(p_1, r_1)$ as a function of r_1, under the assumption that (p_1, r_1) satisfies (2.5.C). The bottom of the diagram is intended to represent the relation between p_1 and r_1 that this assumption implies.

---

[21] That sort of continuity argument is of course only *heuristic*. It neglects in particular the complications that arise from the fact that (2.5.C) may have multiple solutions in p_1 for a given r_1. The reader will find a rigorous argument in Appendix C.

The neoclassical argument for asserting that the Bank indeed has full control over the money supply in the present context, was briefly reviewed in Section 2.2. It relies essentially, we recall, upon the presence and intensity of the real balance effect resulting from a change of current prices of goods, and of the intertemporal substitution effect generated by a variation of the nominal interest rate. The first effect ensures, according to neoclassical theorists, that the goods markets can be brought into equilibrium for each r_1 by movements of current prices, at least when outside money is positive. The second effect is claimed by this school to ensure enough variation of $\Delta M(p_1, r_1)$, when r_1 varies, so as to produce the qualitative picture described in Figure 2.5.

The neoclassical argument was already found to be faulty on one count, since we saw in the preceding section that the real balance effect could be too weak to bring the good markets into equilibrium, given the interest rate. As a matter of fact, examples were provided showing that there may be no pair (p_1, r_1) that satisfies equation (2.5.C). In such a case, the system (2.5.C), (2.5.D), (2.5.E) has no solution, no matter which money supply ΔM is chosen by the Bank.

We will see that there is another important source of disequilibrium in the present model, which can occur in the favorable case in which the goods markets equation (2.5.C) has a solution in current prices for each interest rate. The Bank then has full control over the interest rate, and the relation between r_1 and the money issue $\Delta M(p_1, r_1)$, which is implied by (2.5.C), can be meaningfully defined. It will be found, however, that the range of variation of $\Delta M(p_1, r_1)$, may be quite small when (p_1, r_1) move together so as to maintain the equilibrium of the real sector, if the intertemporal substitution effect resulting from a change of r_1 is weak. Such a circumstance will occur whenever a rise of the nominal rate of interest is offset, partially or completely, by an increase of the traders' expected prices, so that their expected real interest rates are more or less independent of r_1. In such a case, the Bank has little if any control over the money supply at date 1. The likelihood that the Bank mistakenly chooses a value of ΔM that is incompatible with the equilibrium of the goods markets – i.e., for which a solution to the system (2.5.C), (2.5.D), (2.5.E) does not exist – is then great.

The invariance of the money supply
and of equilibrium prices

We now wish to describe a case in which the Bank is unable to exercise *any* influence on the money supply at date 1, although it may have full control over the interest rate.

Let us consider the case where the goods markets equation (2.5.C) can be solved in current prices p_1 for every interest rate because, for instance, the assumptions of (2.4.1) are satisfied for each r_1. Suppose in addition that every consumer's expected discounted prices $\psi_{at}^*(p_1,r_1)/(1+r_1)$ are independent of r_1. Every trader believes then that the only consequences of a change of the interest rate from 0 to r_1 is to multiply equilibrium prices of goods by $1+r_1$ in all subsequent periods, so that expected real interest rates are left invariant. It was shown in Section 2.3 that a consumer's excess demands for goods, his money demand, the amount of money he borrows, as well as his reimbursement to the Bank, depended solely on his initial net money wealth $\bar{\mu}_a$ and on current and expected discounted prices. Under our assumption, therefore, the functions $z_a(p_1,r_1,\bar{\mu}_a)$, $m_a^d(p_1,r_1,\bar{\mu}_a)$, $b_a^s(p_1,r_1,\bar{\mu}_a)/(1+r_1)$, and $R_a(p_1,r_1,\bar{\mu}_a)$ are actually independent of the interest rate.

This fact immediately implies that the equilibrium prices p_1 that satisfy (2.5.C) for a given r_1, and the corresponding money issue $\Delta M(p_1,r_1)$, are also independent of the interest rate. Qualitatively, what happens is that the curves described in Figure 2.5 become completely "flat," i.e., horizontal. Any attempt from the Bank to set the money supply ΔM at a different level will be defeated by the market, in the sense that the system (2.5.C), (2.5.D), (2.5.E) will then have no solution. On the other hand, if ΔM was set by coincidence at a level compatible with the equilibrium of the goods markets, a solution to the whole system of equations would then indeed exist, but the equilibrium nominal interest rate would be indeterminate.

(2.5.1) *Assume that the expected discounted prices $\psi_{at}^*(p_1,r_1)/(1 + r_1)$ are independent of the interest rate, for every t. Then the functions $z_a(p_1,r_1,\bar{\mu}_a)$, $m_a^d(p_1,r_1,\bar{\mu}_a)$, $b_a^s(p_1,r_1,\bar{\mu}_a)/(1 + r_1)$, and $R_a(p_1,r_1,\bar{\mu}_a)$ do not vary with r_1. As a consequence, if p_1 brings the goods markets into equilibrium for a particular interest rate, then (p_1,r_1) is a solution of (2.5.C) for all r_1, and the associated money creation $\Delta M(p_1,r_1) = B^s(p_1,r_1)/(1 + r_1)$ is independent of the rate of interest.*

In this example, the Bank has full control over the interest rate, but is unable to have any influence on the current money supply, or on current equilibrium prices. The origin of the phenomenon is evidently the fact that the intertemporal substitution effect generated by a change of the interest rate vanishes in this case. Such a circumstance will obtain whenever a modification of the nominal rate r_1 is offset by a compensating change of the traders' expected prices, so that their expected real interest rates are in fact invariant.

It is not implausible that the traders' expectations exhibit such a property, at least approximately, in actual economies, since private economic units may interpret an increase of the nominal rate set by monetary authorities as a sign that inflationary tensions are building up in the economy, and conversely. A related justification is that, as we shall see in the next chapter, a permanent increase of the nominal rate r_1 leads, in the long run, to an offsetting move of the rate of growth of prices, so that long-run equilibrium real interest rates are indeed invariant.

The assumption that the traders' expected real interest rates are to some extent independent of the nominal rate in the short run, is thus not implausible. In that case, *the range of money supplies ΔM that the Bank can successfully impose, i.e., for which the system (2.5.C), (2.5.D), (2.5.E) has a solution, will be quite small. The Bank then has little influence on the money supply, although it may have full control over the interest rate.*

An existence result

The foregoing discussion shows that the set of money supplies ΔM for which the system of equations (2.5.C), (2.5.D), (2.5.E) has a solution, may be empty, when it is impossible to find a couple (p_1, r_1) that brings the goods markets into equilibrium, or quite small, when the intertemporal substitution effect generated by a variation of the nominal interest rate is weak. We now wish to study the conditions on expectations that ensure that the Bank has full control over the money supply, i.e., that guarantee the existence of a solution of the system (2.5.C), (2.5.D), (2.5.E) for every $\Delta M > 0$. In view of our previous analysis, these conditions will be quite strong, and cannot be expected to prevail in actual credit money economies.

To discuss this problem, we shall look at a value of current prices p_1 that solves (2.5.C) for a given r_1, and consider the Bank's corresponding money issue $\Delta M(p_1, r_1)$, which is then given by the two following and – according to Walras's Law – equivalent expressions:

$$\Delta M(p_1, r_1) = B^s(p_1, r_1)/(1 + r_1)$$

$$\Delta M(p_1, r_1) = M^d(p_1, r_1) - M + R(p_1, r_1)$$

Such a procedure will be valid, provided that we assume, for instance, that the conditions of (2.4.1) are satisfied for every r_1.

Our strategy, as we recall, is to find conditions that guarantee that $\Delta M(p_1, r_1)$ tends to 0 when the interest rate increases without bound, and that $\Delta M(p_1, r_1)$ tends to $+\infty$ as the interest rate approaches -1, the prices system p_1 moving at the same time so as to maintain the equilibrium on the goods markets. Intuitively, there should then exist, by continuity, a value of the interest rate r_1^*, and an associated prices system p_1^*, that achieves the equality of $\Delta M(p_1^*,r_1^*)$ with the given money supply ΔM, and that thus satisfies the entire system of equations (2.5.C), (2.5.D), (2.5.E).

In order to look at this issue more closely, it is useful to consider again the simple case that we have repeatedly employed, in which there is only one good, and in which every consumer makes plans for the current period and the next one only.

In such a framework, we recall, a typical consumer's optimum current and future consumptions are obtained by the maximization of his utility function under the intertemporal budget constraint:

$$p_1 c_1 + [p_2/(1+r_1)]\, c_2 = \text{Max}(\bar{\mu} + p_1 e_1 + [p_2/(1+r_1)]\, e_2, 0)$$

where $p_2 = \psi^*(p_1,r_1)$. His corresponding money demand and bond supply are in turn given by consideration of the current budget constraint, or equivalently, by looking at the expected budget constraint:

$$p_2 c_2 = p_2 e_2 + (1+r_1)\, m_1 - b_1$$

together with the condition that either m_1 or b_1 is equal to 0.

In the following discussion, it will be assumed without any further explicit reference that movements of the nominal rate r_1 are met by compensating moves of the price p_1 so as to maintain the equilibrium on the good market, i.e., so as to satisfy (2.5.C).

If we want to be sure that $\Delta M(p_1,r_1)$ tends to 0 as r_1 goes to infinity, we need a condition on expectations that guarantees that an increase of the interest rate is not hampered by an offsetting rise of expected prices, so as to avoid the phenomenon of the invariance of the money creation that we described above. To do this, it suffices, as we are going to see, to strengthen the conditions of (2.4.1) by assuming that *all consumers' expected prices* $\psi_a^*(p_1,r_1)$ *are uniformly bounded above by some positive number* η.

Indeed, a typical consumer's expected budget constraint implies that his bond supply b_1 must not exceed his expected income $p_2 e_2$. Under the new assumption, therefore, the aggregate bond supply must be less than or equal to $\eta \sum_a e_{a2}$. The money issue $\Delta M(p_1,r_1)$ cannot exceed $(\eta \sum_a e_{a2})/(1+r_1)$, which tends evidently to 0 when the interest rate increases without bound. Actually, a stronger result is true, since then $\Delta M(p_1,r_1)$ *tends to 0 at least as fast as* $1/(1+r_1)$, *when* r_1 *goes to* $+\infty$.

It remains to look at the conditions that ensure that $\Delta M(p_1,r_1)$ increases without bound when the interest rate tends to -1. Now, we know that since p_1 and r_1 satisfy (2.5.C), $\Delta M(p_1,r_1)$ is given by the two equivalent expressions:

$$\Delta M(p_1,r_1) = B^s(p_1,r_1)/(1+r_1)$$

$$\Delta M(p_1,r_1) = M^d(p_1,r_1) - M + R(p_1,r_1)$$

The second relation shows that whenever $\Delta M(p_1,r_1)$ goes to $+\infty$, the corresponding aggregate demand for money $M^d(p_1,r_1)$ tends to infinity too, and conversely. Thus in order to get the result we are looking for, we may try directly to find conditions that ensure the presence of a consumer willing to borrow larger and larger amounts of money from the Bank as the interest rate approaches -1. Alternatively, we may look for conditions that guarantee the presence of a consumer who is demanding more and more money as r_1 decreases. That will imply that the aggregate money demand $M^d(p_1,r_1)$, and thus the money creation $\Delta M(p_1,r_1)$, tends to infinity. This is the route that we shall follow in the sequel.

A moment of reflection shows that in order to achieve our goal, we shall need two different sorts of conditions. Indeed, the preceding argument shows that if we are successful, both $M^d(p_1,r_1)$ and $\Delta M(p_1,r_1)$ will tend to infinity as r_1 decreases to -1. Hence, there will necessarily exist (at least) two different consumers in the economy who display opposite behaviors, since one of them will borrow a lot from the Bank, whereas the other will hold increasing amounts of money. These two consumers therefore must have different characteristics. There would be no hope of getting the desired result if all consumers living at date 1 were identical. Indeed, in that case, they would be either all savers or all borrowers. Thus either $\Delta M(p_1,r_1)$ or $M^d(p_1,r_1)$ would be zero. This would mean that either:

$$\Delta M(p_1,r_1) = 0 \quad \text{and} \quad M^d(p_1,r_1) = M - R(p_1,r_1)$$

or:

$$\Delta M(p_1,r_1) = - [M - R(p_1,r_1)] \quad \text{and} \quad M^d(p_1,r_1) = 0$$

Hence $M^d(p_1,r_1)$ and $\Delta M(p_1,r_1)$ would be bounded above by M and $(-\Sigma_a\bar{\mu}_a)$ respectively, and these expressions could not go to infinity. As a matter of fact, the argument shows that if all consumers were identical, and if initial outside money $\Sigma_a\bar{\mu}_a$ was nonnegative, one would have $\Delta M(p_1,r_1) = 0$ for all pairs (p_1,r_1) that satisfy (2.5.C).

The two conditions that we shall employ in the sequel are the following. First, we must clearly ensure that a decrease of the nominal rate r_1 is not hampered by an offsetting decrease of expected prices, in order to avoid here too the phenomenon of the invariance of the money creation that we presented before. This will be achieved by strengthening the conditions of (2.4.1), that is, by assuming that *there is a consumer* a *, who is not* *a debtor, whose expected prices* $\psi_a^*(p_1,r_1)$ *are uniformly bounded below by some positive number* ϵ.

The second assumption that we shall need is that *there is a consumer* b *whose expected discounted price* $\psi_b^*(p_1,r_1)/(1+r_1)$ *is uniformly bounded away from infinity and from zero when the interest rate goes to* -1. Or more precisely, for every sequence $(p_1^k \cdot r_1^k)$ such that r_1^k tends to -1, there exist two positive numbers η' and ϵ', which may depend on the sequence, such that $\epsilon' \leqq \psi_b^*(p_1^k r_1^k)/(1+r_1^k) \leqq \eta'$ for all k.

We will first show that, owing to the presence of consumer a, when r_1 tends to -1, the associated price p_1 that achieves equilibrium of the good market goes to infinity. We shall next show that consumer b's demand for money then increases indefinitely. That will imply that $M^d(p_1,r_1)$, and thus $\Delta M(p_1,r_1)$, increase without bound when the interest rate approaches -1, as we wanted.[22]

Let us first show that p_1 goes to $+\infty$ when r_1 tends to -1, the pair (p_1,r_1) being constrained to satisfy the good market equation (2.5.C). To this effect, let us represent consumer a's intertemporal budget constraint in the plane (c_1,c_2) (Figure 2.6). If the price p_1 remained bounded away from infinity when the interest rate r_1 went to -1, the product $(1+r_1)p_1$ would tend to 0. Since this particular consumer's expected price $\psi_a^*(p_1,r_1)$ is bounded below by ϵ, the ratio $p_2/(1+r_1)p_1$ would then go to infinity. The point α on the diagram would tend to the endowment point (e_1,e_2), and the intertemporal budget line would eventually become horizontal. By substitution between current and future goods, the consumer a's optimum current consumption would increase without bound, thereby ultimately generating an aggregate excess demand on the good market. This would violate the assumption that the couple (p_1,r_1) always satisfies equation (2.5.C).

Therefore, when r_1 converges to -1, the corresponding equilibrium price p_1 tends to $+\infty$.[23] We well next check to see if, following our

---

[22] As we said, this will imply the existence of a consumer willing to borrow increasing amounts of money from the Bank. This "borrower" cannot be, of course, consumer b. But he may be someone other than consumer a.

[23] The foregoing argument shows in fact that the product $(1 + r_1)p_1$ must be bounded away from zero when r_1 tends to -1. It is not difficult to see that according to our assumptions, $(1 + r_1)p_1$ also must be bounded above. Here is a sketch of the argument. If on the contrary, $(1 + r_1)p_1$ tended to $+\infty$, the consumer a's intertemporal budget line would eventually become vertical, in which case his planned consumption c_2 would go to $+\infty$. According to the consumer's expected budget constraint, the product of his money demand m_1 and of $(1 + r_1)$ should also increase without bound. Thus $(1 + r_1)M^d(p_1,r_1)$, and therefore $B^s(p_1,r_1)$, would tend to $+\infty$. But this is impossible, for $B^s(p_1,r_1)$ cannot exceed

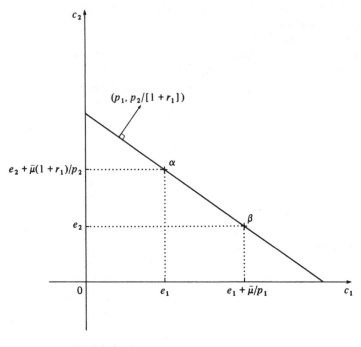

FIGURE 2.6.

assumptions, the consumer b's demand for money then increases without bound.

In order to verify this claim, let us look at the graphical representation of consumer b's decision-making problem as shown in Figure 2.6.[24] Since p_1 tends to $+\infty$ when r_1 decreases to -1, the point β in the diagram approaches the endowment point (e_1,e_2). On the other hand, the inter-temporal budget line eventually becomes vertical, since the ratio $p_2/(1+r_1) p_1$ tends to zero. Hence, the consumer b's optimum future con-sumption c_2 increases without limit. It follows then from the consumer's expected budget constraint:

$$[p_2/(1+r_1)] c_2 = [p_2/(1+r_1)] e_2 + m_1 - b_1/(1+r_1)$$

that his demand for money m_1 also increases without bound, since the

$\eta \Sigma_a e_{a2}$, since we assumed all consumers' expected prices to be uniformly bounded above by η.

[24] If the consumer is initially a debtor, we are sure that he is not bankrupt eventually, since p_1 tends to infinity. Figure 2.6 then applies, with $\bar{\mu} < 0$.

consumer's expected discounted price $p_2/(1 + r_1)$ is, under our assumptions, bounded away from infinity and from zero.

Accordingly, the aggregate demand for money $M_d(p_1,r_1)$, and thus $\Delta M(p_1,r_1)$, tends to infinity when the interest rate r_1 approaches -1, and when p_1 moves correlatively so as to maintain the equilibrium of the good market.

The heuristic discussion has permitted us to discover the kind of conditions we needed to ensure the existence of a solution to the system (2.5.C), (2.5.D), (2.5.E) for each positive money supply ΔM. In order to state a formal result along these lines, it is first necessary to give a few precise definitions.

Let us say that a consumer's price expectations are *continuous* if the functions $\psi_{at}^*(p_1,r_1)$ are continuous with respect to p_1 and r_1, for every t. We shall say that a consumer's *expected prices are uniformly bounded above* if a vector η exists, with all its components positive, such that $\psi_{at}^*(p_1,r_1) \leqq \eta$ for all p_1 and r_1, and every t. A consumer's expected prices will be said to be *uniformly bounded away from zero* if a vector ϵ exists, with all its components positive, such that $\psi_{at}^*(p_1,r_1) \geqq \epsilon$ for all p_1 and r_1, and every t. Finally, let us say that a consumer's *expected discounted prices are uniformly bounded away from infinity and from zero when the interest rate tends to -1*, if for each sequence (p_1^k,r_1^k) such that r_1^k converges to -1, two vectors η' and ϵ' exist, with all their components positive, which may depend upon the sequence, such that:

$$\eta' \geqq \psi_{at}^*(p_1^k,r_1^k)/(1 + r_1^k) \geqq \epsilon'$$

for every k and all t.

Our existence result can now be stated, with these definitions[25]:

(2.5.2) *Assume (a) and (b) of Section 2.1, and that every consumer's price expectations are continuous. Assume moreover that every consumer's expected prices ψ_{at}^* are uniformly bounded above, and that there is at least one consumer a with $n_a \geqq 2$ and $\bar{\mu}_a \geqq 0$, whose expected prices ψ_{at}^* are uniformly bounded away from zero. Assume finally that there is at least another consumer b, with $n_b \geqq 2$, whose expected discounted prices are uniformly bounded away from infinity and from zero when the interest rate tends to -1.*

    Then, the system (2.5.C), (2.5.D), (2.5.E) has a solution for each $\Delta M > 0$, i.e., the Bank has full control over the money supply.

It goes without saying that these conditions are extremely specific, and that they cannot be expected to prevail in reality. Our analysis shows in particular that the effectiveness of large increases of the rate of interest

---

[25] A rigorous proof of the result is given in Appendix C.

as an antiinflationary measure, by reducing the money supply, is subordinated to the condition that *all* traders' expected prices are uniformly bounded above – a condition that is quite unlikely to exist in an inflationary environment.

On the other hand, the effectiveness of large decreases of the interest rate, as a reflationary measure, was subject to conditions less stringent but nevertheless quite specific. But a much more severe limitation exists to the scope of such a policy in actual economies. For in the real world the mere presence of paper money imposes, as we have seen, the additional restriction that the nominal interest rate must be nonnegative.[26] By contrast, in the foregoing analysis, the nominal rate of interest r_1 had to tend to -1 in order to make the Bank's money creation to go to infinity.

Lastly, we wish to mention another limitation to the Bank's ability to manipulate the money supply through its credit operations. All that preceded concerned the Bank's money creation at date 1. Remember now that each trader's net credit position grows at the rate r_1 from the end of period 1, i.e., before interest payments, to the beginning of period 2, where interest payments have to be included. Thus a rise of the nominal rate of interest r_1, even if it generates a reduction of the Bank's money creation at date 1, will increase mechanically, through interest payments, the rate of growth of the money stock from date 1 to date 2. The "dynamic" consequences of a variation of r_1 are thus ambiguous.

This finding will be confirmed by our study of the steady states of this credit money economy in the next chapter, where it will be shown that a *permanent* variation of the nominal interest rate induces, in the long run, only an offsetting change of the rate of inflation – and of the rate of growth of the money stock – leaving steady-state equilibrium "real variables" unaffected.

The qualitative conclusion that emerges from this analysis is therefore that *the abililty of monetary authorities to have a significant influence, in the short run, on the money supply or on equilibrium prices, by manipulating the nominal cost of credit, appears somewhat problematic.*

Remark. In the foregoing investigation, the traders' expectations depended solely on p_1 and r_1. Accordingly, the implicit assumption was that the consumers had no direct information about the Bank's policy. The analysis can however, be transposed, trivially indeed, to the case in which some or all traders have some knowledge of the Bank's policy. Let us assume for instance that a target money supply ΔM^* is publicy announced by the Bank. The consumers' anticipations are then functions not only of p_1

---

[26] See footnote 2 at the beginning of Section 2.1.

and r_1, but of ΔM^* too, and may be written $\psi_{at}^*(p_1,r_1,\Delta M^*)$. The study of this section is still valid for a fixed signal ΔM^*. In particular, if the traders' expectations satisfy the assumptions of (2.5.2) *for a given signal* ΔM^*, the Bank can peg its money supply at the preannounced level ΔM^*, and in fact, at any other arbitrary level $\Delta M > 0$, provided that the consumers do not know that the Bank is actually implementing a policy that differs from the one announced.

2.6   The neutrality of money

All of the preceding discussions concerned the possibility of the Bank controlling the nominal rate of interest or the money supply through its credit operations. We now wish to analyze how the variations of the money supply influence equilibrium magnitudes at date 1. We will verify that a publicly announced once-and-for-all scalar change of all traders' initial balances and of the Bank's money creation is neutral if private units believe in its neutrality. But it will be argued that, apart from this very special case, variations of the money supply have typically real effects in the short run.

We shall concentrate, to fix the ideas, on the case in which the Bank pegs its money creation ΔM.[27] Let us consider the "traditional" proposition that a scalar change of all traders' initial balances from $\bar{\mu}_a$ to $\lambda_1\bar{\mu}_a$, through lump-sum transfers, and of the Bank's money issue from ΔM to $\lambda_1\Delta M$, is neutral, for all positive real numbers λ_1.

The neoclassical viewpoint on this matter, which we recalled briefly in Section 2.2, relies upon the assumption that each trader's excess demand for goods $z_a(p_1,r_1,\bar{\mu}_a)$ is homogenous of degree 0 in $(p_1,\bar{\mu}_a)$, whereas his demand for money $m_a^d(p_1,r_1,\bar{\mu}_a)$, his bond supply $b_a^s(p_1,r_1,\bar{\mu}_a)$, and his reimbursement to the Bank $R_a(p_1,r_1,\bar{\mu}_a)$, are homogenous of degree 1 in these variables. Then examination of the system (2.5.C), (2.5.D), (2.5.E) of the preceding section, which describes the determination of the equilibrium at date 1 for a given money supply, shows immediately that, under the neoclassical homogeneity postulates, short-run equilibrium prices p_1 should move proportionally to the parameter λ_1, whereas the nominal interest rate r_1 and equilibrium real magnitudes should remain unaffected. A variation of λ_1 would be neutral.

By contrast, in our analysis, we have been led to take into account intertemporal substitution effects, and thus to abandon the neoclassical

---

[27] The arguments that follow can easily be transposed to the case in which the Bank pegs the interest rate, and in which money creation is accordingly endogenous. This is left as an exercise to the reader.

homogeneity postulates, in order to ensure the short-run consistency of the model. So it would seem that under our assumptions, the change of the money supply that we consider is no longer neutral. This is of course wrong, and we are going to see that one can still preserve neutrality, if one properly incorporates in the analysis the information generated by the Government's policy. This will be established by adapting the methods developed in the first chapter (see Section 1.7) to the case at hand.

Let us assume that the policy parameter λ_1 is *publicly* announced. Each trader's expected discounted prices now depend on λ_1, as well as on p_1 and r_1. They will be denoted $\psi_{at}^*(p_1,r_1,\lambda_1)/(1+r_1)$. If one looks back at the formulation of a trader's behavior made in Section 2.3, it is clear that each trader's short-run demand and supply functions z_a, m_a^d, b_a^s, R_a are then functions of p_1, r_1, and $\bar{\mu}_a$ as before, and of the policy parameter λ_1. By aggregating over all consumers, as we did in Section 2.3, we can therefore describe with obvious notations the equilibrium prices and interest rates that are associated with a given λ_1, as the outcome of the following system of equations:

(2.6.C) $Z(p_1,r_1,\lambda_1) = 0$

(2.6.D) $M^d(p_1,r_1,\lambda_1) = \lambda_1 M + \lambda_1 \Delta M - R(p_1,r_1,\lambda_1)$

(2.6.E) $(1+r_1) \lambda_1 \Delta M = B^s(p_1,r_1,\lambda_1)$

Let us assume now that each trader believes that a variation of λ_1 is neutral. Or more precisely, that *all forecasts* $\psi_{at}^*(p_1,r_1,\lambda_1)$ *are homogenous of degree 1 with respect to current prices* p_1 *and the policy parameter* λ_1.[28] Since each trader's behavior is free of money illusion – see (2.3.1) – this implies, as the reader can easily check, that $Z(p_1,r_1,\lambda_1)$ is homogenous of degree 0 in (p_1,λ_1), whereas $M^d(p_1,r_1,\lambda_1)$, $B^s(p_1,r_1,\lambda_1)$, and $R(p_1,r_1,\lambda_1)$ are homogenous of degree 1 in these variables. Under the new assumption, therefore, a variation of λ_1 is indeed neutral.

To sum up, *a publicly announced once-and-for-all scalar change of all traders' initial balances* $\bar{\mu}_a$, *and of the Bank's money creation* ΔM, *is neutral if private units believe in the neutrality of this change.* In contrast with the neoclassical approach, this neutrality proposition has been reached by relying on certain homogeneity properties of the consumers' forecasts with respect to current prices p_1, and the publicly announced policy parameter λ_1, and *not* on the homogeneity of a trader's behavior with respect to p_1 and his initial money balance $\bar{\mu}_a$.

---

[28] Here as in Section 1.7, it must be emphasized that this assumption relates expectations with p_1 *and* λ_1, and that it is therefore compatible with anticipations that are not unit elastic with respect to p_1 alone, for a given λ_1.

In the foregoing statement, all underlying assumptions are important. For instance, if we abandon the assumption of a *scalar* change, i.e., if the initial balances $\bar{\mu}_a$ are not modified proportionally, there will be "distribution effects" among traders that are likely to influence equilibrium real magnitudes at date 1. Such distribution effects are presumably important in practice.

If, on the other hand, we keep the assumption of a scalar change of the $\bar{\mu}_a$'s and of ΔM, but discard the assumption that the size λ_1 of the policy move is publicly announced, we open the door, as in Section 1.7, to an informational nonneutrality of the Lucas type, which is so dear to the new classical macroeconomists.[29] Now, the traders who initially have a balance $\bar{\mu}_a \neq 0$ observe the size λ_1 of the Government's policy through the lump-sum transfers $(\lambda_1 - 1)\bar{\mu}_a$ that they receive. Thus the only consumers who can generate that kind of nonneutrality are those for whom $\bar{\mu}_a = 0$, since they may not be able to infer the true value of λ_1 from the sole observation of the current price system p_1 and of the current interest rate r_1. The practical relevance of that sort of informational nonneutrality may appear somewhat weak, however, since it relies upon the presence of traders who have an initial balance $\bar{\mu}_a$ just equal to zero, and who have presumably only a small weight in actual economies.

But the important and the most novel point, by comparison with our analysis of the outside money case of Chapter 1, is that we have considered, in the foregoing neutrality result, two policy instruments that are in fact independent, since we changed simultaneously all traders' initial balances $\bar{\mu}_a$ by means of lump-sum transfers, and the Bank's money issue ΔM on the credit market. The first type of operation pertains actually to *fiscal* policy, while only the second one, strictly speaking, can be considered as *monetary* policy.

Economic policy does not usually work in so special a way. We must therefore ask a more relevant question, namely, whether *monetary policy alone* is neutral. Or more precisely, whether changes of the Bank's money supply ΔM through credit operations, *the initial balances $\bar{\mu}_a$ being fixed*, have an influence on real equilibrium magnitudes at date 1.

Our analysis of the preceding section showed that such a manipulation of the Bank's money issue ΔM might be very problematic. It is not difficult to verify, nonetheless, that *any change of ΔM*, ceteris paribus, *will typically produce real effects at date 1 whenever it can be actually implemented.*

To see this point, let us look at a short-run equilibrium corresponding to a given money supply ΔM. Let us assume that the initial balances $\bar{\mu}_a$ all differ from zero, and that no consumer is bankrupt at the equilibrium

---

[29] See Lucas (1972) in a context involving only outside money.

that we consider. Thus a typical trader's intertemporal consumption program is given by the maximization of his utility function under his intertemporal budget constraint:

$$\Sigma_1^n \beta_t p_t (c_t - e_t) \lessgtr \bar{\mu}$$

where p_t stands for the price that he expects to prevail at each date $t \geq 2$, and β_t is his subjective discount factor:

$$\beta_t = 1/[(1 + r_1) \ldots (1 + r_{t-1})]$$

Consider now a change of ΔM alone, and let us assume – for a moment – that this modification has no real effects. Each trader's intertemporal consumption program should then be invariant. Since the initial balances $\bar{\mu}_a$ differ from 0 and are not modified, that should imply, in view of the traders' intertemporal budget constraints, that current equilibrium prices p_1, and the traders' expected discounted prices $\beta_t p_t$, do not move. Let us look next at a typical trader's current budget constraint, which reads, since by assumption no consumer is bankrupt, as follows:

$$p_1 c_1 + \mu_1 = \bar{\mu} + p_1 e_1$$

Each trader's equilibrium net credit position $\mu_1 = m_1 - b_1/(1 + r_1)$ would then remain unaltered. But we would get a contradiction, since the aggregate desired amount of borrowing would then stay the same while the Bank's money supply has changed. The bond and the money markets could no longer be in equilibrium.

This simple argument therefore shows that a variation of the Bank's money creation ΔM on the credit market, the initial balances $\bar{\mu}_a$ being fixed, does have real effects in the short run. It also shows that the phenomenon occurs whether the policy move is known by the public or not, and that it is independent of the way in which expectations are formed. By similar reasoning, which is left up to the reader, *a once-and-for-all scalar modification of the initial balances $\bar{\mu}_a$ through lump-sum transfers, the Bank's money supply ΔM being kept fixed, would produce real effects too, whenever this policy can be implemented.*

Remark. It should be noted that the neutrality proposition that was established in this section is valid if, and in general only if, no lump-sum transfers are expected to take place at future dates (or are preannounced by the Government). By contrast, a scalar change, at date 1, of the initial balances $\bar{\mu}_a$ and of ΔM would produce typically real effects if the traders expect (or if the Government preannounces) lump-sum transfers of a fixed size to be carried out at later dates. More generally, altering the intertemporal time profile of the changes of the money stock (or of its rate of growth) through lump-sum taxes or subsidies, would not be neutral in the model under consideration. The basic reason that underlies this conclusion is that all traders who live at date 1 typically have different (lifetime) planning horizons (compare to the arguments developed in Section 1.7 in the case of an outside money economy).

Notes on the literature

This chapter evolved from a joint research paper by Grandmont and Laroque (1975). As a matter of fact, (2.4.1) is a direct extension of their analysis for the case in which the Bank pegs the interest rate. The results in Section 2.5 for the case in which the Bank controls the money supply, are new. Grandmont and Laroque also considered the case in which the interest rates charged on loans and paid on deposits may differ.

The analysis has been deliberately restricted in this chapter to point expectations, essentially to permit a diagrammatic exposition. It could be extended – although this has not yet been done formally in the literature, apparently – to the case where expectations take the form of probability distributions.[30] This would require the use of the techniques of dynamic programming under uncertainty. The various "boundedness" conditions on anticipations that have been used in the text would take then the form of some "uniform tightness" conditions, as was done in Grandmont (1974) for an outside money economy. There would accordingly be an additional cost in terms of greater mathematical complexity, but the spirit of the economic argument would be the same.

Suggested reading

Friedman, M., *The Optimum Quantity of Money*, Aldine, Chicago, 1969, Chap. 5.

Gurley, J. G., and E. S. Shaw, *Money in a Theory of Finance*, The Brookings Institution, Washington, 1960, Chaps. 1–3.

Hicks, J., *Critical Essays in Monetary Theory*, Oxford University Press, London, 1967, Chap. 1.

Johnson, H. G., *Essays in Monetary Economics*, Allen & Unwin, London, 1967, Chap. 4.

Patinkin, D., *Money, Interest and Prices*, 2nd ed., Harper & Row, New York, 1965, Chaps. 4–6 and Note E.

Sargent, T. J., *Macroeconomic Theory*, Academic Press, New York, 1979, Chap. 1.

Tobin, J., *Asset Accumulation and Economic Activity*, Yrjö Jahnsson Lectures, Blackwell Publisher, Oxford, 1980, Chap. 1.

[30] See, Akashi (1981), however, for a study of credit economies using probabilistic expectations, in a related but different framework.

CHAPTER 3

Classical stationary states with money and credit

The aim of this chapter is to study the existence and the properties of steady states in the credit money economy that was analyzed in the preceding chapter, when population is stationary. Such steady states are defined as sequences of short-run equilibria (in the sense of the previous chapter), where the nominal interest rate, the relative prices of goods, and the rate of inflation – and more generally all "real" equilibrium magnitudes – are constant over time. Moreover, traders are assumed to forecast future prices and interest rates correctly at every moment. Although we have shown that the existence of a short-run equilibrium was doubtful in economies of this type, steady states are of independent interest because they may obtain as long-run equilibria of other dynamic (e.g., disequilibrium) processes.

It will be established that quantity theory and the classical dichotomy are valid propositions when applied to steady states. Real magnitudes (the relative prices of goods, the real rate of interest, the traders' consumptions) are determined by the equilibrium conditions of the goods markets. Nominal values (the money prices of goods, the rate of inflation, the nominal interest rate) are determined in turn by looking at the money sector, including the Bank's monetary policy. In particular, when population is stationary, the money prices of goods are proportional at any time to the level of monetary aggregates such as outside money or the Bank's money supply. In other words, prices and monetary aggregates grow at the same rate.

These findings imply that the Bank cannot peg in the long run a real variable such as the real interest rate by its interventions on the credit market. Any attempt to do so is self-defeating, in the sense that the economy will never be able then to approach a monetary steady state. In such circumstances, the only stationary equilibrium that can obtain must be a nonmonetary one. This would mean the eventual breakdown of the monetary institution.

If the Bank wishes to preserve the monetary character of the economy, it must therefore control nominal variables only, e.g., by pegging the nominal interest rate at a constant level, or the rate growth of its money supply. These interventions on the credit market are, however, neutral in the long run, in the sense that they will have no influence on the set of steady-state real equilibrium quantities.

It will be shown that there are two types of monetary steady states that typically coexist in a credit money economy, namely, *Golden Rule steady states*, where the real interest rate is equal to the rate of population growth, which is here 0, and where the consumers' aggregate net credit position is permanently positive or permanently negative; and *Balanced steady states*, where outside money is zero at any time, and where the real interest rate differs typically from 0.

The reasons underlying this result are easily understood by using the following heuristic argument. We have shown in the preceding chapter that outside money increases within each period by the extent of bankruptcies, and that it grows mechanically from the end of a given period to the beginning of the next at a rate equal to the nominal interest rate – see the discussion of equations (2.2.C), (2.2.D), and (2.2.E). Next note that consumers do not make forecasting errors, and thus that bankruptcies do not occur along a steady state. Therefore, outside money grows at a rate equal to the nominal interest rate along a steady state. On the other hand, when population is stationary, quantity theory implies that outside money and the prices of goods grow at the same rate along a steady state. Putting together these two facts shows that either the nominal rate of interest is equal to the rate of inflation – one then gets a Golden Rule steady state; or that outside money is permanently equal to 0 – in which case a Balanced steady state obtains.

Two important classes of economies will be distinguished. When consumers have larger real incomes in the late periods of their lives, every Golden Rule steady state involves negative outside money. In "well-behaved" economies, the real interest rate should then be positive for all Balanced steady states. This is sometimes called the *classical* case, since it is the kind of situation described by classical theorists such as I. Fisher. On the other hand, if the consumers have larger real incomes in their youth, and if they do not discount the future too much, every Golden Rule steady state implies positive outside money, whereas the real interest rate should be negative for all balanced steady states. This is sometimes called the *Samuelson* case, as such situations were considered by this author in his seminal paper on the "social contrivance" of money.[1] If r and π denote respectively the nominal interest rate and the rate of inflation associated with a particular steady state, the real interest rate ρ is then given by $1 + \rho = (1 + r)/(1 + \pi)$. The qualitative picture we shall arrive at may then be described by the following table:

Characteristics of the economy	Golden Rule steady states	Balanced steady states
Classical	$\rho = 0$; outside money is negative, and grows at the rate $r = \pi$	$\rho > 0$; outside money is equal to 0
Samuelson	$\rho = 0$; outside money is positive, and grows at the rate $r = \pi$	$\rho < 0$; outside money is equal to 0

3.1   Consumers' characteristics

The institutional setup of the economy that we will consider is the same as that of the preceding chapter. Since we wish to study steady states, however, the demographic structure of the model has to be made precise.

In order to fix the ideas, we shall use the framework of an overlapping generation model without bequest and with a constant population, as in Section 1.6. This is merely a convenience, however, as the structure of the results that we shall obtain does not depend crucially on this specification. We recall briefly the characteristics of the overlapping generation model.

There are various "types" of consumers. A consumer of type i is described by:

(i)   the number of periods of his lifetime, $n_i \geq 2$;

(ii) his real income, or endowments of goods during his lifetime. His endowment of goods when he is of age τ, i.e., in the τth period of his life, is described by a vector $e_{i\tau}$, with l components;

(iii) his intertemporal preferences, which are represented by a utility function $u_i(c_{i1}, \ldots, c_{in_i})$, where $c_{i\tau} \geq 0$ is the trader's vector of consumption goods when he is of age τ.

---

[1]   The terminology is borrowed from D. Gale's excellent article on the subject (1973). The reader may wish to begin with a reading of that paper.

At each date, a newborn consumer of each type comes into the market. Thus there are n_i consumers of type i in activity in any period, each of them being in a different period of his life. The characteristics of a consumer are supposed to be independent of time, that is, they are independent of the date of his "birth."

We shall make the following assumptions throughout this chapter (the same as assumptions *(a)* and *(b)* of Section 1.6).

> *(a) The utility function u_i is continuous, increasing, and strictly quasiconcave for every i.*
>
> *(b) The endowment vectors $e_{i\tau}$ have all their components positive, for all i and τ.*

3.2   Long-run demands and supplies

Steady states are characterized by the fact that the relative prices of goods and the nominal rate of interest are constant over time, and that all money prices of goods are growing at a constant rate. The purpose of the present section is to look at the consumers' behavior in such an environment.

To this effect, consider the economy at some date, which we shall call the "current period," when the price system for goods is p, and the nominal interest rate r. Assume moreover that the interest rate was constant and equal to r in the past, and that prices of goods have been growing at a constant rate π. In other words, past prices of goods were equal to $(1+\pi)^{-1} p$, $(1+\pi)^{-2} p$, and so on. All components of the price system p are assumed to be positive, whereas the interest rate r and the rate of inflation π are both greater than -1.

We shall assume that in such a situation, a consumer, no matter which type he belongs to and of which age he is, forecasts that the same interest rate r will prevail and that prices will continue to grow at the rate π in the future. This assumption is natural, and means that consumers have "rational" or correct expectations along a steady state.[2]

Consider a consumer of a given type, say i, who is just "born" at the date under consideration. This consumer must choose, for every period τ of his life, his consumption $c_\tau \geqq 0$, his money balance $m_\tau \geqq 0$, and his supply of bonds $b_\tau \geqq 0$, or more concisely his net credit position at the Bank before interest payments, $\mu_\tau = m_\tau - b_\tau/(1 + r)$. We shall assume,

---

[2]   Note that the assumption concerns the dependence of a consumer's forecasts with respect to the *sequence* of current and past prices and interest rates. It is thus compatible, as the reader can check, with the conditions that were used in the preceding chapter to guarantee the existence of a short-run monetary equilibrium, since these conditions concerned the dependence of a consumer's expectations with respect to the *current* prices and interest rate only.

as in the preceding chapter, that a trader is either a creditor or a debtor, but not both. Thus either m_τ or b_τ will be zero. The net credit position the trader plans to have at the end of his life must be nonnegative, i.e., $\mu_\tau \geq 0$ for $\tau = n_i$. On the other hand, he begins his life without any credit or any debt at the Bank, since there are no bequests in the model.

The consumer seeks to maximize his lifetime utility under his current and expected budget constraints. His behavior is thus described by the following program, which is simply the transposition of (2.3.I) to the case at hand.

(3.2.I)   *Maximize* u_i *with respect to* $c_\tau \geq 0$ *and* μ_τ, *for* $\tau = 1, \ldots, n_i$, *subject to* $\mu_{n_i} \geq 0$ *and to the budget constraints*

$$(1+\pi)^{\tau-1} pc_\tau + \mu_\tau = (1+\pi)^{\tau-1} pe_{i\tau} + (1+r)\,\mu_{\tau-1}$$

for $\tau = 1, \ldots, n_i$, *(with the convention* $\mu_0 = 0$*)*

For reasons that will become clear shortly, it is convenient to reformulate this problem by dividing each budget constraint by $(1+\pi)^{\tau-1}$. If one defines the real rate of interest ρ by $1+\rho = (1+r)/(1+\pi)$, and if one sets $\mu'_\tau = \mu_\tau/(1+\pi)^{\tau-1}$, this yields:

$$pc_\tau + \mu'_\tau = pe_{i\tau} + (1+\rho)\mu'_{\tau-1}$$

for every τ. This way of looking at the consumer's decision problem makes clear that the optimum values of $c_\tau - e_{i\tau}$ and of $\mu'_\tau = \mu_\tau/(1+\pi)^{\tau-1}$ that arise from (3.2.I) depend only on the price system p, and on the real interest rate ρ. These optimum values will be denoted $z_{i\tau}(p,\rho)$ and $\mu_{i\tau}(p,\rho)$, respectively.

The homogeneity properties of the budget constraints imply immediately that the functions $z_{i\tau}(p,\rho)$ and $\mu_{i\tau}(p,\rho)$ are homogenous of degree 0 and 1 respectively, with respect to p. Moreover, by construction, they are linked by:

$$pz_{i\tau}(p,\rho) + \mu_{i\tau}(p,\rho) = (1+\rho)\,\mu_{i\tau-1}(p,\rho)$$

for every p and ρ, and all τ (with the convention $\mu_{i0}(p,\rho) = 0$).

With this notation, the excess demands for goods and the net credit position that our newborn consumer plans to have in the τth period of his life, are given by $z_{i\tau}(p,\rho)$ and $(1+\pi)^{\tau-1}\mu_{i\tau}(p,\rho)$. Now, according to our assumptions on expectations, consumers make no forecasting errors when the prices of goods are growing at a constant rate π, and when the interest rate r is constant over time. In such an environment, consumers do carry out, during their lifetime, the plans they made at the date of their "birth." What a consumer of type i and of age τ actually does in the current period is therefore what he intended to do during that period, when he formulated his plans as a newborn consumer, $\tau - 1$ periods before. At that time the prevailing price system was $p/(1+\pi)^{\tau-1}$. What such a consumer does in the current period is thus given by the values of $z_{i\tau}(p,\rho)$ and of $(1+\pi)^{\tau-1} \mu_{i\tau}(p,\rho)$, when p is replaced by $p/(1+\pi)^{\tau-1}$. In view of the homogeneity properties of these functions, the excess demands for goods and the desired net credit position of a consumer of type i and of age τ, in the current period, are thus equal to $z_{i\tau}(p,\rho)$ and $\mu_{i\tau}(p,\rho)$ respectively.

An equivalent way to get the functions $z_{i\tau}(p,\rho)$ and $\mu_{i\tau}(p,\rho)$, which we shall use later on, is to remark that the optimum consumption program which arises from (3.2.1) – hence the functions $z_{i\tau}(p,\rho)$ – can be computed by maximizing u_i under the intertemporal budget constraint:

$$\sum_\tau pc_\tau/(1+\rho)^{\tau-1} = \sum_\tau pe_{i\tau}/(1+\rho)^{\tau-1}$$

which is obtained by eliminating the financial variables from the sequence of budget constraints that appear in that problem, and by taking into account the fact that it is never optimal for a consumer to keep a positive money balance at the end of his life. The expressions $\mu_{i\tau}(p,\rho)$ are then determined recursively from the relations:

$$pz_{i\tau}(p,\rho) + \mu_{i\tau}(p,\rho) = (1+\rho)\mu_{i,\tau-1}(p,\rho)$$

Consider now all consumers of type i who participate in the market in the current period. The demographic structure that was postulated implies that there are n_i of them, each of whom is in a different period of his life. The excess of their aggregate consumption over their aggregate endowment of goods in the current period (their "long-run" excess demand for goods) is simply:

$$z_i(p,\rho) = \sum_\tau z_{i\tau}(p,\rho)$$

where the summation sign runs from $\tau = 1$ to $\tau = n_i$. Similarly, their desired net credit position is:

$$\mu_i(p,\rho) = \sum_\tau \mu_{i\tau}(p,\rho)$$

The net credit position that a consumer of type i and of age τ wishes to have at the end of the current period determines his corresponding money demand $m_{i\tau}$ and his bond supply $b_{i\tau}$ by the relation:

$$\mu_{i\tau}(p,\rho) = m_{i\tau} - b_{i\tau}/(1+r)$$

together with the condition that either $m_{i\tau}$ or $b_{i\tau}$ is equal to 0. Summing over all consumers of type i who live in the current period shows that their aggregate demand for money is a function of p and ρ, which will be noted $m_i(p,\rho)$. The amount of money that they wish to borrow in the aggregate (the sum of the $b_{i\tau}/(1+r)$) is also a function of p and ρ:

$$\beta_i(p,\rho) = m_i(p,\rho) - \mu_i(p,\rho)$$

and thus, their corresponding aggregate bond supply is $(1+r)\,\beta_i(p,\rho)$.

To sum up, these expressions define the aggregate behaviour of all consumers of a given type who participate in the market in a given period when prices are growing at a constant rate and when the nominal interest rate is constant over time, in function of the prices of goods p that prevail at the date under consideration and of the real rate of interest ρ. The homogeneity properties of the consumers' budget constraints imply, as we have already noted, that *the long-run excess demands for goods $z_i(p,\rho)$ and the desired net credit positions $\mu_i(p,\rho)$ are homogenous of degree 0 and 1 respectively, with respect to the prices of goods.*

In addition, these functions are linked by:

$$pz_{i\tau}(p,\rho) + \mu_{i\tau}(p,\rho) = (1+\rho)\,\mu_{i,\tau-1}(p,\rho)$$

for every τ. Adding these relations, while taking into account the fact that $\mu_{i\tau}(p,\rho) = 0$ for $\tau = n_i$, yields:

$$pz_i(p,\rho) + \mu_i(p,\rho) = (1+\rho)\,\mu_i(p,\rho)$$

for every p and ρ. Summing over all types i shows that the consumers' long-run demands and supplies satisfy what can be called the *generalized Say's Law*, that is:

$$p\sum_i z_i(p,\rho) - \rho\sum_i \mu_i(p,\rho) = 0$$

for every price system p and every real interest rate ρ.

To conclude, we wish to emphasize that, although the traders' long-run demand and supplies have been formally derived here within the framework of an overlapping generation model without bequests, their properties do not depend on this particular specification. The homogeneity properties of $z_i(p,\rho)$ and of $\mu_i(p,\rho)$ should hold in any model where traders are free of money illusion. On the other hand, the identities:

$$pz_i(p,\mu) + \mu_i(p,\rho) = (1+\rho)\,\mu_i(p,\rho)$$

for all p and ρ, which are the basis of the generalized Say's Law, can be interpreted as an aggregate budget restraint for the consumers of type i, and are thus pretty general. As a matter of fact, the expression $pz_i(p,\rho) + \mu_i(p,\rho)$ should be equal, for every p and ρ, to these consumers' aggregate net monetary wealth at the beginning of the period, including interest payments. This aggregate monetary wealth is given by $(1+r)\,\mu_i(p/(1+\pi), \rho)$, since $p/(1+\pi)$ is the price system that prevailed at the preceding date. Taking into account the homogeneity of degree 1 of μ_i with respect to the prices of goods yields the result. The generalized Say's Law is thus based on a very simple accounting argument, and should accordingly hold in any model with a stationary population.

3.3 The equations of steady states

We now wish to specify the system of equations that characterizes steady states and to study its properties.[3] It will be established in particular that the classical dichotomy and quantity theory are valid propositions when applied to steady states. Relative prices of goods and the real rate of interest are determined by the equilibrium of the goods markets. Nominal magnitudes such as the level of money prices, the nominal rate of interest, and the rate of inflation are in turn determined by the consideration of the monetary sector. In particular, the level of money prices will be shown to be proportional to monetary aggregates such as outside money, the Bank's money supply, and so on. This findings will imply that monetary authorities cannot influence, in the long run, the set of "real" equilibrium magnitudes by manipulating the nominal rate of interest or the rate of growth of the money supply. In this sense, pure monetary policy is *neutral* in the long run.

It will be shown in addition that there are two different sorts of (monetary!) steady states that coexist in a credit money economy: Golden Rule steady states, where the real rate of interest is equal to the rate of population growth, which is here equal to zero, and where outside money typically differs from zero at any point of time; and Balanced steady states, where the aggregate net credit position of the private sector is permanently 0, and where the real interest rate typically differs from the population growth rate.

A steady state is defined, we recall, as a sequence of short-run equilibria in which the nominal rate of interest is constant over time, say r, and in which prices of goods as well as monetary aggregates grow at a common constant rate (the "rate of inflation"), say π. If p denotes the vector of goods prices that prevail at the date $t = 1$, the price system at date t is

---

[3] It must be emphasized that the steady states that are analyzed in the sequel are *monetary* steady states, i.e., money has positive value in exchange at every date. Under the assumptions *(a)* and *(b)* of Section 3.1, *nonmonetary* steady states also exist, in which the price of money is zero in every period. Nonmonetary steady states are characterized by the fact that individual consumers cannot make any intertemporal value transfers. In the particular case in which there is only one good, a nonmonetary steady state is the autarkic one, where every consumer consumes his own endowment of good in each period of his life.

thus equal to

$$p_t = (1 + \pi)^{t-1} p$$

for every t. According to our assumptions on anticipations, consumers then have rational or correct expectations along a steady state.

As we have seen in the preceding section, in such an environment the aggregate behavior of the consumers of type i can be described in any period t by their excess demands for goods $z_i(p_t, \rho)$, where ρ is the real interest rate determined by r and π, and by their desired net credit position at that time, excluding the payment of the interest r, i.e., $\mu_i(p_t, \rho)$, or more precisely, their demand for money $m_i(p_t, \rho)$ and their bond supply $(1 + r)\ \beta_i(p_t, \rho)$.

The conditions that describe the equilibrium of the various markets along a steady state are then easily expressed by using these "long-run" demands and supplies. Indeed, equilibrium of the goods markets requires that aggregate excess demands for goods is zero in every period, that is:

(3.3.A$_t$) $\Sigma z_i(p_t, \rho) = 0$

for every t, where the summation sign runs over all types i of consumers.

The condition for money states that the aggregate long-run demand for money at date t, i.e., $\Sigma_i m_i(p_t, \rho)$, is equal to the outstanding money stock at that time, M_t. It is in fact convenient to express the money stock M_t as a function of the value of outside money at the beginning of the period, and of the amount of money created by the Bank when granting loans to consumers at date t, i.e., $\Delta M_t \geqq 0$. A moment of reflection shows that M_t is equal to the initial money stock at the date under consideration, including the payment of the interest rate r, i.e., to $(1 + r)\ M_{t-1}$, to which is added the Bank's money issue ΔM_t, net of the consumers' reimbursements of their past debts. As there are no forecasting errors along a steady state according to our assumptions on the consumers' expectations, the aggregate reimbursement is indeed equal to the aggregate bond supply at the preceding date B_{t-1}. One therefore obtains:

$$M_t = (1 + r)\ M_{t-1} + \Delta M_t - B_{t-1}$$

or equivalently:

$$M_t = (1 + r)\mu_{t-1} + \Delta M_t$$

where μ_{t-1} is the value of outside money at the beginning of period t, before interest payments. With this notation, the equilibrium condition for money reads:

(3.3.B$_t$) $\sum\limits_i m_i(p_t, \rho) = (1 + r)\ \mu_{t-1} + \Delta M_t$

for every t.

The Bank's demand for bonds is given by $(1+r) \Delta M_t$ in every period, whereas the consumers' aggregate bond supply is $(1+r)\Sigma_i \beta_i(p_t, \rho)$. Equilibrium of the bond market at each date thus necessitates:

$(3.3.B_{t2})$ $\Delta M_t = \sum_i \beta_i(p_t, \rho)$

for every t.

It is clear from the homogeneity of degree 1 of the functions $m_i(p_t, \rho)$ and $\beta_i(p_t, \rho)$ with respect to the prices of goods, that the monetary aggregates ΔM_t and μ_t must grow at the rate π over time. This is obvious for ΔM_t, in view of the bond market conditions $(3.3.B_{t2})$. On the other hand, the value of μ_t is given along a steady state by:

$$\sum_i \mu_i(p_t, \rho) = \sum_i [m_i(p_t, \rho) - \beta_i(p_t, \rho)]$$

which evidently also grows at the rate π.[4] The dynamic evolution of the two monetary aggregates ΔM_t and μ_t is thus determined once one specifies their values at some date. For notational convenience, we shall denote by μ the value of outside money at the beginning of period 1, before interest payments, and by ΔM the Bank's money creation on the credit market at that date.

A steady state is therefore characterized by a set of parameters $(p, \pi, r, \mu, \Delta M)$ such that the associated prices $p_t = (1+\pi)^{t-1}p$, as well as the monetary aggregates $\mu_t = (1+\pi)^t \mu$ and $\Delta M_t = (1+\pi)^{t-1} \Delta M$, satisfy the equilibrium conditions $(3.3.A_t)$, $(3.3.B_{t1})$, and $(3.3.B_{t2})$ for every t. By virtue of the homogeneity properties of the consumers' long-run demands and supplies, these equilibrium conditions are fulfilled in every period if and only if they are satisfied at a single date, say date 1. Accordingly, one can state:

A steady state is characterized by the set of parameters $(p, \pi, r, \mu, \Delta M)$ *that satisfy:*

$(3.3.A)$ $\sum_i z_i(p, \rho) = 0$

$(3.3.B_1)$ $\sum_i m_i(p, \rho) = (1+r) \mu + \Delta M$

$(3.3.B_2)$ $\Delta M = \sum_i \beta_i(p, \rho)$

where the real interest rate ρ *is given by* $1 + \rho = (1+r)/(1+\pi)$.

---

[4] It is intuitively clear how these statements must be modified when the population grows at the rate γ. For then the aggregate demand for money and the aggregate bond supply should grow at a rate λ given by $1 + \lambda = (1+\gamma)(1+\pi)$. The monetary aggregates ΔM_t and μ_t then also grow at the rate λ. In that case, per capita monetary aggregates and prices of goods grow at the rate π along the steady state.

The foregoing equilibrium conditions characterize a steady state without making any reference to the monetary policy the Bank may wish to implement. They must therefore be supplemented by a specification of the parameters that the Bank seeks to control, in the long run, by its interventions on the credit market. Examination of the system (3.3.A), (3.3.B_1), (3.3.B_2) shows that the monetary authority can a priori hope to control at most two variables among those that define a steady state, since this system involves $(l+2)$ equations whereas there are $(l+4)$ unknowns. For instance, the Bank may choose to peg the level and the rate of growth of its money supply: this would fix exogenously the parameters ΔM and π in the above system. Or alternatively, it may choose to peg the nominal interest rate permanently at the level r. The Bank's money issue ΔM_t would then be endogenous at every date. The Bank may even try to peg a "long-run" real variable such as the real interest rate ρ, by, for instance, linking the nominal rate of interest r with the observed rate of inflation π.

The system of equations (3.3.A), (3.3.B_1), (3.3.B_2), together with a specification of the values of the parameters that the Bank seeks to control in the long run by its intervention on the credit market, define completely steady states that are associated with the Bank's policy.

We proceed now to the study of the qualitative properties of the system (3.3.A), (3.3.B_1), (3.3.B_2). As we have seen, the long-run excess demands $z_i(p,\rho)$ appearing in this system are homogenous of degree 0, whereas the functions $m_i(p,\rho)$ and $\beta_i(p,\rho)$ are homogenous of degree 1 with respect to the prices p of goods. Moreover, these long-run demands and supplies satisfy the generalized Say's Law, that is:

$$p\sum_i z_i(p,\rho) - \rho \sum_i \mu_i(p,\rho) = 0$$

for every p and ρ.

These properties imply that the classical dichotomy and quantity theory are valid propositions in the present model. The l equations (3.3.A) for the goods markets are homogenous of degree 0 with respect to p, and thus define a priori the set of equilibrium relative prices of goods and of equilibrium real interest rates. Equilibrium of the real sector determines real equilibrium magnitudes. Once a particular solution of (3.3.A) has been selected, the corresponding equilibrium nominal values can be determined in turn by looking at the monetary part of the model. Indeed, the homogeneity properties of (3.3.B_1) and (3.3.B_2) show that the equilibrium level of money prices of goods is proportional to the level of the monetary aggregates μ and ΔM. Finally, the determination of the nominal rate of interest r and of the rate of inflation π (or equivalently, the rate of growth of the monetary aggregates), given the real interest rate ρ

obtained from (3.3.A), may be achieved by taking into account the Bank's monetary policy. For instance, if the Bank chooses to peg the nominal rate, this determines r, and thus the inflation rate π by $1 + \rho = (1 + r)/(1 + \pi)$. If the Bank chooses to peg the rate of growth of its money supply, this determines π, and thus the nominal interest rate r by the same relation.

These considerations have important implications concerning what monetary policy can achieve and also, most significantly, what it cannot. If one takes for granted the existence of a solution to (3.3.A) (we shall see that this can be done under quite general conditions), long-run real equilibrium magnitudes (the relative prices of goods, the real rate of interest, the traders' consumptions) are determined by the equilibrium of the real sector, independently of the Bank's monetary policy. The Bank can in principle manipulate the level of money prices of goods and the rate of inflation π (or alternatively, the nominal interest rate r), either by pegging the level and the growth of its money supply ΔM_t or by permanently fixing the nominal rate of interest r at an appropriate level.[5] Such a control is purely nominal, however, in the sense that it does not affect real equilibrium quantities in the long run. In particular, given a particular solution of (3.3.A), and thus a real interest rate ρ, a permanent increase of the nominal rate r induces only in the long run an offsetting increase of the rate of inflation π so as to leave the real rate $(1 + r)/(1 + \pi)$ unchanged. Similarly, a permanent increase of the rate of growth of the money supply ΔM_t leads only in the long run to an equal increase of the rate of inflation π, and to a correlative rise of the nominal rate r so as to maintain the ratio $(1 + r)/(1 + \pi)$ constant. Variations of the nominal rate r, or of the growth rate of the money supply, are *neutral* in the long run.[6]

---

[5] The Bank has full control over the rate of inflation only if the nominal rate r can assume any value between -1 and $+\infty$. If r cannot be negative (we saw in Section 2.1 that this is the case if paper money is assumed to be present in the model), there is a lower bound on the rate of inflation, given a particular solution of (3.3.A), since it must then satisfy $1 + \pi \geqq 1/(1 + \rho)$.

[6] This statement concerns only the consequence of a change of the growth rate of the money supply by means of monetary policy on the credit market. *If this change were brought about by means of fiscal policy, i.e., by levying taxes from and paying subsidies to consumers, it would have typically real effects in the long run.* The reader can easily check this fact by working out the simple example in which there is only one good and in which consumers live two periods, with a Cobb-Douglas utility function, $u(c_1, c_2) = c_1 c_2$. The basic reason for that non-neutrality, here as in Section 1.7, is that in an overlapping generation model, traders living at a given date face different intertemporal "liquidity constraints" because they are of different ages, and thus have different planning horizons.

An immediate corollary of this analysis is that the Bank cannot use its control over nominal magnitudes to peg a real quantity in the long run. Of course, the Bank may always attempt to do so through a deliberate policy on the credit market. For instance, it may decide to peg the real interest rate at some predetermined value $\bar{\rho}$, by setting a nominal interest rate r, in each period that is related to the rate of growth of the money supply observed in the immediate past, e.g., by using the relation:

$$1 + r_t = (1 + \bar{\rho})\, (\Delta M_{t-1}/\Delta M_{t-2})$$

If the chosen value $\bar{\rho}$ is not compatible with the equilibrium of the real sector (3.3.A), such a policy will be defeated by the market, in the sense that the economy will never reach a monetary steady state. If it ever approached a steady state, it should then be a nonmonetary one, in which money has no value in exchange. This would mean a complete breakdown of the monetary institutions under consideration.

The preceding analysis shows that all the information about the real characteristics of steady states is embodied in the equilibrium conditions (3.3.A) for the goods markets. The purpose of the next two sections is to investigate more closely the properties of the solutions of these equations.

It turns out that the set of these solutions displays a remarkable and quite simple structure. This is almost evident if one considers the generalized Say's Law, which claims that:

$$p\sum_i z_i(p,\rho) = \rho\sum_i \mu_i(p,\rho)$$

for every p and ρ. Any solution (p,ρ) of (3.3.A) must therefore satisfy either $\rho = 0$, or $\sum_i \mu_i(p,\rho) = 0$. Another even simpler way to obtain this result is to consider the money and the bond equations (3.3.B$_{t1}$) and (3.3.B$_{t2}$). By adding them and rearranging, one gets:

$$\mu_t = \sum_i [m_i(p_t,\rho) - \beta_i(p_t,\rho)] = (1 + r)\mu_{t-1}$$

for every t. These relations imply that outside money μ_t must grow along a steady state at the rate r as well as at the rate π (by virtue of the homogeneity of degree 1 of the functions m_i and β_i with respect to prices). This apparent contradiction can only be resolved if either the nominal interest rate r is equal to the rate of inflation, in which case the real interest rate ρ is equal to zero, or if outside money μ_t is permanently zero along the steady state.[7]

---

[7]   It is intuitively clear how these statements must be modified when population grows at the rate γ. For then outside money should grow at the same time at the rate r and at the rate λ that is defined by $1 + \lambda = (1 + \pi)(1 + \gamma)$. Thus,

There are therefore at most two types of monetary steady states: Golden Rule steady states, in which the real rate of interest is equal to zero, and in which the consumers' aggregate net credit position is typically permanently positive or permanently negative; and Balanced steady states, in which the consumers' aggregate net credit position is zero at any point in time, and where the real rate of interest typically differs from zero.

These two types of steady states will in fact coexist under quite general conditions, as we will see in the next two sections.

Remark. It should be emphasized that the results of this section borrow very little from the particular features of the overlapping generation model. The general argument used only the homogeneity of the consumers' long-run demands and supplies, and the generalized Say's Law, which is a simple accounting identity. The results should therefore be valid in any well-specified model of a credit money economy with a stationary population.

3.4   Golden Rule steady states

We will first study Golden Rule steady states, which involve by definition a real rate of interest ρ equal to 0. If we set $z_i^*(p) = z_i(p,0)$, the equilibrium of the real sector for such steady states is described by:

$$(3.4.\text{A}^*) \quad \sum_i z_i^*(p) = 0$$

The existence of a solution to this system is really a straightforward matter. Indeed, the functions z_i^* are homogenous of degree 0 with respect to the prices of goods, and the generalized Say's Law reduces here to $p\sum_i z_i^*(p) = 0$ for every p. Equation $(3.4.\text{A}^*)$ looks like a traditional Walrasian system, and accordingly should have a solution under the usual conditions of continuity and convexity of the consumers' preferences.[8]

(3.4.1)   *Assume (a) and (b) of Section 3.1. The system $(3.4.\text{A}^*)$ then has a solution. Every solution p involves positive prices, and is defined up to a positive real number.*

Our main concern in this section will be the study of the conditions that determine the sign of the consumers' aggregate net credit position along Golden Rule steady states. If we denote $\mu_i^*(p) = \mu_i^*(p,0)$, this

---

either the real interest rate is equal to the rate of population growth, or outside money is zero.

[8]   A proof of the result is given in Appendix D.

amounts to looking at the sign of the expression $\Sigma_i \mu_i^*(p)$, where p is a solution of (3.4.A*).

It is clear that the sign of outside money along Golden Rule steady states will depend on the intertemporal profiles of the consumers' real incomes during their lifetime, and on how they discount the future. Intuitively, one should expect that if the consumers have on the average larger real incomes in their "youth" than in their old age, and if they do not discount the future too much, they should be net creditors in the aggregate, that is, Golden Rule outside money should be positive. Conversely, if the consumers are on the average richer in the late periods of their lifes, they should be net debtors in the aggregate, i.e., Golden Rule outside money should be negative.

The remainder of this section is devoted to a precise formulation of these heuristic statements. To this effect, it is useful to begin the analysis by considering the simple case of only one good and consumers who live only two periods. The value of p that arises from (3.4.A*) is then indeterminate, and can be fixed arbitrarily.

According to our previous study of the consumers' behavior along a steady state (Section 3.2), the functions $z_{i1}^*(p) = z_{i1}(p,0)$ and $z_{i2}^*(p) = z_{i2}(p,0)$ are the optimum values of $c_1 - e_{i1}$ and of $c_2 - e_{i2}$ that result from the maximization of the utility function u_i under the consumer's intertemporal budget constraint, which, since $\rho = 0$, here takes the form:

$$p(c_1 + c_2) = p(e_{i1} + e_{i2})$$

Therefore, if the consumer does not discount the future, i.e., if his marginal rate of substitution between present and future consumption is equal to one whenever $c_1 = c_2$, he is going to consume $(e_{i1} + e_{i2})/2$ in every period (see Figure 3.1).

In such a case, $\mu_i^*(p)$ is equal to the consumer's saving when he is young, that is, to:

$$\mu_i^*(p) = p(e_{i1} - c_1) = p(e_{i1} - e_{i2})/2$$

If the consumer's income is larger when he is young than when he is old $(e_{i1} > e_{i2})$, then saving is positive. If he is on the contrary richer in his old age $(e_{i2} > e_{i1})$, then $\mu_i^*(p)$ is negative. On the other hand, discounting of the future generates a clockwise "rotation" of the indifference curves around the points of the figure such that $c_1 = c_2$. This should lead to an increase of c_1, and thus to a decrease of the consumer's desired net credit position $\mu_i^*(p)$.

Therefore, if the consumers are in the aggregate richer in their youth, i.e., if $\Sigma_i e_{i1} > \Sigma_i e_{i2}$, and if they do not discount the future "too much," outside money is positive along the Golden Rule steady state. If the

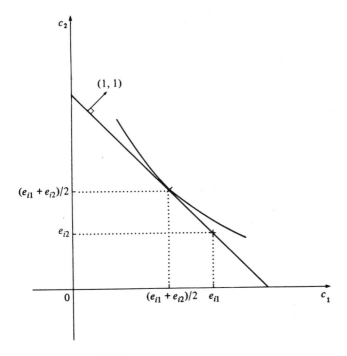

FIGURE 3.1.

consumers are richer when they are old in the aggregate, i.e., if $\Sigma_i e_{i1} < \Sigma_i e_{i2}$, outside money is negative along the Golden Rule steady state.

We turn now to the general case in which there are several goods and in which consumers live for an arbitrary number of periods. First, we must be able to speak in a meaningful way of the consumers' rates of time preference. We shall assume therefore that every consumer's utility function is separable, with a constant discount rate. Specifically, assumption *(a)* of Section 3.1 is replaced by:

> *(a')* The utility function u_i is of the form $\Sigma_\tau \delta_i^{\tau-1} w_i(c_\tau)$, where w_i is increasing, continuous, and strictly concave, and where $0 < \delta_i \leqq 1$ for every i.

We have next to find an appropriate measure of the difference between the consumers' real incomes in their youth and their real incomes in their old age. Consider the consumers of type *i*, and let $\epsilon_{i\tau}$ be the difference between the vectors of their endowments of goods in the τ first periods and in the last τ periods of their life:

$$\epsilon_{i\tau} = (e_{i1} + \ldots + e_{i\tau}) - (e_{n_i-\tau+1} + \ldots + e_{n_i})$$

Next define the vector ϵ_i by:

$$\epsilon_i = \Sigma_1^q \epsilon_{i\tau}$$

when n_i is odd and equal to $2q + 1$, and by:

$$\epsilon_i = \Sigma_1^{q-1} \epsilon_{i\tau} + \tfrac{1}{2} \epsilon_{iq}$$

when n_i is even and equal to $2q$.

This measure is at first sight adequate. If the consumers are richer in their youth, the vectors $\epsilon_{i\tau}$, and thus the vector ϵ_i, will tend to have positive components. Conversely, if they are richer when they are old the components of the vectors $\epsilon_{i\tau}$, and thus those of ϵ_i, will tend to be negative. This measure is further justified by the following fact.[9]

(3.4.2) *Assume (a'). If there is no rate of time preference ($\delta_i = 1$), then $\mu_i^*(p)$ = p ϵ_i for every price system p. If there is a positive rate of time preference ($\delta_i < 1$), then $\mu_i^*(p) \leqq p \, \epsilon_i$ for every p.*[10]

The argument has been developed up to now at the level of a single type of consumer. Finding the sign of outside money along Golden Rule steady states is then easy by considering all types together.

Let us define the vector ϵ as $\Sigma_i \epsilon_i$, and consider first the case in which the consumers have on average larger real incomes in the early periods of their lives, so that the vector ϵ has all its components nonnegative, with some of them positive. In view of (3.4.2), if there is no preference for present consumption ($\delta_i = 1$ for every type), the consumers wish to be net creditors in the aggregate, since $\Sigma_i \mu_i^*(p)$ is equal to $p\epsilon$ and is thus positive for every p. Outside money is then positive for every solution of (3.4.A*). It is intuitively clear that the same conclusion should hold, by continuity, when the consumers do not discount the future too much, i.e., when the parameters δ_i are close to 1. This argument justifies the following proposition.[11]

(3.4.3) *Assume (a') of the present section, and (b) of Section 3.1. If the vector $\epsilon = \Sigma_i \epsilon_i$ has all its components nonnegative, with some of them positive, outside money is positive along every Golden Rule steady state, when the parameters δ_i are close enough to 1.*

When consumers are on average richer when they are old the problem is even simpler. Let us assume that the vector ϵ has all of its components

---

[9] A proof of this fact is given in Appendix D.
[10] Actually, there is strict inequality under assumption *(b)* of Section 3.1, if w is differentiable, and if the partial derivative of w with respect to the hth good $\partial w / \partial c_h$, is infinite whenever $c_h = 0$. See Appendix D.
[11] A proof of the proposition (essentially a continuity argument) is given in Appendix D.

nonpositive, with some of them negative. In view of (3.4.2), the desired aggregate net credit position $\Sigma_i\mu_i^*(p)$ is then negative for every p, independently of the consumers' rates of time preference. Outside money is thus negative for every solution of (3.4.A*).

(3.4.4) *Assume (a') of the present section, and (b) of Section 3.1. If the vector $\epsilon = \Sigma_i\epsilon_i$ has its components nonpositive, with some of them negative, outside money is negative along every Golden Rule steady state.*

3.5   Balanced steady states

We proceed now to the study of balanced steady states, for which outside money is by definition equal to zero in every period. It will be shown that Balanced steady states do exist under quite general conditions, namely, *(a)* and *(b)* of Section 3.1. Moreover, it will be argued that such steady states are likely to involve a negative real rate of interest if consumers have larger real incomes in their youth and if they do not discount the future too much, and that the real interest rate is likely to be positive whenever consumers are richer in the later periods of their lives.

Real equilibrium quantities along a balanced steady state are given by the following set of equations, which express that the goods markets clear and that outside money is equal to zero:

(3.5.A) $\sum_i z_i(p,\rho) = 0$

(3.5.B) $\sum_i \mu_i(p,\rho) = 0$

The functions $z_i(p,\rho)$ and $\mu_i(p,\rho)$ appearing in this system are homogenous of degree 0 and 1 respectively, with respect to p, and they are linked by the generalized Say's Law, that is:

$$p\sum_i z_i(p,\rho) - \rho \sum_i \mu_i(p,\rho) = 0$$

for every p and ρ.

The equations expressing the equilibrium of the goods markets are identical to the system (3.4.A*) when the real interest rate is set equal to 0. Therefore, every $(\bar{p}, 0)$ such that $\bar{p}$ is a solution of (3.4.A*) satisfies (3.5.A). It should be noted, however, that the generalized Say's Law does not generally imply $\Sigma_i\mu_i(\bar{p}, 0) = 0$, since $\rho = 0$. In fact, this circumstance will occur only by an unlikely coincidence. For instance, we know from the analysis of the preceding section that if the consumers have a zero rate of time preference, $\Sigma_i\mu_i(\bar{p}, 0)$ is equal to $\bar{p} \Sigma_i\epsilon_i$ – see (3.4.2). When there is only one good this expression is equal to zero if and only if $\Sigma_i\epsilon_i = 0$, a condition that is satisfied only in very special cases.

This means that if we want to find a solution to the whole system, we must typically look for solutions (p, ρ) of (3.5.A) such that ρ differs from zero. By the generalized Say's Law, such solutions will satisfy the equation (3.5.B) as well.

In order to understand intuitively how changes in the real rate of interest permit us to find a solution to the complete system (3.5.A), (3.5.B), it is convenient to look at the simple case in which there is only one good. The value of p is then indeterminate and can be fixed arbitrarily. We are thus left with two equations to determine the real rate of interest ρ, which is the sole unknown of the system. The previous argument shows that $\rho = 0$ is always a solution of (3.5.A), but that typically it does not satisfy (3.5.B). In that case, finding an equilibrium value of the real interest rate can be achieved by looking for solutions of (3.5.A) such that $\rho \neq 0$, or by looking directly at equation (3.5.B), since by the generalized Say's Law any solution of (3.5.B) satisfies (3.5.A).

A typical heuristic argument for asserting the existence of such a solution is to say that an increase of the real interest rate should favor savings, and should thus lead to an increase of the consumers' desired aggregate net credit position $\Sigma_i \mu_i(p, \rho)$. One can then reasonably expect that this expression is positive for large real rates of interest, and that it becomes negative when ρ approaches -1. By continuity, therefore, a value of the real interest rate should exist in between that satisfies (3.5.2).

The foregoing argument can easily be visualized if one considers the simple case in which consumers live only two periods. According to our analysis of the consumers' behavior along a steady state (Section 3.2), the expressions $z_{i1}(p, \rho)$ and $z_{i2}(p, \rho)$ are the optimum values of $c_1 - e_{i1}$ and of $c_2 - e_{i2}$ that result from the maximization of the utility function u_i under the intertemporal budget constraint:

$$pc_1 + [p/(1 + \rho)] c_2 = pe_{i1} + [p/(1 + \rho)]e_{i2}$$

The desired net credit position $\mu_i(p, \rho)$ is then equal to the value of the consumer's saving when he is young:

$$\mu_i(p, \rho) = -p z_{i1}(p, \rho)$$

As the real rate of interest ρ varies, the line representing the intertemporal budget constraint (see Figure 3.2), rotates around the endowment point (e_{i1}, e_{i2}).

When the real interest rate tends to -1, this line becomes almost horizontal. Optimum consumption c_1 must go to infinity, and thus net saving $\mu_i(p, \rho) = p(e_{i1} - c_1)$ tends eventually to $-\infty$. If the real rate of interest tends to $+\infty$, the intertemporal budget line eventually becomes vertical. Optimum consumption c_1 must ultimately be less then e_{i1}, and

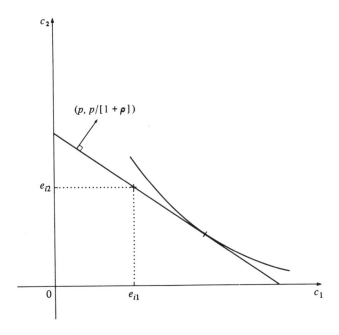

FIGURE 3.2.

therefore $\mu_i(p, \rho)$ becomes positive. Aggregating over all types of consumers yields the desired properties of $\Sigma_i\mu_i(p, \rho)$.

The foregoing heuristic argument shows that one can reasonably expect the system (3.5.A), (3.5.B) to have a solution under rather general conditions. It turns out indeed that it has one under assumptions *(a)* and *(b)* of Section 3.1.[12]

(3.5.1)   *Assume (a) and (b) of Section 3.1. Then (3.5.A), (3.5.B) has a solution. Every solution* (p,ρ) *involves a positive vector of prices, which is defined up to a positive real number, and a real interest rate* $-1 < \rho < +\infty$.

In "well-behaved" economies, one may expect that the expression $\Sigma_i\mu_i(p,\rho)$ increases with the real rate of interest, for each value of p. If this property is taken for granted, it becomes possible to get more information about the sign of the real interest rate associated with a balanced steady state, by relying upon the analysis of the preceding section. We are going to see indeed that in such a circumstance, *if the consumers are richer in their youth, and if they do not discount the future too much,*

---

[12]   A proof of the result is given in Appendix D.

every balanced steady state will involve a negative real rate of interest. On the other hand, if the consumers are richer when they are old, any balanced steady state will then involve a positive real rate of interest.

Let us assume that the consumers have separable utility functions, as in *(a')* of Section 3.4. Consider first the case where the consumers have larger real incomes in their youth, so that the components of the vector $\epsilon = \Sigma_i \epsilon_i$ are all nonnegative, with some of them positive. We know from (3.4.2) that, if the consumers do not discount the future, their desired aggregate net credit position $\Sigma_i \mu_i(p,\rho)$ is equal to $p\epsilon$ and is thus positive for every p whenever $\rho = 0$. Thus, if the expression $\Sigma_i \mu_i(p,\rho)$ is increasing with ρ, any solution of (3.5.A), (3.5.B) should imply a negative real rate of interest. It is intuitively clear that by continuity, the same result should hold when the consumers discount the future, provided that their rates of time preference are close to 0. We can thus state:[13]

(3.5.2) *Assume (a') of Section 3.4 and (b) of Section 3.1, and that the expression $\Sigma_i \mu_i(p,\rho)$ is increasing with ρ. If the vector $\epsilon = \Sigma_i \epsilon_i$ has all its components nonnegative, with some of them positive, any balanced steady state involves a negative real interest rate when the parameters δ_i are close enough to 1.*

Let us consider the other case, in which the consumers are richer in the later periods of their lives, so that the components of the vector ϵ are all nonpositive, with some of them negative. We know from (3.4.2) that $\Sigma_i \mu_i(p,\rho)$ is then equal to $p\epsilon$ and is thus negative for every p, independently of the consumers' rates of time preference, whenever $\rho = 0$. If the expression $\Sigma_i \mu_i(p,\rho)$ is increasing with ρ, any solution of (3.5.A), (3.5.B) therefore implies a positive real interest rate.

(3.5.3) *Assume (a') of Section 3.4 and (b) of Section 3.1, and that the expression $\Sigma_i \mu_i(p,\rho)$ is increasing with ρ. Then if the vector $\epsilon = \Sigma_i \epsilon_i$ has all its components nonpositive, with some of them negative, every balanced steady state involves a positive real rate of interest.*

Remark. It should be emphasized that *balanced steady states are monetary equilibria.* Money has positive value at every date, and is actually used by the consumers to make intertemporal income transfers at the individual level. The fact that outside money is zero simply means that at any point of time, the money balances of the consumers are exactly matched by their debts *in the aggregate.* Balanced steady states are thus essentially different from the long-run equilibria that would arise in this economy

---

[13] We shall not provide a formal proof of (3.5.2), as it reproduces almost exactly the argument that is used in Appendix D to prove (3.4.2). The mathematically oriented reader will easily fill in the details.

if the price of money is zero, since such nonmonetary equilibria are characterized by the fact that no intertemporal income transfers take place at the individual level.

3.6   Remarks on dynamics

Our analysis showed that there are two different sorts of monetary steady states that coexist in a credit money economy. First, there are Golden Rule steady states, in which, when the population is stationary, the rate of inflation equals the nominal interest rate, and in which the consumers' aggregate net credit position is permanently positive or permanently negative. Second, there are balanced steady states, in which outside money is zero at any time, and in which the real interest rate is positive or negative.

Two particular cases were distinguished. Whenever the consumers have larger real incomes in the later periods of their lives, every Golden Rule steady state involves negative outside money. The real interest rate should then be positive for each balanced steady state, at least in "well-behaved" economies. This is sometimes called the *classical* case in the literature, since this is the kind of situation depicted by classical writers such as I. Fisher when arguing that real interest rates should be positive. On the other hand, if the consumers have larger real incomes in their youth, and if they do not discount the future too much, every Golden Rule steady state implies positive outside money, while the real rate of interest should be negative, in well-behaved economies, for all balanced steady states. This is sometimes called the *Samuelson* case, as such situations were considered by this author in his seminal paper (1958) on the "social contrivance" of money. One then gets the following qualitative table:

Characteristics of the economy	Golden Rule steady states	Balanced steady states
Classical	$\rho = 0$ $\mu < 0$	$\rho > 0$ $\mu = 0$
Samuelson	$\rho = 0$ $\mu > 0$	$\rho < 0$ $\mu = 0$

In addition to monetary steady states, there is of course a nonmonetary stationary equilibrium in which money has no value in exchange, and in which there are accordingly no intertemporal income transfers at the individual level, contrary to what happens along a monetary steady state.

The mere multiplicity of possible long-run equilibria raises important questions concerning the nonsteady behavior of the model. More precisely, consider an arbitrary date, where the (nonsteady) past history of the economy is given. Assume that the Government intervenes from now on only on the credit market through its Banking Department, by manipulating the nominal interest rate or the money supply, and that the evolution of the economy is described, following the neoclassical tradition, by a sequence of short-run Walrasian equilibria, subject to the (stationary) monetary policy chosen by the Bank in each period. Will the economy tend to a steady state, and if so, which one?

In view of the validity of the classical dichotomy in the present model, if the Bank implements a policy that aims at pegging a real variable (e.g., the real interest rate) at a predetermined level that is incompatible with the long-run equilibrium of the real sector – that is, with (3.3.A) – the corresponding sequence of short-run equilibria can only tend to a nonmonetary equilibrium if it converges at all toward a steady state. This would mean the eventual breakdown of the monetary institutions. One can therefore hope to preserve the monetary character of the economy only by restricting the attention to the case where the Bank seeks to control nominal variables, e.g., by pegging the nominal interest rate r_t at a constant level r, or alternatively, the level and the rate of growth of the amount of credit distributed ΔM_t at every date.

The dynamics of the model is a complex matter, which will depend, presumably crucially, on how the consumers' forecasts of future prices and interest rates are functions at any moment of their information on the current and past states of the economy. Very little is in fact known about the subject, and it is a topic where a significant research effort is needed in the future. A moment of reflection nevertheless shows that a few dynamic configurations are impossible, or unlikely.

Let us start with the simple remark that along a nonsteady sequence of short-run Walrasian equilibria, outside money increases within each period by the Bank's deficit (the extent of bankruptcy), and that it grows in addition mechanically from the end of a period t to the beginning of the next at a rate equal to the nominal interest rate r_t that prevailed in that period.[14] Therefore if outside money is initially positive, it is bound

---

[14] See the discussion of the equations (2.2.C), (2.2.D), and (2.2.E). It should be noted that this statement relies upon a simple accounting argument that is independent of the particular notion of equilibrium employed in the short run. This statement, and the considerations that follow, are accordingly valid even if

to remain positive afterward. Symmetrically, if outside money is initially negative, it is likely to remain negative from then on, neglecting the possibility that bankruptcies reverse its sign.

Let us assume now that the particular sequence of short-run equilibria approaches in the long run a monetary steady state. That means in particular that the sequence of short-run equilibrium interest rates r_t converges to some level $r > -1$. On the other hand, the time path of outside money μ_t will tend to be eventually of the form $(1 + r)^t \bar{\mu}$, where $\bar{\mu}$ is positive if outside money was initially positive, and negative otherwise.

The immediate conclusion is that *a particular trajectory for which outside money is initially positive cannot converge to a Golden Rule steady state that involves a negative outside money – as occurs in the classical case – and this is independent of the Bank's monetary policy on the credit market. Symmetrically, if one neglects the effect of bankruptcies, a particular trajectory for which outside money is initially negative, must stay away from all Golden Rule steady states that involve a positive outside money – as they do in the Samuelson case.*

Is it possible that a nonsteady trajectory converges toward a Balanced steady state? If one literally interprets the definition of such a steady state to mean that *nominal* outside money must be permanently equal to zero along it, it would seem that such a convergence can occur only by coincidence. Any trajectory for which outside money is initially positive could not conceivably tend to a balanced steady state. If we neglect the effect of bankruptcies, the same would be true for any trajectory initially involving a negative outside money. Convergence toward a balanced steady state could only obtain in the special case of a pure inside money economy, i.e., if nominal outside money was zero at any time.

This view is incorrect, for it is based upon an interpretation of the definition of a balanced steady state that is unduly restrictive. In fact, the condition that outside money is zero along such a steady state will obtain in the long run if the real value of outside money tends to zero. To see this point, consider an arbitrary sequence of short-run equilibria that converges to a steady state, the nominal interest rate is r and the rate of inflation is π. As we said, the time path of nominal outside money will tend to be eventually of the form $(1 + r)^t \bar{\mu}$, where the sign of $\bar{\mu}$ is positive or negative depending upon the sign of outside money initially. On the other hand, prices of goods, as well as the outstanding money stock and the consumers' debt, will ultimately grow at the same rate π. Now, if π exceeds r, i.e., if the real interest rate is negative, the real

the evolution of the economy is governed by a dynamic disequilibrium process in which trade occurs at any moment at nonmarket-clearing prices.

value of outside money will tend to zero. The limiting steady state will indeed be balanced, although nominal outside money differs permanently from zero along the trajectory – it may actually go to infinity if both $\bar{\mu}$ and r are positive. On the other hand, if π is less than r, the real value of outside money along the trajectory would tend to $+\infty$ or $-\infty$, which would contradict our starting assumption that the trajectory converges toward a steady state. To conclude, *a sequence of short-run equilibria for which outside money differs initially from zero may well converge toward a balanced steady state that involves a negative real rate of interest – as occurs in the Samuelson case.*[15] *By contrast, such a trajectory will always stay away from balanced steady states involving a positive real interest rate – as they do in the classical case.*

These heuristic arguments may in some cases give a few qualitative insights about the dynamics of the model. In the classical case, a trajectory for which outside money is initially positive will typically stay away from monetary steady states. If the trajectory approaches in the long run a steady equilibrium, it must then be a nonmonetary one, in which case the monetary institutions are eventually destroyed. In most cases, however, there is still a multiplicity of possible long-run equilibria. The study of the nonsteady behavior of the economy then requires a precise modeling of the consumers' process of expectations formation. As we said, this is an area where our ignorance is great, and where a great deal of research is needed.

Remark. There have been a few studies of the monetary dynamics of the overlapping generation model when expectations are *rational*, i.e., when consumers forecast correctly future prices and interest rates even out of steady states (Cass and Yaari 1966; Gale 1973; Kareken and Wallace 1980; Hahn 1982). Gale's work suggests that in well-behaved environments, assuming a unique steady state in each class and that the Bank pegs the nominal interest rate at a predetermined and constant level:

In the Samuelson case, the balanced steady state is stable;
In the classical case, the Golden Rule path is stable if outside money is initially negative; whereas the only rational expectations equilibrium is the nonmonetary one if outside money is positive.

---

[15] Note that convergence toward a balanced steady state in which the real interest rate is negative is conceivable in particular when the Bank sets a nominal interest rate equal to 0 in every period, in which case nominal outside money is constant over time, if we neglect the effect of bankruptcies. *Sustained inflation is conceivable in that class of models with a constant level of nominal outside money, without implying any disruption of the monetary system.*

Whether or not these qualitative conclusions hold when consumers do not have rational expectations but learn over time the dynamics of prices and interest rates is an unresolved question.

Notes on the literature

This chapter is an extension of ideas developed by David Gale (1973) and by Grandmont and Laroque (1975). The results stated in (3.4.1) and (3.5.1) are generalizations of theorems proved by Grandmont and Laroque within the framework of an overlapping generation model in which traders live only two periods. These authors also considered the case in which the borrowing interest rate may differ from the rate paid on deposits.

For further studies of the overlapping generation model, the reader may consult the recent volumes edited by Kareken and Wallace (1980) and Hahn (1982), and the references contained therein.

Suggested reading

Cass, D. and M. Yaari, "A Re-examination of the Pure Consumption Loans Model," *Journal of Political Economy 74* (1966), 353–67.

Gale, D., "Pure Exchange Equilibrium of Dynamic Economic Models," *Journal of Economic Theory 6* (1973), 12–36.

Hahn, F. H., *Money and Inflation*, Blackwell Publisher, Oxford, 1982.

Kareken, J. H. and N. Wallace (eds.), *Models of Monetary Economies*, Federal Reserve Bank of Minneapolis, Minneapolis, 1980.

Phelps, E. S., *Golden Rules of Economic Growth*, Norton, New York, 1966.

Stein, J. L., "Monetary Growth Theory in Perspective," *American Economic Review*, 60 (1970), 85–106.

CHAPTER 4

Open-market policies and liquidity

In the real world, there are many channels through which a banking system may influence economic activity by implementing a specific monetary policy. One way, which was considered in the previous two chapters, is to intervene on the credit market by trying to manipulate the cost of borrowing, or the amount of money that is created when granting loans to the private sector. Another way, which we shall study presently, is the Bank's attempts to influence the economy's liquidity by exchanging illiquid assets such as long-term bonds for liquid assets such as short-term bonds or money.

The model we shall use to take this kind of phenomenon into account is quite simple, and bears some resemblance to popular Keynesian macroeconomic models. The real part of the model is the same as that in the previous chapters. As in Chapter 1, consumers have to decide in each period how much to consume and to save (no borrowing is allowed). But consumers can now save by holding two sorts of assets instead of one: paper money and perpetuities, both of which are issued by a governmental agency, the Bank. In such a context, the Bank can in principle engage in open-market operations by trading perpetuities for money, and vice versa. In particular, the Bank may wish to peg the interest rate, i.e., the reciprocal of the money price of perpetuities, or the money supply.

We shall be interested here in the determination of short-run equilibrium prices and interest rate at a given date, called the "current" period, subject to the Bank's policy.

Conventional neoclassical theory claims that a short-run equilibrium typically exists, and that, therefore, the Bank has full control over the interest rate or the money supply in a money economy with flexible prices like this one. There is, however, considerable disagreement about the underlying regulating mechanisms. Monetarists underscore the role of wealth effects, and of the intertemporal substitution that is engineered by a variation of the interest rate. Others emphasize the substitution between money and bonds embodied in the Keynesian Liquidity Preference theory. It will be shown, and this should by now be no surprise, that although both viewpoints contain some elements of truth, they miss an important part of the story, i.e., intertemporal substitution effects.

In order to make intertemporal substitution effects operative, we shall have to assume, in the same spirit as before, that some consumers' prices and interest rates forecasts are to a large extent *insensitive* to the current values of these variables. Here again, the restrictive character of such a condition makes the existence of a short-run monetary equilibrium more problematic than neoclassical theorists used to believe. It casts some doubts too on the ability of monetary authorities to fully control the interest rate or the money supply in the short run through open-market operations.

Another issue we shall be concerned with is the presence of a "liquidity trap." It will be shown that such a phenomenon does exist in the present model whenever the Bank has full control over the money stock, in the sense that the lower the interest rate, the less sensitive it becomes to a given variation of the Bank's money supply. More precisely, it will be shown that the short-run *equilibrium* money stock diverges to $+\infty$ if and only if the short-run *equilibrium* interest rate decreases to zero – provided that these variables can be manipulated without bound.

The last issue that we shall analyze is the neutrality of money. It will be shown by adapting the methods developed in the preceding chapters to the case at hand that a publicly announced once-and-for-all scalar change of all traders' initial holdings of money and of perpetuities, and of the Bank's money creation by open market, is neutral in the short run whenever the traders believe in its neutrality. By contrast, a change of the sole Bank's money issue through open-market operations, the traders' initial portfolios being fixed, will be found to produce short-run real effects.

This chapter is organized as follows. Neoclassical theory is briefly reviewed in Section 4.1. The basic assumptions of the model are recalled in Section 4.2, and the behavior of the consumers is made precise in Section 4.3. The question of the existence of a short-run equilibrium is analyzed next, both when the Bank attempts to peg the interest rate (Section 4.4) and when it tries to control the money supply (Section 4.5). The "liquidity trap" phenomenon is studied in Section 4.6. Lastly, the issue of the neutrality of money is taken up in Section 4.7.

4.1   Neoclassical theory revisited

We begin with a brief review of what conventional theory has to say in the present context.

The real part of the model is the same as before. There are thus l nondurable goods available in each period, whose (positive) equilibrium money prices p have to be determined at every date. Consumers decide at each moment how much to consume and to save: For simplicity, borrowing is not allowed. On the other hand, consumers can save by holding two kinds of monetary assets: paper money, on which no interest is paid by assumption[1]; and long-term bonds, which here take the form of perpetuities, i.e., promises to pay to the holder one unit of money in each period. At any date, the (positive) money price of perpetuities s determines the rate of interest, which is defined as the value of the short-term interest rate r that equalizes the discounted value of interest payments with the current price, that is:

$$s = 1/(1 + r) + 1/[(1 + r)^2] + \cdots = 1/r$$

Both assets are issued by a governmental agency, called the Bank. This agency's interventions are by assumption restricted to open-market operations, i.e., to exchanges of bonds for money. An issue of perpetuities by the Bank will reduce the amount of money held by consumers; conversely, the Bank's purchases of bonds will increase the money stock. The Bank can then aim at influencing systematically the economy's liquidity by implementing a specific policy, such as pegging the interest rate or the money supply. We shall be concerned with the existence of a short-run equilibrium at a given date, say date 1, or the "current period," subject to the Bank's policy.

According to neoclassical theorizing, a consumer a's actions at date 1 can be viewed as functions of the current money prices of goods p_1; of the current interest rate on bonds r_1, of his initial money wealth $\bar{m}_a + (\bar{b}_a/r_1)$, where $\bar{m}_a$ is the consumer's initial money holdings (including interest payments on bonds) and $\bar{b}_a$ stands for his initial stock of perpetuities; and of his expectations about future prices and interest rates (p_t, r_t). (We remind the reader that current and future endowments of goods are exogenous here, for the sake of simplicity.).

Following this approach, expectations are viewed in turn as functions of the currently observed prices and interest rate (p_1, r_1), and of the

---

[1]   The assumption that money does not bear interest is made only for convenience. The analysis that follows can be easily transposed to the case in which money is replaced by any safe short-term interest-bearing asset. This is left as an exercise to the reader.

trader's information on past history, which can be kept implicit since it is exogenous at date 1. What characterizes neoclassical theorizing, as we have mentioned several times, is that expected prices of goods are assumed to be unit elastic with respect to current prices p_1. Specifically, the prices that are anticipated by trader a are assumed to be given by $p_t = (1 + \pi_a)^{p-1}p_1$, where the trader's expected rate of inflation π_a is taken as independent of p_1. On the other hand, the influence of the current interest rate r_1 on expected prices is more ambiguous in that class of models, for they do not always make a precise distinction between nominal and real rates. In some cases, the traders' expected rates of inflation π_a are apparently assumed to be independent of r_1. In others, their expected real interest rates ρ_a, which are given by $1 + \rho_a = (1 + r_1)/(1 + \pi_a)$, seem to be exogenous in the short run. Finally, there is a similar imprecision in that sort of model concerning the influence of p_1 and r_1 on expected interest rates r_t. Current prices p_1 are usually assumed, explicitly or implicitly, to have no influence on expected rates of interest r_t. On the other hand, anticipations about future rates r_t are often assumed to be somewhat inelastic with respect to the current rate r_1, as we shall see shortly. But beyond that, these models are not very explicit on this matter.

Explicitly or not, a trader's expectations are functions of current prices p_1 and of the current rate of interest r_1 in neoclassical macroeconomic models. On this approach, therefore, a consumer's excess demand for goods, his money demand, and his bond demand, are written as $z_a[p_1,r_1, \bar{m}_a + (\bar{b}_a/r_1)]$, $m_a^d[p_1,r_1,\bar{m}_a + (\bar{b}_a/r_1)]$, $b_a^d[p_1,r_1,\bar{m}_a + \bar{b}_a/r_1)]$, respectively.

Summing these individual demand functions over all consumers yields an aggregate excess demand for goods, an aggregate demand for money, and an aggregate demand for bonds:

$$Z(p_1,r_1) = \sum_a z_a[p_1,r_1,\bar{m}_a + (\bar{b}_a/r_1)]$$

$$M^d(p_1,r_1) = \sum_a m_a^d[p_1,r_1,\bar{m}_a + (\bar{b}_a/r_1)]$$

$$B^d(p_1,r_1) = \sum_a b_a^d[p_1,r_1,\bar{m}_a + (\bar{b}_a/r_1)]$$

where the influence of initial holdings of money and of perpetuities is kept implicit, for notational convenience.

Writing down the equilibrium conditions for all markets at date 1 is easy by using these expressions. Equilibrium of the goods markets requires as usual:

(4.1.C) $Z(p_1,r_1) = 0$

The equation for money states that the aggregate demand for money must be equal in equilibrium to the initial money stock $M = \Sigma_a \bar{m}_a$, to which is added the Bank's money creation through the purchase of bonds. If we take momentarily this money creation ΔM as a parameter of the system, the money condition reads:

(4.1.D) $M^d(p_1,r_1) = M + \Delta M$

The fact that the Bank is issuing the quantity ΔM of money means that it is purchasing $r_1 \Delta M$ perpetuities on the bond market. Equilibrium of that market therefore requires:

(4.1.E) $B^d(p_1,r_1) + r_1\Delta M = B$

where $B = \Sigma_a \bar{b}_a$ is the initial aggregate stock of bonds.

These equations imply, trivially, that the Bank's money supply ΔM is bounded below by $-M$, and above by (B/r_1). The first inequality simply means that the final money stock has to be nonnegative, and the second that the Bank's money creation cannot exceed the value of outstanding bonds. Moreover, if one eliminates ΔM from equations (4.1.D) and (4.1.E), one gets:

(4.1.D$_1$) $M^d(p_1,r_1) = M + (1/r_1)[B - B^d(p_1,r_1)]$

This equality implies that the Bank's open market interventions do influence in the present model the economy's liquidity, i.e., the composition of the consumers' portfolios; but cannot alter, within the period, private aggregate money wealth.[2]

Examination of the above equations (4.1.C), (4.1.D), and (4.1.E) shows that the Bank has, as usual, one degree of freedom when choosing its money supply, and that it can try to influence the current short-run equilibrium position by linking ΔM with current economic observables (p_1,r_1). We shall restrict ourselves, for simplicity, to two specific policies, one in which the Bank pegs the interest rate, and the other in which it pegs the money supply ΔM.

Before looking at what conventional neoclassical theory has to say in such cases, we will review the particular properties of individual demand functions that are usually postulated in that kind of theorizing. The first property is Walras's Law, which states that the sum across markets of the values of excess demands is identically zero:

$$p_1 Z(p_1,r_1) + [M^d(p_1,r_1) - M - \Delta M] + (1/r_1)[B^d(p_1,r_1) + r_1\Delta M - B] = 0$$

for every p_1 and r_1. This identity is a consequence of the consumers' budget constraints.

---

[2] Aggregate money wealth will increase, however, from one period to the next, owing to interest payments made by the Bank on outstanding bonds.

The second property is, as usual, a homogeneity property stating that, for each consumer a, *the excess demand functions* z_a, *and the demands for money and for bonds* m_a^d *and* b_a^d, *are homogenous of degree 0 and 1 respectively, with respect to the current prices of goods* p_1 *and the money wealth* $\bar{m}_a + (\bar{b}_a/r_1)$. Such a property is traditionally justified by the assumption that expected prices of goods are unit elastic with respect to current prices p_1, and that expected interest rates are independent of them. In that case indeed a scalar change of current prices generates a proportional variation of expected prices, leaving expected interest rates unchanged. If the initial money wealth moves in proportion to p_1, the "real" opportunities of the trader are unaltered. His "real behavior" should accordingly remain the same.

Pegging the interest rate

We will first consider the case in which the Bank pegs the interest rate r_1, and thus has an infinitely elastic demand (supply) of perpetuities. The Bank's money supply ΔM is then endogenously determined by the equilibrium condition (4.1.E) of the bond market. Putting this value of ΔM into the money-market equation (4.1.D) yields, as we have seen, the equilibrium condition (4.1.D$_1$).

The short-run equilibrium of the system is thus described by the equations (4.1.C) and (4.1.D$_1$), where r_1 is fixed and the vector p_1 is variable. As a matter of fact, Walras's Law implies that one of these equations is redundant, so that we can focus the attention on the goods markets condition (4.1.C).

The neoclassical homogeneity postulates imply the short-run quantity theory: a doubling of all initial money stocks $\bar{m}_a$ and bond holdings $\bar{b}_a$, the interest rate r_1 being fixed, doubles the equilibrium prices p_1, but has no influence upon equilibrium "real" magnitudes.

On the other hand, the same postulates imply that, given r_1, the main regulating mechanism in the short run is the real balance effect. Indeed, if the model is specialized to the case in which there is one good, each individual's excess demand for the good can be written as $z_a(1, r_1, (\bar{m}_a/p_1) + (\bar{b}_a/p_1 r_1))$. A variation of p_1 thus influences the excess demand for the good exclusively by changing the "real" value of every individual's portfolio.

If the good is not inferior, every consumer's excess demand, and thus the aggregate excess demand $Z(p_1, r_1)$, is a decreasing function of p_1. The neoclassical argument for asserting the existence of an equilibrium, given the interest rate, is then, as usual, that a large (or small) value of p_1 should lead to an aggregate excess supply (or demand) on the good market. By continuity, there must be an equilibrium in between. Moreover, the equilibrium is unique, and stable in any *tâtonnement* process in which prices respond positively to excess demands.

As we have seen before, the theoretical validity of this sort of argument appears to have been accepted by many theorists today, but its empirical relevance has been seriously disputed. We shall see – and this should be no surprise to the reader – that the argument is in fact theoretically incorrect, because it neglects an important regulating mechanism, namely, the intertemporal substitution effects that are generated by a variation of current prices.

Pegging the money supply

We now turn to the case in which the Bank pegs its money supply ΔM at a value such that $\Delta M + M > 0$. This condition means that the final money stock must be positive. The associated equilibrium values of p_1 and r_1 are then defined by the system of equations:

(4.1.C) $Z(p_1,r_1) = 0$

(4.1.D) $M^d(p_1,r_1) = M + \Delta M$

(4.1.E) $B^d(p_1,r_1) + r_1\Delta M = B$

in which ΔM is given exogenously.

As an incidental remark, it is easily checked that the neoclassical homogeneity postulates imply the following version of the short-run quantity theory: a doubling of all initial money stocks $\bar{m}_a$ and bond holdings $\bar{b}_a$, and of the Bank's money supply ΔM, leads to a doubling of the equilibrium prices p_1, but leaves unchanged the equilibrium interest rate r_1 and all equilibrium real magnitudes. By contrast, a change of ΔM alone will have real effects, according to this viewpoint.

Most theorists would be willing to readily admit that the above system of equations has a solution for arbitrary values of ΔM, i.e., that the Bank has full control over the money supply, at least in this simple context in which there is no private banking sector. There is considerable disagreement, however, about the mechanisms that make an equilibrium possible. We briefly reviewed the debate concerning the real balance effect associated with a variation of current prices. The variety of opinions on the possible consequences of a variation of the interest rate is even more confusing.

The origin of this variety can be understood if one considers the possible impacts on demand functions of an increase of r_1 that are often referred to in that sort of model. First, there is a real balance effect, since each consumer's money wealth $\bar{m}_a + (\bar{b}_a/r_1)$ goes down, which should decrease both consumption and savings. On the other hand, it is often argued, an increase of r_1 alters the terms at which present goods can be exchanged for future goods. This intertemporal substitution effect should decrease current consumption, and increase savings: the demands for money and for bonds should both go up. Lastly, some theorists claim that the increase of the interest rate should make perpetuities more attractive in comparison with money. Substitution between bonds and money should accordingly yield an increase of the demand for bonds, and a decrease of the demand for money.

According to such heuristic arguments, the aggregate excess demand for goods $Z(p_1,r_1)$ should be inversely related to the interest rate. The impact of a variation of r_1 on the demands for money and for bonds is more ambiguous, as it depends on the importance given to the various effects we just discussed.

At one end of the spectrum, there is the "monetarist" view that money demand displays little sensitivity to the interest rate. An extreme version of a model of this type would be to say that $M^d(p_1,r_1)$ is actually independent of r_1. In the simple macroeconomic case in which there is one good, the equilibrium price p_1 could be viewed as determined by the money equation (4.1.D). The equilibrium level of r_1 would be found in turn by looking, say, at the good equation (4.1.C). From such a viewpoint, variations of the interest rate make an equilibrium possible essentially through wealth and intertemporal substitution effects.

At the other end of the spectrum, there are a number of economists who discount the wealth and intertemporal substitution effects of a variation of the interest rate, and who believe that substitution between money and bonds, which is at the heart of the Keynesian Liquidity Preference theory, is an important part of the story. An extreme version of this viewpoint would be to say that $Z(p_1,r_1)$ is actually independent of r_1. When there is one good, the equilibrium price p_1 can then be found by solving the good market equation (4.1.C). The existence of such a solution is asserted by appealing to the real balance effect associated with a variation of p_1. Given such a value of p_1, and an arbitrary rate of interest r_1, the equilibrium of the other markets would require a money creation by the Bank, say $\Delta M(p_1,r_1)$, which is given by the two following expressions which, according to Walras's Law, are equivalent:

$$\Delta M(p_1,r_1) = M^d(p_1,r_1) - M$$
$$= (1/r_1)[B - B^d(p_1,r_1)]$$

The problem is then to find a value of r_1 such that $\Delta M(p_1,r_1)$ is equal to the given money supply ΔM. The argument here rests essentially upon an alleged substitution between money and bonds. Since an increase of

r_1 should make bonds more attractive relatively to money, $\Delta M(p_1, r_1)$ should be a decreasing function of the rate of interest. Moreover, if r_1 is close to zero, "almost everybody prefers cash to holding a debt that yields so low a rate of interest."[3] The product $r_1 \Delta M(p_1, r_1)$ should then be approximately equal to B, implying that $\Delta M(p_1, r_1)$ largely exceeds ΔM. On the other hand, if r_1 is large, almost nobody should hold money. The value of $\Delta M(p_1, r_1)$ would then be close to $-M$, which is less than the money supply ΔM. It is clear that, by continuity, an equilibrium value of r_1 should then exist in between, and that furthermore such an equilibrium value is stable in any Walrasian *tâtonnement* process. As the argument applies to an arbitrary value of ΔM, the Bank would in fact have full control over the money supply.[4]

Most economists fall in between these two categories, and believe that an equilibrium can be achieved as a result of the various mechanisms that we described. Most theories give a more or less predominant role to the substitution between money and bonds engineered by a variation of the rate of interest. It is therefore worthwhile to have a quick look at the usual microeconomic explanations of the phenomenon.

The first explanation was provided by Keynes himself when introducing the notion of liquidity preference, and is based on the assumption that consumers have certain and inelastic expectations about future interest rates.[5] The explanation is in fact still popular in modern macroeconomic textbooks.[6]

The argument is quite simple. Consider a consumer who has to decide in which form to hold his savings. If the current interest rate is r_1, and if the consumer expects with certainty the interest rate r_2 to prevail in the future, it is clear that savings will be invested wholly in bonds if $(1/r_2) + 1 > (1/r_1)$, and wholly in money if the inequality is reversed. Now suppose that there is a continuum of infinitesimal consumers who hold different expectations, and that these expectations do not depend upon the current rate because, for instance, consumers believe that current variations of r_1 are only transitory. The aggregate demand for money will then be a smooth, decreasing function of the current interest rate, since as r_1 rises there will be more transactors who switch from money into bonds. Moreover, if r_1 is close to zero, almost everybody prefers cash, whereas nobody wishes to hold money when r_1 is large.

---

[3] See Keynes (1936, Chap. 15).

[4] However, in this extreme "Keynesian" version, a variation of ΔM has no effect upon the equilibrium of the real sector.

[5] See Keynes (1936, Chaps. 13 and 15).

[6] See, e.g., Branson (1972, Chap. 12), or Crouch (1972, Chap. 4).

This explanation is useful in the sense that it provides a justification of the theory of liquidity preference at the macroeconomic level. It has some drawbacks at the microeconomic level, since it predicts that every individual holds either bonds or money, but never both assets. The difficulty has been eliminated by Tobin's seminal contribution; Tobin showed that an expected utility-maximizing risk-averse transactor would diversify his portfolio if he is uncertain about the future interest rate.[7] Assuming that all consumers' probability distributions over future bond prices are inelastic with respect to the current rate of interest yields then the desired properties of the aggregate demand for money.

Both explanations give a rationale to the Keynesian Liquidity Preference theory via inelastic expectations. As appealing as it is, the argument has been criticized, however, on the ground that it requires exceedingly strong assumptions, since *all* consumers' interest rate expectations must apparently be inelastic.

More importantly, from our viewpoint, all the arguments that we reviewed suffer from the defect of being of a partial equilibrium nature. The widespread belief that monetary authorities can control the money supply through open-market operations is, accordingly, to be taken at best as an act of faith, for it is not the result of a coherent general equilibrium analysis. Our purpose in the sequel is to build such a theory, by adapting the methods that we developed in the previous chapters, thereby uncovering the sort of assumptions that are needed in order to ensure the existence of a short-run monetary equilibrium in the simple economy under consideration.

4.2 Consumers' characteristics

The real part of the model is, as we indicated, the same as in the previous chapters. The consumers' real characteristics at date 1 are thus as before the length n_a of their remaining lifetimes, their preferences u_a among consumption streams, and their endowments of goods e_{at}, where $t = 1, \ldots, n_a$.[8]

We make the usual assumptions:

(a) *The utility function* u_a *is continuous, increasing, and strictly quasi-concave, for each* a.
(b) *All components of the endowments vectors* e_{at} *are positive, for each* a *and* t.

[7] See J. Tobin (1958), and also K. Arrow (1970, Chap. 3).
[8] The usual caveat applies here. It is assumed that there are consumers whose lifetimes extend beyond the current period ($n_a \geq 2$). There may be consumers for whom $n_a = 1$, but the present short-run analysis will not rely on them explicitly.

Each consumer owns at the beginning of date 1 a stock of money $\bar{m}_a \geqq 0$, which is assumed to include interest payments on bonds, and a stock of perpetuities $\bar{b}_a \geqq 0$. The initial aggregate stocks of money $M = \Sigma_a \bar{m}_a$, and of bonds $B = \Sigma_a \bar{b}_a$, will be assumed to be *positive* in the sequel.

4.3   Short-run demands

We begin the analysis by looking at an individual's behavior, and consider to this effect a typical consumer (we drop the index a momentarily), who is faced at date 1 by the price system p_1 and the interest rate r_1 (or equivalently, the price of bonds $s_1 = 1/r_1$). We wish to describe how the consumer chooses his current consumption $c_1 \geqq 0$, and his demands for money $m_1 \geqq 0$, and for perpetuities $b_1 \geqq 0$.

The consumer must also plan his demands $(c_t, m_t, b_t) \geqq 0$ over his horizon, for $t = 2, \ldots, n$. His choices will thus depend crucially on how his expectations are formulated. We noticed already when reviewing the literature that a consumer will decide to hold either bonds or money but not both when he has certain expectations about future interest rates, and that on the contrary he may diversify his portfolio if he has uncertain expectations. Although the latter assumption is surely more realistic, we shall work nonetheless with deterministic expectations in the sequel. This is merely a convenience that keeps the mathematical exposition as simple as possible. Assuming probabilistic expectations would indeed yield the same qualitative conclusions.[9]

Let p_t be the consumer's expected prices of goods, and let r_t stand for his forecasts of future interest rates (or equivalently, $s_t = 1/r_t$, the expected prices of perpetuities). The consumer will seek to maximize his utility under the current and expected budget constraints. This decision problem can be formulated as:

(4.3.I)   *Maximize* u *with respect to* $(c_t, m_t, b_t) \geqq 0$ *for* t $= 1, \ldots,$ n, *subject to the budget constraints:*

$$p_1 c_1 + m_1 + s_1 b_1 = p_1 e_1 + \bar{m} + s_1 \bar{b}$$

$$p_t c_t + m_t + s_t b_t = p_t e_t + m_{t-1} + (s_t + 1)b_{t-1}$$

for t $= 2, \ldots,$ n.

This problem has a solution when current and expected prices and current and expected interest rates are positive. Moreover, the utility

---

[9] For a mathematical analysis of a similar model with probabilistic expectations, the reader may consult Grandmont and Laroque (1976a), or Grandmont (1977, Section 3.3).

function being strictly quasi-concave, the optimum consumption program, and thus the current consumption c_1, is uniquely determined. Consider now the expected yield g of perpetuities at date 1 that is implied by the consumer's expectations, and that is defined by:

$$1 + g = (s_2 + 1)/s_1$$

It is clear that if $g > 0$, the consumer prefers to hold his savings, if any, in the form of bonds. The corresponding optimum current portfolio is unique, and involves a money demand m_1 equal to zero. If on the other hand $g < 0$, the optimum current portfolio is again unique, but this time involves a zero demand for bonds. Lastly, when the expected yield g is zero, the optimum value of current savings $m_1 + s_1b_1$ is uniquely defined, but the consumer is indifferent about which he holds, money or bonds.

The absence of money illusion property here takes the following simple form, as the reader will easily check. If (c_t, m_t, b_t) is a solution of (4.3.I), then $(c_t, \lambda m_t, \lambda b_t)$ will be a solution of (4.3.I) too whenever the initial stocks of assets $\bar{m}$ and $\bar{b}$, and current and expected prices $p_1, \ldots, p_n$ are multiplied by the positive parameter λ.

In order to complete the description of the consumer's behavior, the dependence of expectations upon the trader's information has to be specified. As in the previous models, we shall keep implicit the influence of his information on past history, and single out the impact of current prices and the current interest rate. Expected prices and expected interest rates will thus be denoted $\psi_t(p_1, r_1)$ and $\rho_t(p_1, r_1)$ respectively, for $t = 2, \ldots, n$.

When expectations are replaced by these expressions, the solutions of (4.3.I) depend only on initial money wealth $\bar{m} + (\bar{b}/r_1)$, and on p_1 and r_1. If one reintroduces at this stage the consumer's index a, this yields an excess demand function for goods $z_a[p_1, r_1, \bar{m}_a + (\bar{b}_a/r_1)]$. The corresponding demands for money and bonds will be denoted $m_a^d[p_1, r_1, \bar{m}_a + (\bar{b}_a/r_1)]$, and $b_a^d[p_1, r_1, \bar{m}_a + (\bar{b}_a/r_1)]$, respectively. We remarked previously that the solution of (4.3.I) exhibited some indetermination when the expected yield on bonds was zero. In that case, the preceding expressions will represent an arbitrary member of the solution set.

In view of the absence of money illusion property stated above, it is clear that the neoclassical homogeneity postulates, i.e., the homogeneity of degree 0 (or 1) of the excess demand for goods (or the demands for money and bonds) with respect to the initial money wealth $\bar{m}_a + (\bar{b}_a/r_1)$ and current prices p_1, hold if, and in general only if, expected prices p_t are proportional to current prices and if expected interest rates are independent of them. These assumptions will not be retained here, however, as they will be shown to be typically inconsistent with the existence of a short-run monetary equilibrium.

A proportional increase of current prices from p_1 to λp_1 will thus have more complex consequences on a consumer's behavior than is usually posited in a neoclassical world. First there is a real balance effect, which is due to the change in the purchasing power of initial money wealth $\bar{m}_a + (\bar{b}_a/r_1)$. This real balance effect would occur alone if expected prices moved proportionately to current prices and if expected interest rates were unchanged. As these assumptions on expectations are typically not satisfied, the change of current prices will yield an additional intertemporal substitution effect due to the alteration of the terms at which future goods can be exchanged for current ones, i.e., to the change of the consumer's expected rate of inflation. Lastly, there may be a substitution between money and bonds caused by a relative variation of the expected rates of return on the two assets, i.e., by a change of the consumer's expected yield on perpetuities.[10] Similarly, an increase of the current interest rate will yield a real balance effect, through the change of the initial money wealth $\bar{m}_a + (\bar{b}_a/r_1)$, as well as an intertemporal substitution effect and a possible substitution between bonds and money.

Summing all individual demands over all consumers gives an aggregate excess demand for goods, and an aggregate demand for money and bonds:

$$Z(p_1,r_1) = \sum_a z_a[p_1,r_1,\bar{m}_a + (\bar{b}_a/r_1)]$$

$$M^d(p_1,r_1) = \sum_a m_a^d[p_1,r_1,\bar{m}_a + (\bar{b}_a/r_1)]$$

$$B^d(p_1,r_1) = \sum_a b_a^d[p_1,r_1,\bar{m}_a + (\bar{b}_a/r_1)]$$

where the influence of the initial stocks of assets is kept implicit.

If one momentarily takes the Bank's money creation through the purchase of perpetuities as a parameter ΔM, the market-clearing conditions at date 1 then read[11]:

(4.3.C) $Z(p_1,r_1) = 0$

(4.3.D) $M^d(p_1,r_1) = M + \Delta M$

(4.3.E) $B^d(p_1,r_1) + r_1\Delta M = B$

---

[10] In this particular version of the model, where traders hold certain expectations, such a substitution will occur if and only if the sign of the consumer's expected yield on perpetuities is reversed. In a more general version where anticipations would take the form of probability distributions and where traders would diversify their portfolios, any variation of a trader's subjective probability distribution over future interest rates would induce "smoothly" a substitution between the two assets.

[11] The conditions (4.3.D) and (4.3.E), and in fact any condition involving $M^d(p_1,r_1)$ and/or $B^d(p_1,r_1)$, have to be interpreted with some care, since with a finite number

This system is formally identical to the neoclassical system discussed in Section 4.1 when reviewing the literature. In view of the consumers' current budget constraints, it satisfies Walras's Law:

$$p_1 Z(p_1,r_1) + [M^d(p_1,r_1) - M - \Delta M] + (1/r_1)[B^d(p_1,r_1) + r_1 \Delta MB] = 0$$

for every p_1 and r_1. It differs from the neoclassical system in one important respect, however, for we did not assume any homogeneity properties. We shall see that in order to ensure the existence of a short-run equilibrium, one has to make assumptions on expectations that violate the neoclassical homogeneity postulates.[12]

4.4   Pegging the interest rate

We are interested first in the case of the Bank pegging the interest rate r_1. The Bank's supply or demand of perpetuities is then assumed to be infinitely elastic: the money creation ΔM becomes endogenously determined by the equilibrium of the bond market. The equilibrium conditions associated with this policy are thus obtained by eliminating ΔM between (4.3.D) and (4.3.E), which yields:

(4.4.C) $Z(p_1,r_1) = 0$

(4.4.D$_1$) $M^d(p_1,r_1) = M + (1/r_1)[B - B^d(p_1,r_1)]$

where the interest rate is fixed. By Walras's Law, one of these conditions is actually redundant, and attention can be focused on the real sector (4.4.C) when looking for an equilibrium.

Neoclassical theorists claim that a short-run monetary equilibrium typically exists in such case by appealing to the real balance effect that results from a variation of the current prices p_1. We shall see that such a statement is theoretically incorrect, and that one must reinforce the real balance effect with a strong stabilizing intertemporal substitution

of consumers, the aggregate demands for money and bonds may exhibit some degree of indeterminacy. They mean that particular choices exist from every individual's set of solutions of (4.3.I) for the given configuration (p_1,r_1), such that the market-clearing conditions are satisfied. It is possible to remove this aggregate indeterminacy by assuming, as it is often done in macroeconomic textbooks, a continuum of infinitesimal consumers who hold diverse expectations about future interest rates. This approach would have yielded the same results. We preferred not to use it, in order to avoid unnecessary technicalities.

[12] Accordingly, it would seem that the various versions of the short-run quantity theory that were discussed in Section 4.1 are no longer valid. Here again, this is not true (see Section 4.7).

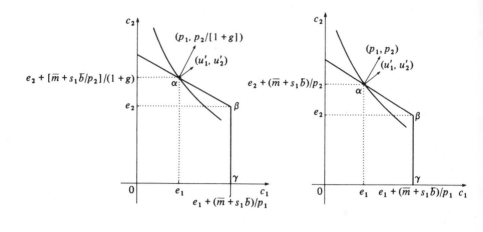

FIGURE 4.1.

effect to guarantee the existence of a monetary equilibrium. This will be shown by adapting the methods we developed in the previous chapters to the model at hand.

In order to see this point, it is convenient here again to look at the simple case in which there is only one good, and in which each transactor makes plans for the current and the next periods only. A typical consumer's current and expected budget constraints then read:

$$p_1 c_1 + m_1 + s_1 b_1 = p_1 e_1 + \bar{m} + s_1 \bar{b}$$
$$p_2 c_2 + m_2 + s_2 b_2 = p_2 e_2 + m_1 + (s_2 + 1) b_1$$

If the consumer's expected yield on perpetuities g, which is defined by $1 + g = (s_2 + 1)/s_1$, is positive, he will decide to hold his savings wholly in bonds. One can then set without any loss of generality $m_1 = 0$ in the foregoing constraints. The optimum consumption program is obtained in such a case by maximizing the trader's utility function subject to the following inequalities, which are obtained from the budget constraints by eliminating the asset variables:

$$p_1 c_1 + p_2 c_2/(1 + g) \leqq p_1 e_1 + [p_2 e_2/(1 + g)] + \bar{m} + s_1 \bar{b}$$
$$p_1 c_1 \leqq p_1 e_1 + \bar{m} + s_1 \bar{b}$$

The corresponding region of feasible current and future consumptions is shown in Figure 4.1a.

When the expected yield g is negative, the same procedure applies with $b_1 = 0$. The associated feasible region for (c_1, c_2) is then given by:

$$p_1 c_1 + p_2 c_2 \leqq p_1 e_1 + p_2 e_2 + \bar{m} + s_1 \bar{b}$$

$$p_1 c_1 \leqq p_1 e_1 + \bar{m} + s_1 \bar{b}$$

and is represented in Figure 4.1b.[13]

Suppose now that the consumer's initial wealth $\bar{m} + s_1 \bar{b}$ is positive. It is clear from Figure 4.1a that, when the expected yield g is positive, the optimum current consumption will exceed e_1 if and only if the ratio $p_2/(1 + g)p_1$ is greater than the marginal rate of substitution u'_2/u'_1 at the point α. Since p_2/p_1 exceeds $p_2/(1 + g)p_1$ in such a case, this condition reads:

$$(p_2/p_1) > p_2/(1 + g)p_1 > (u'_2/u'_1)|\alpha$$

A similar reasoning for Figure 4.1b shows that when g is negative, $c_1 > e_1$ if and only if:

$$p_2/(1 + g)p_1 > (p_2/p_1) > (u'_2/u'_1)|\alpha$$

It is easy to construct from these premises an example in which there is an *aggregate excess demand* on the good market at all current prices. Assume that the typical consumer's utility function is of the form $w(c_1) + \delta w(c_2)$, where w is strictly concave and differentiable, and $0 < \delta \leqq 1$. This implies that the marginal rate of substitution u'_2/u'_1 is a decreasing function of future consumption. Whether g is positive or not, the individual desired consumption c_1 then exceeds e_1 if both ratios p_2/p_1 and $p_2/(1 + g)p_1$ are greater than or equal to the marginal rate of substitution at the endowment point, i.e., $\delta w'(e_2)/w'(e_1)$. If all consumers' expectations concerning future prices and interest rates, as functions of p_1 and r_1, are biased upward in this way, there will be an aggregate excess demand on the good market at all current prices p_1. One can then make the size of aggregate excess demand arbitrarily small, through the real balance effect, by increasing the current price p_1, since the point β on the diagrams converge to the endowment point (e_1, e_2) as p_1 tends to infinity. But a short-run equilibrium does not exist in which money has positive value.

It is equally easy to construct an example of a persistent *aggregate excess supply* on the good market. Assume that for all consumers, the marginal rate of substitution is bounded below by $\nu > 0$ when one moves up the vertical line going through the endowment point (e_1, e_2). It is

---

[13] Both diagrams apply of course when $g = 0$.

straightforward to check that, if each consumer's ratio p_2/p_1, as a function of p_1 and r_1, is bounded above by v, there is an aggregate excess supply of the good at all values of p_1.[14] Again, there can be no short-run equilibrium.

The two examples apply in particular in the neoclassical case, where expected prices are unit elastic with respect to current prices, and expected interest rates are independent of them. They are, in addition, independent of the sizes of the initial stocks of assets M and B. They invalidate, therefore, the neoclassical position, which claims that one should be able, given the interest rate, to equilibrate the market through the real balance effect engineered by a variation of current prices.

The origin of the inexistence phenomenon we just described is to be found, of course, in the rigidities of the individual ratios p_2/p_1 and $p_2/(1 + g)p_1$, i.e., in the absence of a strong, stabilizing substitution between current and future consumption. In order to make such a substitution effect operational, what is needed, here again, is some insensitivity of expectations with respect to current prices.

In order to check this point, let us go back to the simple case represented in the foregoing diagrams, and look at what happens when p_1 tends to infinity. Each consumer's excess demand $c_1 - e_1$ is bounded above by his initial real wealth $(\bar{m} + s_1\bar{b})/p_1$, which goes to 0. It suffices therefore that $c_1 - e_1$ becomes negative for at least one consumer to eventually get an aggregate excess supply on the good market. Now suppose that there is an insensitive consumer whose expected price p_2 and expected interest rate r_2 do not vary with the current price p_1. This consumer's expected yield g is then actually independent of p_1, which leads to considering Figure 4.1a if it is positive, and Figure 4.1b otherwise. In either case, the intertemporal budget line $\alpha\beta$ rotates around the point α, and tends to be almost vertical, which yields the desired result. More precisely, the insensitive consumer's planned consumption c_2 goes to infinity. In view of his expected budget constraint:

$$p_2c_2 = p_2e_2 + m_1 + (s_2 + 1)b_1$$

(where m_2 and b_2 have been set equal to 0 without any loss of generality), either his demand for money m_1 or his demand for funds b_1 increases without bound. Thus either $M^d(p_1,r_1)$ or $B^d(p_1,r_1)$ diverges to infinity. If one looks back at the money-market equation $(4.4.D_1)$, this means that there is eventually an aggregate excess demand on that market. By Walras's Law, there must be an aggregate excess supply for the good. Intertemporal substitution, together with the real balance effect, ensures indeed the

[14] The argument works equally well by using the ratio $p_2/(1 + g)\,p_1$.

appearance of an aggregate excess supply on the good market as p_1 tends to $+\infty$.

Consider next the case in which p_1 tends to 0. The insensitive consumer's intertemporal budget line rotates again around α and becomes almost horizontal. If $\bar{m} + s_1\bar{b}$ is positive, this trader's desired current consumption is then bound to go to infinity, thereby generating an aggregate excess demand on the good market. Thus, by continuity, one should be able to equilibrate the good market, and therefore the whole system.

The insensitive consumer ensures the presence of a stabilizing intertemporal substitution which, together with the real balance effect, guarantees the existence of a short-run monetary equilibrium for a given interest rate.[15] We will now give a general result along these lines.

Consider a consumer a whose horizon extends beyond the current period ($n_a \geqq 2$). We shall say that his expectations are *continuous in current prices* if the functions $\psi_{at}(p_1,r_1)$ and $\rho_{at}(p_1,r_1)$ are continuous, given r_1, with respect to p_1, for every t. Expectations will be said to be *bounded with respect to current prices* if, given r_1, there are two vectors $\epsilon(r_1)$ and $\eta(r_1)$, with all their components positive, such that $\epsilon(r_1) \leqq \psi_{at}(p_1,r_1) \leqq \eta(r_1)$, and if there are two positive numbers $\epsilon'(r_1)$ and $\eta'(r_1)$ such that $\epsilon'(r_1) \leqq \rho_{at}(p_1,r_1) \leqq \eta'(r_1)$, for all p_1 and t. Such boundedness conditions lead of course to a violation of the neoclassical homogeneity postulates, and are the key for the following existence result.[16]

(4.4.1) *Let the interest rate* r_1 *be fixed. Assume (a) and (b) of Section 4.2, and that every consumer's expectations are continuous in current prices. Assume moreover that there is a consumer with* $n_a \geqq 2$ *and* $\bar{m}_a + (\bar{b}_a/r_1) > 0$, *whose expectations are bounded with respect to current prices.*
Then, given r_1, *the system (4.4.C), (4.4.D_1) has a solution, i.e., the Bank can peg the interest rate at the level* r_1.

To sum up, this analysis has shown that, in contradiction to conventional theory, the real balance effect resulting from a variation of current prices, the interest rate being fixed, may be too weak to equilibrate the market; and that intertemporal substitution effects must be taken into account. However, in order to make such substitutions operational, we had to make the strong assumption that some consumers' expectations are to a large extent insensitive to a variation of current prices. Here again, one is entitled to conclude from the restrictive character of that kind of assumption that the existence of a short-run monetary equilibrium is problematic.

---

[15] The argument shows too that substitution between money and bonds need not play any role in the equilibrating process if the interest rate is given.
[16] A proof of this result is given in Appendix E.

4.5   Controlling the money supply

We now turn to the situation where the Bank attempts to peg its money creation at a given level $\Delta M > -M$. The short-run equilibrium current prices and interest rate (p_1, r_1) are then the solutions of the following set of conditions:

(4.5.C) $Z(p_1, r_1) = 0$

(4.5.D) $M^d(p_1, r_1) = M + \Delta M$

(4.5.E) $B^d(p_1, r_1) + r_1 \Delta M = B$

where ΔM is given.

This system, of course, need not admit of a solution. The examples developed in the preceding section showed that an equilibrium might not exist on the goods markets for a given interest rate if the consumers' expectations were biased upward or downward. These inexistence examples can be extended, trivially, so as to be valid for all interest rates. In that case, there can be no pair (p_1, r_1) that satisfies (4.5.C).

Conventional theory nevertheless asserts that the foregoing system has a solution for every ΔM, i.e., that the monetary authority has complete control of the money supply. The purpose of the present section is to uncover the kind of assumptions that validate such a proposition.

It is convenient, to this effect, to use once again the following heuristic procedure. Given an arbitrary r_1, let p_1 be a corresponding solution of (4.5.C). As this configuration (p_1, r_1), one needs a creation of money $\Delta M(p_1, r_1)$ by the Bank in order to bring the two other markets into equilibrium, which is given by the following and, according to Walras's Law, equivalent expressions:

$$\Delta M(p_1, r_1) = M^d(p_1, r_1) - M$$

$$= (1/r_1)[B - B^d(p_1, r_1)]$$

Solving the whole system then amounts to finding a value of r_1, and a corresponding solution p_1 of (4.5.C), such that $\Delta M(p_1, r_1)$ equals the given money supply ΔM.

The validity of the procedure presupposes that (4.5.C) can be solved in p_1 for each interest rate. We shall assume that it is indeed the case because, for instance, the conditions of (4.4.1) are fulfilled for each r_1.

Our strategy will be to find conditions that ensure that $\Delta M(p_1, r_1)$ approaches $-M$ when the interest rate is large, and conversely, that $\Delta M(p_1, r_1)$ becomes very large when r_1 tends to 0, the prices p_1 moving correlatively in each case so as to maintain the equilibrium of the real sector.[17] Intuitively, by continuity, one should then be able to equilibrate the entire system.

It is easily seen that $\Delta M(p_1, r_1)$ is equal to $-M$, or equivalently that $M^d(p_1, r_1)$ is equal to 0 in the present model, when the interest rate is large. Indeed, if $r_1 \geqq 1$, or alternatively if the price s_1 of perpetuities is less than or equal to unity, every consumer's expected yield on bonds is positive. Accordingly, nobody wishes to hold money.

It remains to see when $\Delta M(p_1, r_1)$ has the desired property as r_1 gets close to zero. The Keynesian viewpoint of this matter was reviewed in Section 4.1. It supposes that *all* consumers' interest rate expectations are inelastic with respect to a variation of the current rate. With a finite number of transactors as here, every individual's expected yield on perpetuities then becomes negative as r_1 goes to 0. Everyone eventually switches from bonds into money, in which case $\Delta M(p_1, r_1)$ is equal to B/r_1, and thus tends to infinity.

Some substitution between money and bonds is clearly needed in order to get the desired result as the interest rate goes down. Otherwise, $\Delta M(p_1, r_1)$ would be equal to $-M$ for all r_1. The foregoing Liquidity Preference theory is, however, too demanding, and is accordingly based upon exceedingly strong assumptions on expectations, for it requires *full* substitution between money and perpetuities eventually. But this is obviously asking too much. The money creation:

$$\Delta M(p_1, r_1) = (1/r_1)[B - B^d(p_1, r_1)]$$

may well tend to infinity as r_1 decreases, without the aggregate demand for bonds going to 0.

One may therefore expect to be able to significantly weaken the assumptions underlying the Keynesian Liquidity Preference theory. It will be shown that it is indeed the case, provided that real balance and intertemporal substitution effects are properly integrated into the analysis. In fact, it will be enough to strengthen the conditions of (4.4.1) by postulating the presence of *a single consumer who intially holds some bonds, and whose price and interest rate expectations are insensitive to variations of* p_1 *and of* r_1.

In order to see this point more precisely, it is convenient to specialize the model to the case in which there is one good, and in which all consumers make plans for the current and the next dates only. Assume that there is a particular consumer (we will drop his index a for simplicity) with $\bar{b} >$

---

[17] In the remainder of this section, it will be always assumed that changes of the interest rate are accompanied by such compensating moves of prices.

0, whose price and interest rate expectations p_2 and r_2 are actually independent of p_1 and r_1.

Substitution between bonds and money evidently occurs at the level of this particular consumer. If r_1 is large enough, this consumer's demand for money, like everyone else's, is equal to zero. If r_1 gets close to 0, this consumer's demand for bonds vanishes (but others may behave differently).

At such low interest rates r_1, given p_1, the insensitive trader's optimum actions result from the maximization of his utility function under the budget constraints:

$$p_1 c_1 + m_1 = p_1 e_1 + \bar{m} + \bar{b}/r_1$$

$$p_2 c_2 = p_2 e_2 + m_1$$

where the demand for bonds b_1, as well as final money and bond holdings m_2 and b_2, have been set equal to zero, without any loss of generality.

We shall show now that under our assumption this particular consumer's money demand m_1 tends to infinity as r_1 goes to 0, and p_1 moves to maintain the equilibrium of the good market. This will imply that under these circumstances, aggregate money demand $M^d(p_1, r_1)$, and thus $\Delta M(p_1, r_1)$, tends to infinity as well.

We will distinguish two cases.

The product $p_1 r_1$ *tends to 0.* The insensitive consumer's current budget constraint can then be written:

$$p_1 r_1 c_1 + r_1 m_1 = p_1 r_1 e_1 + r_1 \bar{m} + \bar{b}$$

The individual's current consumption c_1 is surely bounded, since the good market has to be in equilibrium. Thus the product $r_1 m_1$ approaches $\bar{b}$, which is positive: the consumer's demand for money m_1 goes to $+\infty$. The essential mechanism here is the real balance effect induced by a variation of r_1.

The product $p_1 r_1$ *is bounded away from 0.* Then, the region of the feasible consumption programs (c_1, c_2) is obtained by eliminating the variable m_1 from the budget constraints. It is thus defined by:

$$p_1 c_1 + p_2 c_2 = p_1 e_1 + p_2 e_2 + \bar{m} + (\bar{b}/r_1)$$

$$p_1 c_1 \leqq p_1 e_1 + \bar{m} + \bar{b}/r_1$$

and is represented in Figure 4.2.

Since $p_1 r_1$ is bounded away from 0, the price p_1 tends to infinity. Hence the ratio $\bar{m}/p_1$ goes to zero, whereas $\bar{b}/p_1 r_1$ remains bounded. The point

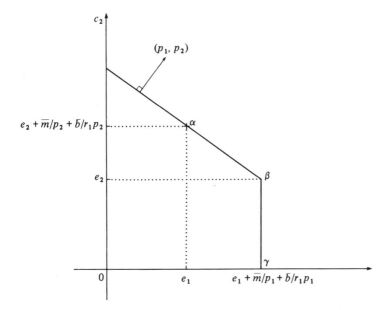

FIGURE 4.2.

β therefore stays at a finite distance on the diagram. On the other hand, since $\bar{b}$ is positive, the ratio $\bar{b}/r_1 p_2$ increases without bound, and thus the point α moves vertically toward infinity. The intertemporal budget line $\alpha\beta$ eventually becomes vertical, implying that the individual's planned consumption c_2 tends to $+\infty$. Since:

$$m_1 = p_2(c_2 - e_2)$$

this consumer's demand for money goes to infinity as well. The essential mechanism here is the intertemporal substitution effect.

The foregoing heuristic analysis shows that the monetary authority has complete control over the money supply in the present model, provided that there is a consumer with $\bar{b}_a > 0$ whose interest rate and price expectations are insensitive to a variation of p_1 and r_1. We will now give a general result along this line.

We shall say that a consumer's expectations are *continuous* if the functions $\psi_{at}(p_1, r_1)$ and $\rho_{at}(p_1, r_1)$ are continuous with respect to p_1 and r_1, for all t. They will be said to be *bounded* if there are two vectors ϵ and η, with all their components positive, such that $\epsilon \leqq \psi_{at}(p_1, r_1) \leqq \eta$, and two positive numbers ϵ' and η' such that $\epsilon' \leqq \rho_{at}(p_1, r_1) \leqq \eta'$, for all p_1 and r_1, and all t. This inelasticity condition, which violates the neoclassical homogeneity postulates, is essential for the following existence result.[18]

(4.5.1)   *Assume (a) and (b) of Section 4.2, and that all consumers' expectations are continuous. Assume moreover that there is a consumer with $n_a \geqq 2$ and $\bar{b}_a > 0$ whose expectations are bounded.*

   Then the system (4.5.C), (4.5.D), (4.5.E) has a solution for every $\Delta M > -M$, i.e., the Bank has complete control over the money supply.

This result shows that the inelasticity assumptions underlying the Keynesian Liquidity Preference theory can be much weakened. One needs only a limited substitution between money and bonds if proper account is taken of real balance and intertemporal substitution effects. Full control of the money supply by means of an open-market policy still requires, apparently, very strong assumptions on expectations. The qualitative conclusion of our analysis is thus, once again, that the possibility of such control seems quite problematic.

Remark. The analysis of this section has been carried out under the implicit assumption that traders have no direct knowledge of the Bank's policy. It can be transposed, trivially, to the case in which some or all traders have some information about it – for instance, when a target money supply ΔM^* is publicly announced by the Bank. The argument is actually the same as for the case in which money is created through loans to the private sector (see the "Remark" at the end of Section 2.5). The traders' expectations – hence their behavior – are then functions not only of p_1 and r_1 but of the signal ΔM^* too. Our analysis is still valid for a fixed ΔM^*. In particular, if the traders' anticipations satisfy the assumption of (4.5.1) given the signal ΔM^*, the result implies that the Bank can indeed peg its money supply at the preannounced level ΔM^*. As a matter of fact, (4.5.1) shows that the Bank could then peg the money supply at any other level $\Delta M \neq \Delta M^*$, provided that the consumers do not know that the Bank actually pursues a policy that differs from the one that has been announced.

4.6   The liquidity trap

It is sometimes claimed by Keynesian theorists than open-market policies are ineffective when the interest rate is close to zero. We will show in this section that such a "liquidity trap" phenomenon does exist in the present model whenever the Bank has full control over the money supply,

---

[18]   A formal proof of the result is given in Appendix E.

in the sense that the lower the interest rate, the less sensitive it becomes to a given variation of the Bank's money supply.

The liquidity trap phenomenon is often viewed as a property of the aggregate demand for money, which is supposed to tend to infinity as the interest rate goes to zero. This assertion is usually justified by appealing to Liquidity Preference theory. At low interest rates, it is argued, almost everyone switches from bonds into cash, and thus aggregate money demand increases without bound.

That sort of argument is at best partial. It first contemplates only the consumers' choices between money and bonds, and thus neglects consumption savings decisions. A related point is that it does not say anything about how the prices of goods are supposed to behave when the interest rate goes down. Finally, it is based upon the assumptions underlying the Liquidity Preference theory, which, as we have seen, are unnecessarily strong.

There is in the literature another interpretation of the liquidity trap, which views it as a property of the relation between short-run *equilibrium* interest rates and *equilibrium* money stocks.[19] We are going to see that, with this interpretation, there is indeed a liquidity trap in the present model whenever the Bank has full control of the money supply.

The property can be stated differently if the Bank pegs the interest rate, or if it controls the money supply. In the first case, given r_1, one looks at the price system p_1 that satisfies the goods markets clearing conditions (4.5.C). The corresponding equilibrium money stock is then $M^d(p_1,r_1)$, and the associated Bank's equilibrium money creation $\Delta M(p_1,r_1)$ is given by:

$$\Delta M(p_1,r_1) = M^d(p_1,r_1) - M$$
$$= (1/r_1)\,[B - B^d(p_1,r_1)]$$

One can say that there is a liquidity trap if $M^d(p_1,r_1)$ or equivalently $\Delta M(p_1,r_1)$ tends to infinity as the interest rate decreases to 0, the prices p_1 adjusting to clear the goods markets. But we have seen in the preceding section that such a property was true precisely under the conditions that gave the Bank complete control of the money supply, namely, under the assumptions of (4.5.1). We can therefore state without further argument:[20]

(4.6.1) *Consider an infinite sequence of prices and interest rates (p_1^k, r_1^k) that satisfies the goods markets equations (4.5.C) for all k, such that r_1^k tends to 0. Let $M^d(p_1^k, r_1^k)$ be a corresponding sequence of equilibrium money stocks.*

Then, under the assumptions of (4.5.1), $M^d(p_1^k, r_1^k)$ tends to $+\infty$.

[19] See, e.g., Patinkin (1965, Chap. 14, Section 3).
[20] A proof of this statement is given in Appendix E.

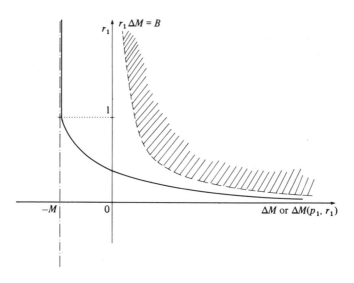

FIGURE 4.3.

When the Bank pegs its money supply, ΔM is given, and one looks at a corresponding solution (p_1, r_1) of the system (4.5.C), (4.5.D), (4.5.E). One can say then that a liquidity trap exists if equilibrium interest rates r_1 tend to 0 when the money creation ΔM increases indefinitely.

That statement obviously presupposes that a short-run equilibrium indeed exists as the money supply tends to infinity. In that case, the argument is almost trivial. For the money creation ΔM is bounded above by the money value of the initial stock of bonds B/r_1. Thus interest rates must go to 0 (at least as fast as $B/\Delta M$) when ΔM tends to infinity. Formally:

(4.6.2) *Consider an infinite sequence of money supplies ΔM^k that tends to $+\infty$ and let (p_1^k, r_1^k) be a corresponding sequence of equilibrium prices and interest rates. Then r_1^k tends to 0.*

The above two statements show that if one is willing to admit that the Bank can fully control the money stock, then a liquidity trap phenomenon exists in principle, in the sense that the relation between the Bank's equilibrium creation of money ΔM and the equilibrium interest rate r_1 becomes almost "flat" when ΔM is large or when r_1 is low (see Figure 4.3). In such circumstances, the impact of open-market policies on interest rates, or on the economy's liquidity, becomes relatively weak. In this model, the liquidity trap is however a limit phenomenon, which occurs asymptotically when the interest rate gets close to zero or the money supply is large. The model has little to say about its actual strength, and thus about its practical relevance. One can remark nevertheless that the product of r_1 with ΔM, or with $\Delta M(p_1, r_1)$, cannot exceed in equilibrium the initial stock of bonds B. The curve representing the relation between equilibrium interest rates and equilibrium money creations is thus bound to lie below the hatched region in Figure 4.3.

Remark. There is a stronger version of the liquidity trap, which claims that the aggregate demand for money – or the equilibrium money stock – goes to infinity when the interest rate decreases to a low but *positive* level. That sort of phenomenon, obviously, cannot occur here. The aggregate demand for money is indeed defined in the present model for *all* positive r_1. On the other hand, if the Bank has complete control over the money supply, (4.6.2) shows that the equilibrium interest rate cannot be bounded away from zero as the Bank's money supply ΔM increases without limit.

4.7 The neutrality of money

We will now analyze the consequences of changes of the money supply on the short-run equilibrium at date 1. We shall employ the methods of the previous chapters – see in particular Section 2.6 – to determine that a publicly announced once-and-for-all scalar change of the consumers' initial stocks of money and of perpetuities, and of the Bank's money creation by means of open-market operations, is neutral provided that traders believe this change to be neutral. By contrast, a change of the Bank's money creation ΔM through the purchase of perpetuities, the consumers' initial portfolios being fixed, will be found to produce generally short-run real effects.

We shall focus our attention, in order to make some ideas clear, on the case in which the Bank pegs its money supply ΔM. Consider first a once-and-for-all scalar change of the traders' initial holdings of money and of bonds, from $\bar{m}_a$ and $\bar{b}_a$ to $\lambda_1 \bar{m}_a$ and $\lambda_1 \bar{b}_a$, through lump-sum transfers, and assume that the Bank's money creation changes proportionally from ΔM to $\lambda_1 \Delta M$. If the policy parameter λ_1 is *publicly announced*, it becomes an argument of the consumers' expectations functions, in addition to the current price system p_1 and interest rate r_1. Expectations can then be written $\psi_{at}(p_1, r_1, \lambda_1)$ and $\rho_{at}(p_1, r_1, \lambda_1)$. Every consumer's short-run demand functions thus depend on λ_1 too. If we aggregate them as we did in Section 4.3, a short-run equilibrium associated with the policy parameter λ_1 is the outcome of the following system, with obvious notation:

(4.7.C) $Z(p_1, r_1, \lambda_1) = 0$

(4.7.D) $M^d(p_1,r_1,\lambda_1) = \lambda_1 M + \lambda_1 \Delta M$

(4.7.E) $B^d(p_1,r_1,\lambda_1) + r_1 \lambda_1 \Delta M = \lambda_1 B$

Let us now assume that all traders believe that a change of λ_1 is neutral. Specifically, *expected prices* $\psi_{at}(p_1,r_1,\lambda_1)$ *and expected interest rates* $\rho_{at}(p_1,r_1,\lambda_1)$ *are assumed to be homogenous of degree 1 and 0, respectively, in* (p_1,λ_1). It is straightforward to verify that the aggregate excess demands $Z(p_1,r_1,\lambda_1)$ are then homogenous of degree 0 in (p_1,λ_1), and that the aggregate demands for money and for perpetuities $M^d(p_1,r_1,\lambda_1)$ and $B^d(p_1,r_1,\lambda_1)$, are homogenous of degree 1 in these variables. All that is involved here is simply that the consumers are free of money illusion. It is then obvious from the foregoing system of equations that any change of the publicly announced policy parameter λ_1 has no real effects.

By contrast, changes of the money supply that depart from the above assumptions will modify typically real equilibrium magnitudes at date 1. Changes of the traders' portfolios that are not proportional to their initial holdings will generate distribution effects among consumers. If changes of the money supply are not made public, there may be an "informational nonneutrality" of the Lucas type, which we have already encountered in the preceding chapters. Moreover, if changes of the traders' initial portfolios by means of lump-sum transfers, and of the Bank's money supply, are preannounced at date 1 not only for that date but also for other dates in the future, any alteration of the Government's policy parameter at a *single* date – and more generally, of the time profile of the Government's changes of the money stock – will generally produce real effects at date 1. The basic mechanism, here as in Chapter 1, is that traders face liquidity constraints since their portfolios cannot be negative in the present model, and that they have different lifetime planning horizons (the reader can easily adapt the arguments given at the end of Section 1.7 to the case at hand).

But the most important source of the nonneutrality of money in the present context is the fact that *monetary policy usually aims at changing the Bank's money creation* ΔM *through open-market operations, without altering the traders' initial portfolios*. Our analysis in Section 4.5 cast some doubts about the Bank's ability to have complete control over its money supply. It is nonetheless straightforward to check that *any change of the money supply* ΔM *alone will typically produce real effects, whenever such changes can be implemented*.

Consider a variation of ΔM, the traders' initial holdings $\bar{m}_a$ and $\bar{b}_a$ being fixed. If this move had no "real" consequences at date 1, every trader's equilibrium intertemporal consumption program should be unaffected. This would imply that current equilibrium prices p_1 and the current equilibrium interest rate r_1 stay the same, if the initial stock of perpetuities B is positive, in order to avoid a modification of the real value of the traders' portfolios, $\bar{m}_a + s_1\bar{b}_a$. This would imply in turn that every consumer's forecast of future prices and future interest rates should remain invariant, in order to prevent the occurrence of intertemporal substitution effects. But we would then get a contradiction. For that would mean that the aggregate demands for money and for bonds have not changed, while the Bank's money creation ΔM has been modified. The money and the bond markets could no longer be in equilibrium.

A change of ΔM alone is therefore bound to generate real effects at date 1. A similar argument, which is left to the reader, would show that a scalar variation of the consumers' initial holdings $\bar{m}_a$ and $\bar{b}_a$, the Bank's money creation ΔM being fixed, will also be nonneutral. As the foregoing argument makes clear, that sort of result is true whether or not the policy move is made public, and is independent of the way in which private economic units form their anticipations about the future.

Notes on the literature

This chapter is an extension of a study by Grandmont and Laroque (1976a). These authors considered a framework in which the traders have probabilistic expectations, but in which they make plans for the current and the next dates only. For an extension of the model to the case in which consumers face intraperiod constraints on their transactions, see Hool (1979).

Suggested reading

Branson, W. H., *Macroeconomic Theory and Policy*, Harper & Row, New York, 1972, Chap. 12.

Crouch, R. L., *Macroeconomics*, Harcourt Brace Jovanovich, New York, 1972, Chaps. 4, 6, 7, and 12.

Hool, B., "Liquidity, Speculation, and the Demand for Money," *Journal of Economic Theory 21* (1979), 73–87.

Keynes, J. M., *The General Theory of Employment, Interest, and Money*, Harcourt Brace Jovanovich, New York, 1936, Chaps. 13 and 15.

Leijonhufvud, A., *On Keynesian Economics and the Economics of Keynes*, Oxford University Press, London, 1966, Chaps. 4, 5.

Patinkin, D., *Money, Interest, and Prices*, 2nd ed., Harper & Row, New York, 1965, Chaps. 9–12, 14:3, and 15.

Tobin, J., "Liquidity Preference as Behavior Towards Risk," *Review of Economic Studies 67* (1958), 65–86.

Conclusion

A significant outcome of this analysis concerns the existence of a monetary Walrasian equilibrium in the short run. We found indeed that whenever the traders' learning processes involve short-run rigidities of their expected real interest rates – which is the case in traditional neoclassical macro-economic models – a short-run Walrasian equilibrium in which money has positive value may not exist. Real balance effects are then the essential regulating mechanisms of the economy, but they may be too weak to equilibrate the markets. As a corollary, in order to guarantee the existence of a short-run monetary equilibrium, one has to appeal to a stabilizing mechanism that was neglected by conventional neoclassical monetary theorists, namely, the intertemporal substitution effects that are induced by a variation of the traders' expected real interest rates. In the class of models that we have considered, this required basically that some or all traders' expectations about future prices and interest rates are to a large extent insensitive to the variations of current prices and rates of interest. The fact that such restrictions on anticipations are rather implausible shows that the existence of a short-run Walrasian monetary equilibrium raises more problems that neoclassical theorists like to believe.

This study therefore supports one of the views of Keynesian economists: full price flexibility may not lead to market clearing after all, for the quite simple reason that there may not exist a set of prices and interest rates that would equate Walrasian demands and supplies.

Another important outcome of the analysis concerned the possibility for monetary authorities to manipulate interest rates or the money supply through their credit or open-market operations. Here again, the main finding was that such a control could well be problematic if the traders'

150

expected real interest rates were to some extent rigid in the short run. In the light of such results, one is entitled to be suspicious about traditional monetarist policy recommendations, which advocate controlling the money supply to regulate economic activity.

These conclusions have been reached by studying models deliberately kept simple. Important features of modern monetary economies have been taken into account, in particular the fact that money is usually created by banking institutions by granting loans to the private sector, and/or by open-market operations. It is desirable, evidently, to extend the analysis to a more general framework, which would include production activities, and, in particular, the intertemporal choices of the firm, and which would take into account a function of money that economists believe to be important, i.e., its role in the exchange process. There have indeed been a few studies that aimed at incorporating these features in the models.[1] They confirm the qualitative finding of this inquiry, namely, that real balances effects may be too weak to equilibrate the markets, and that intertemporal substitution effects must be brought in if one wishes to be sure of the existence of a short-run monetary equilibrium.

The other results that we obtained concerned the neutrality of money. Changes of the money stock or of the nominal rate of interest were found to be neutral in the long run, thereby supporting the classical view on this matter. As for the short run, it was checked that a publicly announced once-and-for-all scalar change of all traders' initial holdings of money and of assets denominated in money, and of the banking institutions' money creation through loans or by means of open-market operations, was neutral indeed if all agents believed this policy move to be neutral. By contrast, preannounced changes of the time profile money stock by means of lump-sum transfers were shown to generate real effects, owing to the various liquidity constraints that the agents face. Finally, changes of the money creation at some date through credit or open-market policies, the traders' initial balances of monetary assets being held fixed, were found to be nonneutral as well, whenever such changes of the money supply could be implemented. Needless to say, these results cast serious doubts upon the validity of some recent claims by quite a few new classical macroeconomists concerning the neutrality of perfectly anticipated, deterministic changes of the money supply.[2]

[1]   Production activities were considered by Sondermann (1974), and Grandmont and Laroque (1976b). The role of money in the exchange process has been studied with the methods of this book by Grandmont and Younès (1972), and by Hool (1976, 1979), by introducing a cash-in-advance constraint of the Clower type on transactions at every date.

One lesson of this analysis is the fact that the traders' learning processes are among the important characteristics of an economy, and that accordingly they must be carefully studied, both from a theoretical and an empirical viewpoint. Postulating rational expectations, as has become fashionable recently in some academic circles, is an elegant way to avoid the issue rather than to face it. By endogenizing anticipations, rational-expectations market-clearing models do incorporate intertemporal substitution effects, the importance of which we have emphasized at length. But our investigation shows how dangerous the blind use of that sort of assumption can be. For it seriously discounts the origins of the possible disequilibria that can exist in actual monetary economies, since it ignores the short-run rigidities of expected real interest rates that the traders' learning processes may involve in the world in which we actually live.

[2]   See, e.g., Sargent and Wallace (1975).

Appendixes

The purpose of the following appendixes is to prove the theorems that were stated in the text. Appendix A reviews the mathematical notions and results that are required. Appendixes B, C, D, and E are devoted to the proofs of the propositions of Chapters 1, 2, 3, and 4, respectively.

Although the exposition is intended to be self-contained, a fair knowledge of real analysis, as exemplified by Bartle (1964, Sections 1–8, 11, 15, and 16), is required from the reader. Some familiarity with conventional general equilibrium theory, as provided by a graduate course in mathematical economics, is not necessary but is nevertheless recommended.

APPENDIX A

Preliminaries

This appendix gives the terminology and the facts that will be used later on. Some results are stated in italics and numbered for later reference. Other facts will be used freely in the other appendixes without specific reference.

We shall deal exclusively in the sequel with elements or subsets of finite Euclidean spaces. It is assumed that the reader already has some familiarity with the elementary properties of such spaces, and with the essential notions of real analysis (see, e.g., Bartle 1964). A more detailed review of most of the material present here can be found in Debreu (1959, Chapter 1), or in Hildenbrand (1974, part 1, Sections A, B, and C).

A.1 Basic notions

An element of a Euclidean space of dimension s, say $\mathbb{R}^s$, is described by a vector $x = (x_1, \ldots, x_h, \ldots, x_s)$, where every component x_h is a real number. Given two vectors x and y of $\mathbb{R}^s$, $x \geqq y$ means that $x_h \geqq y_h$ for all h, $x > y$ stands for $x \geqq y$ and $x \neq y$, and $x >> y$ means $x_h > y_h$ for all h. The vector whose components are all zero will be denoted by 0. We shall then speak of the *origin* of $\mathbb{R}^s$. The set of elements x of $\mathbb{R}^s$ such that $x \geqq 0$ is denoted $\mathbb{R}^s_+$. The set of vectors x of $\mathbb{R}^s$ satisfying $x >> 0$ is denoted Int $\mathbb{R}^s_+$.

The *scalar product* of two vectors x and y of $\mathbb{R}^s$ is denoted:

$$xy = \sum_h x_h y_h$$

Given two arbitrary real numbers λ_1 and λ_2, the notation $\lambda_1 x + \lambda_2 y$ stands for the vector whose components are $\lambda_1 x_h + \lambda_2 y_h$, for all h. When λ_1

155

and λ_2 are both positive and when their sum is equal to 1, we shall say that $\lambda_1 x + \lambda_2 y$ is a *convex combination of x and y*.

The *distance* of two points x and y in $\mathbb{R}^s$ is:

$$d(x,y) = [\sum_h (x_h - y_h)^2]^{1/2}$$

An (infinite) *sequence* of elements of $\mathbb{R}^s$, $(x^1, x^2, \ldots)$, or in short, (x^k), is said to *converge* to y if the distance of x^k to y tends to 0 as k increases indefinitely, or more precisely, if for every real number $\epsilon > 0$, there is an integer $K(\epsilon)$ such that $d(x^k,y) < \epsilon$ for all $k > K(\epsilon)$. The sequence is *bounded* if a real number λ exists such that the distance between the zero vector and x^k is less than λ for all k. The sequence is *unbounded* otherwise. It is easily verified that an unbounded sequence (x^k) in $\mathbb{R}^s$ contains a subsequence $(x^{k'})$ such that the sequence $(d(0,x^{k'}))$ diverges to $+\infty$, i.e., such that for every real number $\eta > 0$, an integer $K'(\eta)$ exists such that $d(0,x^{k'}) \geqq \eta$ for all $k' \geqq K'(\eta)$.

A *set* or a *subset* X of $\mathbb{R}^s$ is a collection of elements of $\mathbb{R}^s$. The fact that x belongs to (is a member of) X is denoted $x \in X$. The empty set is a set that has no element. A set that has at least one member is said to be nonempty. A set X is *convex* if $\lambda x + (1 - \lambda) y$ belongs to X whenever $x \in X$, $y \in Y$, and λ is a real number in the interval $(0,1)$. A particular case of a convex set is a hyperplane H of dimension $s - 1$, which is defined by the following property: There is a unique vector q of $\mathbb{R}^s$ that satisfies $\sum_h q_h = 1$, and a unique real number c such that x belongs to H if and only if $qx = c$. The set X is *closed* if, for every sequence (x^k) of elements of X that converges to x, then $x \in X$. The set X is *bounded* if there is a real number K such that $d(0,x) \leqq K$ for all x in X.

A set is *compact* if it is both closed and bounded. A fundamental property of compact sets is the *Bolzano–Weierstrass theorem*: A set X is compact if and only if every sequence (x^k) of elements of X contains a subsequence $(x^{k'})$ that converges to an element of X. This result will be applied to the following special case. Consider a sequence (x^k) in $\mathbb{R}^s$ that is bounded. That is, there is a real number K such that x^k belongs to the set X of all vectors x of $\mathbb{R}^s$ satisfying $d(0,x) \leqq K$. It is easily verified that X is compact. The Bolzano–Weierstrass theorem then implies that there is a subsequence $(x^{k'})$ that converges to some element of X. In other words:

(A.1.1) *Every bounded sequence in $\mathbb{R}^s$ contains a convergent subsequence.*

Given two sets X and Y of $\mathbb{R}^s$, X is a *subset of Y* if every element of X belongs to Y. The *complement* of X in Y is the set of elements y of Y that do not belong to X, and is noted $Y \backslash X$. X is a proper subset of Y if $Y \backslash X$ is nonempty. A subset X of Y is *closed in Y* if for every sequence (x^k) of elements of X that converges to an element y of Y, then y belongs to X. X is *open in Y* if its complement in Y is closed in Y.

Given two sets X and Y of $\mathbb{R}^s$ and $\mathbb{R}^u$, respectively, the product of X and Y, which is denoted $X \times Y$, is the set of elements $z = (x, y)$ of $\mathbb{R}^{s+u}$ such that $x \in X$ and $y \in Y$. The product of finitely many sets is defined in a similar way.

A.2   Functions and correspondences

Consider two subsets X and Y of $\mathbb{R}^s$ and $\mathbb{R}^u$, respectively. A *function f from X into Y* associates to every member x of X an element $y = f(x)$ of Y. It is denoted $f:X \rightarrow Y$. In the particular case where y is a real number ($u = 1$), the function is said to be *real-valued*.

A function $f:X \rightarrow Y$ is continuous at $x \in X$ if for each sequence (x^k) of elements of X that converges to x, the sequence $[y^k = f(x^k)]$ of elements of Y converges to $y = f(x)$. If f is continuous at every $x \in X^*$, where X^* is a subset of X, we shall say that f is continuous on X^*. If $X^* = X$, we shall say simply that f is continuous. The following characterization is useful.

(A.2.1)   *Consider two subsets* X *and* Y *of* $\mathbb{R}^s$ *and* $\mathbb{R}^u$, *respectively. The function* f:X $\rightarrow$ Y *is continuous at* x $\in$ X *if and only if for every sequence* (x^k) *of elements of* X *that converges to* x, *the associated sequence* $[y^k = f(x^k)]$ *of elements of* y *contains a subsequence* (y^k) *that converges to* y = f(x).

By using (A.2.1), it is not difficult to check the following result.

(A.2.2)   *Consider a continuous function* f:X $\rightarrow$ Y *where* X *is closed. If the sequence* (x^k) *of elements of* X *is bounded, then the sequence* $(f(x^k))$ *is bounded.*

The notion of a correspondence is a direct extension of the concept of a function. Given two subsets X and Y of $\mathbb{R}^s$ and $\mathbb{R}^u$, respectively, a *correspondence ϕ from X into Y* associates to every member x of X a *nonempty subset* $\phi(x)$ of Y. It is denoted $\phi: X \rightarrow Y$. In the particular case where the set $\phi(x)$ has a single element for all x, we shall identify the correspondence ϕ and the function $f:X \rightarrow Y$ that associates to each x the unique member of $\phi(x)$, and conversely. If $\phi(x)$ is compact we shall say that the correspondence ϕ is *compact-valued at x*. If $\phi(x)$ is convex, we shall say that ϕ is *convex-valued at x*.

The notion of a continuous function extends here to the concept of an *upper hemicontinuous (UHC)* correspondence. The following statement, which generalizes the characterization given in (A.2.1), will be taken as a definition.

(A.2.3)   *Consider two subsets* X *and* Y *of* $\mathbb{R}^s$ *and* $\mathbb{R}^u$, *respectively. The correspondence* ϕ:X $\rightarrow$ Y *is UHC and compact-valued at* x $\in$ X, *if and only if for every sequence* (x^k) *of elements of* X *that converges to* x, *then every associated sequence* (y^k) *of elements of* Y *such that* $y^k \in \phi(x^k)$ *for all* k *contains a subsequence* (y^k) *that converges to a member* y *of* $\phi(x)$.

If the correspondence ϕ is compact-valued and UHC (convex-valued) at every x in some subset X^* of X, we shall say that ϕ is compact-valued and UHC (convex-valued) on X^*. If $X^* = X$, we shall say, simply, that ϕ is compact-valued and UHC (convex-valued).

The "summation" of several compact-valued UHC correspondences preserves upper hemicontinuity. More precisely, consider a finite collection $(\phi_a)_{a \in A}$ of correspondences from a subset X of $\mathbb{R}^s$ to $\mathbb{R}^u$. Then, by definition, the correspondence $\phi = \Sigma_a \phi_a$ associates to every x in X the set of $y \in \mathbb{R}^u$ such that $y = \Sigma_a y_a$, where $y_a \in \phi_a(x)$ for all a. By applying (A.2.3), if each ϕ_a is compact-valued and UHC, the correspondence ϕ is compact-valued and UHC as well. If each ϕ_a is convex-valued, so is ϕ.

The composition of a continuous function and of a compact-valued UHC correspondence preserves upper hemicontinuity too. More precisely, consider a function $f:X \to Y$, where X and Y are subsets of $\mathbb{R}^s$ and $\mathbb{R}^u$, respectively, and a correspondence $\phi: Y \to Z$, where Z is a subset of $\mathbb{R}^v$. The *composition of* ϕ *by* f is denoted $(\phi \circ f)$, and is defined as the correspondence from X to Z that associates to every x in X the set $\phi(f(x))$. By applying (A.2.3), if f is continuous, and if ϕ is UHC and compact-valued, then $(\phi \circ f)$ is compact-valued and UHC as well.

We will next look at a few useful definitions concerning *real-valued functions*. Consider a function $f: X \to \mathbb{R}$ in which X is a subset of $\mathbb{R}^s$. The function is *nondecreasing* if $f(x_2) \geq f(x_1)$ whenever $x_2 > x_1$. It is *increasing* if one has actually $f(x_2) > f(x_1)$ for all $x_2 > x_1$. When X is *convex*, the function is *quasi-concave* if for every x_1 and x_2 in X, and every real number λ in the open interval $(0,1)$, one has $f[\lambda x_1 + (1 - \lambda)x_2] \geq f(x)$ whenever $f(x_1) \geq f(x)$ and $f(x_2) \geq f(x)$. It is *strictly quasi-concave* if one has actually $f(\lambda x_1 + (1 - \lambda)x_2) > f(x)$ whenever x_1 and x_2 differ. The function f is *(strictly) quasi-convex* if $(-f)$ is (strictly) quasi-concave.

The function f is *concave* if for every x_1 and x_2 in X, and every real number λ in the open interval $(0,1)$, one has:

$$f[\lambda x_1 + (1 - \lambda)x_2] \geq \lambda f(x_1) + (1 - \lambda)f(x_2)$$

It is *strictly concave* if one has actually a strict inequality whenever x_1 and x_2 differ. A function f is *(strictly) convex* if $(-f)$ is (strictly) concave. A function that is (strictly) concave is (strictly) quasi-concave.

Finally, it is not difficult to check the following result.

(A.2.4) *Consider a real-valued function* f $: X \to \mathbb{R}$. *If* f *is continuous and* X *is compact, the function* f *reaches its maximum on* X, *i.e., there exists* x^* *in* X *such that* $f(x^*) \geq f(x)$ *for all* x *in* X. *The set of such maximizers* x* *is then compact. If* X *is convex and* f *quasi-concave, the set of maximizers* x* *is convex. If* X *is convex and* f *is strictly quasi-concave, the set of maximizers contains at most one element.*

As an incidental remark, the functions we shall consider later on will often be defined on the product of two sets, $X \times Z$, where X and Z are subsets of $\mathbb{R}^s$ and $\mathbb{R}^v$ respectively. In such a case we shall say that the function $f : X \times Z \rightarrow Y$ has some specific property (such as continuity or concavity) with respect to the variable x whenever, for each $z \in Z$, the function f_z that associates to every $x \in X$ the element $f(x,z)$ has indeed this property. The same semantic remark will apply to correspondences.

A.3   Competitive equilibrium

When looking for a Walrasian equilibrium, we shall have to deal with the following typical situation. Let us suppose that there are s "commodities" (some of them may be financial assets), whose prices are described by a vector q in $\mathbb{R}^s$. These prices may be positive or negative. By a suitable normalization, we shall restrict ourselves to situations in which the price system q belongs to a subset Q of a *hyperplane H of* $\mathbb{R}^s$ of dimension $s - 1$, which does not contain the origin of $\mathbb{R}^s$. To each q in Q is associated a set of aggregate excess demands for all commodities, which is described by a nonempty subset $\zeta(q)$ of $\mathbb{R}^s$. A Walrasian equilibrium price vector q^* must then satisfy the requirement that all markets clear. This means here that $0 \in \zeta(q^*)$.

Apart from some continuity and convexity requirements, the usual arguments for asserting the existence of a Walrasian equilibrium rest, explicity or implicitly, on the behavior of aggregate excess demand when the price system q approaches the boundary of the admissible set Q. For instance, if the relative price of some, or several, commodities goes down to zero, it is required that a positive aggregate excess demand appears in one of the corresponding markets. The following version of such a boundary condition will be used below.

(A.3.B) *For every sequence* (q^k) *of elements of* Q *that either tends to a vector* $q \in H\backslash Q$, *or is unbounded, and for every sequence* $[z^k \in \zeta(q^k)]$, *there exists an element* q̄ *of* Q *such that* q̄$z^k > 0$ *for infinitely many* k.

The following existence result will be our basic tool in the sequel.

Market equilibrium lemma[1]

Let H *be a hyperplane of* $\mathbb{R}^s$ *of dimension* s $- 1$ *that does not contain the origin. Let* ζ:Q→$\mathbb{R}^s$ *be an aggregate excess demand correspondence,*

[1]   The interested reader may look at the proof given in Grandmont (1977, Section 3.1) which applies to the case at hand. However, the proof uses Kakutani's fixed-

where the set of admissible prices Q is a nonempty, convex subset of
H, which is open in H. Assume that ζ is compact-valued, convex-valued
and UHC, and that it satisfies qz = 0 for any z $\in$ ζ(q) and all q in Q.
Then, under the boundary condition (A.3.B), there exists q* $\in$ Q
such that 0 $\in$ ζ(q*).

The above boundary condition (A.3.B) will often be used in the particular context where the correspondence ζ is the sum of finitely many
correspondences $\zeta_a : Q \rightarrow \mathbb{R}^s$:

$$\zeta = \sum_a \zeta_a$$

each of which is *bounded below*, i.e., has the property that $\zeta_a(q) \geqq \bar{\zeta}_a$ for
some $\bar{\zeta}_a \in \mathbb{R}^s$, for all $q \in Q$. Then we get the following fact, the proof of
which is straightforward and is left as an exercise to the reader:

(A.3.1) *Assume that ζ is the sum of finitely many correspondences $\zeta_a : Q \rightarrow \mathbb{R}^s$,*
each of which is bounded below. Consider a sequence (q^k) in Q that
either tends to q $\in$ H\Q, or is unbounded. Assume that there is an a
such that every sequence [z$_a^k \in \zeta_a$(q^k)] is unbounded. Then the sequence
($\bar{q}$z^k) diverges to +∞ for all $\bar{q} \in Q$ such that $\bar{q} >> 0$, and all sequences
[z$^k \in \zeta$(q^k)].

A.4   Demand correspondences

Our strategy in the following will be to apply the foregoing market equilibrium lemma. In doing so, we shall encounter the following typical
situation. An individual agent has to make decisions for the current date
($t = 1$) and for the remainder of his planning horizon ($t = 2, \ldots, n$),
with $n \geqq 1$. Decision variables in each period are purchases of various
commodities (real goods and services, financial assets), whose number
is s. For each t, the *decision variable* is a vector x_t of $\mathbb{R}_+^s$. The whole
intertemporal decision vector $x = (x_1, \ldots, x_n)$ is thus a member of X
$= \mathbb{R}_+^{ns}$. The *prices* of these s commodities at t are described by a vector
q_t, an element of $\mathbb{R}_+^s$ too. We shall be especially interested in vector
prices $q = (q_1, \ldots, q_n)$ that satisfy $q >> 0$, that is, that belong to Q
$= \text{Int } \mathbb{R}_+^{ns}$.

The *constraints* faced by the agent are budget constraints. They state
that the value of his purchases at date t, $q_t x_t$, cannot exceed his wealth
at that date. His wealth at date 1 is viewed as a function of q_1, and is
denoted $w_1(q_1)$. The agent's wealth at subsequent dates $t \geqq 2$ may depend
upon his preceding decisions as well as on all prices that prevailed up

point theorem, which has not been included in this brief presentation, but which
can be found in Debreu (1959) or Hildenbrand (1974).

to that date. It will be denoted $w_t(x_1, \ldots, x_{t-1}, q_1, \ldots, q_t)$. It is assumed that the value of these functions is nonnegative for any value of x, and of q_t in $\mathbb{R}_+^s$. This defines *wealth functions* $w_1: \mathbb{R}_+^s \to \mathbb{R}_+$ and $w_t: \mathbb{R}^{(2t-1)s} \to \mathbb{R}_+$, for $t = 2, \ldots, n$.

Finally, the agent's objective is to maximize, under these constraints, a *utility function* that depends upon the decision vector $x = (x_1, \ldots, x_n) \in X$, and (in some cases) on some "taste" parameters, which are described by a vector δ in a subset Δ of an arbitrary Euclidean space. The utility function $u(x, \delta)$ defines a function $u: X \times \Delta \to \mathbb{R}$.

The agent's decision problem can be summarized as:

(A.4.I) *Given* $q = (q_1, \ldots, q_n)$ *in* $\mathbb{R}_+^{ns}$ *and* δ *in* Δ, *maximize* $u(x, \delta)$ *with respect to* $x = (x_1, \ldots, x_n) \in X$, *subject to:*

$$q_1 x_1 \leqq w_1(q_1)$$

$$q_t x_t \leqq w_t(x_1, \ldots, x_{t-1}, q_1, \ldots, q_t)$$

for $t = 2, \ldots, n$. .

The problem has a well-defined solution whenever the price system q *satisfies* $q \gg 0$, *i.e., when it belongs to* $Q = \text{Int } \mathbb{R}_+^{ns}$, *if the utility function* u *and the wealth functions* w_t *are continuous*. For then, the set of decision vectors x meeting the constraints of (A.4.I) is clearly closed (it is certainly nonempty since it contains $x = 0$). We wish to show that this set is bounded and thus compact. Suppose that this is not true. That would mean that there is an unbounded sequence (x^k) of vectors satisfying the constraints of (A.4.I). But since $q_1 \gg 0$, (x_1^k) must be bounded, for otherwise the constraint:

$$0 \leqq q_1 x_1^k \leqq w_1(q_1)$$

would ultimately be violated. According to (A.2.2), this implies that the sequence $[w_2(x_1^k, q_1, q_2)]$ is itself bounded. Since $q_2 \gg 0$, the constraints:

$$0 \leqq q_2 x_2^k \leqq w_2(x_1^k, q_1, q_2)$$

imply that the sequence (x_2^k) is also bounded. By recurrence on t, the whole sequence (x^k) is in fact bounded. One gets a contradiction.

The set of vectors x meeting the constraints of (A.4.I) is thus compact. By applying (A.2.4), the set of solutions of (A.4.I), say $\xi(q, \delta)$, is non-empty. This defines a *correspondence* $\xi: Q \times \Delta \to X$. The next result gives more information about the properties of ξ.

(A.4.1) *Assume that the utility function* $u: X \times \Delta \to \mathbb{R}$ *and the wealth functions* $w_1: \mathbb{R}_+^s \to \mathbb{R}_+$ *and* $w^t: \mathbb{R}_+^{(2t-1)s} \to \mathbb{R}_+$ *are continuous for all* t. *Assume moreover that the* w_t *values are concave with respect to* $(x_1, \ldots, x_{t-1})$.

(i) Let Q^* be the set of all $q^* \in Q$ such that $w_1(q_1^*) > 0$ and $w_t(0, \ldots, 0, q_1^*, \ldots, q_t^*) > 0$ for all t. Then the correspondence ξ is compact-valued and UHC on $Q^* \times \Delta$.

(ii) If u is quasi-concave with respect to x, the correspondence ξ is convex-valued on $Q \times \Delta$.

Proof. In order to show that ξ is compact-valued and UHC on Q^*, we seek to apply (A.2.3). Consider a sequence (q^k) of elements of Q that converges to $q^* \in Q^*$, a sequence (δ^k) of elements of Δ that converges to $\delta^* \in \Delta$, and look at a sequence $[x^k \in \xi(q^k, \delta^k)]$. Since $q_1^* >> 0$ and w_1 is continuous, the sequence (x_1^k) must be bounded, for otherwise the constraint:

$$0 \leq q_1^k x_1^k \leq w_1(q_1^k)$$

would ultimately be violated. Since w_2 is continuous, the sequence $[w_2(x_1^k, q_1^k, q_2^k)]$ is bounded by (A.2.2). This implies that the sequence (x_2^k) is bounded, since $q_1^* >> 0$, if one takes into account the constraint:

$$0 \leq q_2^k x_2^k \leq w_2(x_1^k, q_1^k, q_2^k)$$

By recurrence, the sequence (x^k) is thus bounded. By (A.1.1), it contains a subsequence $(x^{k'})$, which converges to an element x^* of $\mathbb{R}^{ns}$. Since X is closed, x^* actually belongs to X. In fact, by continuity of the functions w_t, x^* satisfies the constraints of (A.4.I) for $q = q^*$ and $\delta = \delta^*$.

We will next show that x^* is indeed a solution of (A.4.I) for these particular values of q and δ. Consider an arbitrary $\bar{x}$ in X that satisfies the constraints of (A.4.I) for $q = q^*$ and $\delta = \delta^*$. Take an arbitrary real number λ in the open interval $(0,1)$, and define $x^\lambda = \lambda \bar{x}$. This vector is in fact a convex combination of $\bar{x}$ and of the origin of $\mathbb{R}^{ns}$, with respective weights λ and $(1 - \lambda)$. Since $w_1(q_1^*) > 0$ and $w_t(0, \ldots, 0, q_1^*, \ldots, q_t^*) > 0$, and since the w_t's are concave in $(x_1, \ldots, x_{t-1})$, x^λ satisfies the budget constraints of (A.4.I) for $q = q^*$ with a *strict* inequality sign for all t. By continuity, x^λ satisfies the same constraints with strict inequality for $q = q^{k'}$ if k' is large enough. For such a k', one has:

$$u(x^{k'}, \delta^{k'}) \geq u(x^\lambda, \delta^{k'})$$

This yields, by continuity of u, when k' tends to infinity:

$$u(x^*, \delta^*) \geq u(x^\lambda, \delta^*)$$

This is true for any λ in $(0,1)$. If one takes a sequence of such λ values that converges to 1, x^λ tends to $\bar{x}$ and the continuity of u implies:

$$u(x^*, \delta^*) \geq u(\bar{x}, \delta^*)$$

The decision vector x^* is thus a solution of (A.4.I) for $q = q^*$ and

$\delta = \delta^*$. According to (A.2.3), the correspondence ξ is compact-valued and UHC.

The fact that ξ is convex-valued when u is quasi-concave with respect to x is easy to verify. Indeed, when each w_t is concave with respect to the decision variables $(x_1, \ldots, x_{t-1})$, the set of x satisfying the constraints of (A.4.I) is convex. Then the convexity of $\xi(q,\delta)$ follows from (A.2.4).

Q. E. D.

While proving that ξ is compact-valued and UHC, we have in fact shown the following proposition, which will often be useful in the sequel.

(A.4.2) *Under the assumptions of (A.4.1) (except the quasi-concavity of* u*), consider a sequence* (q^k) *of price vectors in* Q *converging to* $q^* \in \mathbb{R}_+^{ns}$, *a sequence* (δ^k) *of elements of* Δ, *and a sequence* $[x^k \in \xi(q^k,\delta^k)]$ *that tends to* $x^* \in X$.
    Then x^* *is a solution of (A.4.I) for* q $= q^*$ *and* $\delta = \delta^*$ *provided that*

$$w_1(q_1^*) > 0 \text{ and } w_t(0, \ldots, 0, q_1^*, \ldots, q_t^*) > 0$$

    for all t.

Expectations and the real balance effect

The aim of this appendix is to prove the existence results stated in Chapter 1. Section B.1 deals with the properties of an individual household's demands functions. The existence of a short-run Walrasian equilibrium is studied in Section B.2, and the existence of a stationary state is taken up in Section B.3.

B.1   Demand functions

We will first consider the decision problem of a typical consumer at date 1 (the current period), as it was described in (1.3.I). Assumptions *(a)* and *(b)* of Section 1.2 are thus postulated. Since the utility function is increasing, the equality signs appearing in the budget constraints of that problem can be replaced by inequality signs without changing the outcome. This yields:

(B.1.I)   *Given* $(p_1, \ldots, p_n) \in \mathbb{R}_+^{nl}$, *maximize* $u(c_1, \ldots, c_n)$ *with respect to* $(c_1, \ldots, c_n) \in \mathbb{R}_+^{nl}$ *and* $(m_1, \ldots, m_n) \in \mathbb{R}_+^n$, *subject to:*

$$p_1 c_1 + m_1 \leqq p_1 e_1 + \bar{m}$$

$$p_t c_t + m_t \leqq p_t e_t + m_{t-1} \qquad (t = 2, \ldots, n)$$

This problem is a particular case of (A.4.I), where the taste parameter δ is left implicit, and can thus be considered as fixed. To see this, it suffices to take $s = l + 1$, $x_1 = (c_t, m_t) \in \mathbb{R}_+^s$, $q_t = (p_t, 1) \in \mathbb{R}_+^s$, and to define the values of the w_t's wealth functions as the right-hand sides of the budget constraints.

Problem (B.1.I) thus has a well-defined solution whenever $p_t >> 0$ for all t. The solution is then in fact unique. Indeed, in order to solve

(B.1.I) for an optimum consumption program, it is necessary and sufficient to maximize u on the set of all $(c_1, \ldots, c_n) \in \mathbb{R}^{nl}_+$ for which there exists a choice of $(m_1, \ldots, m_n) \in \mathbb{R}^n_+$ that meets the budget constraints. This set is convex. Since u is strictly quasi-concave, the optimum consumption program is unique, according to (A.2.4). But at the optimum of (B.1.I), the budget constraints are satisfied as equalities. The optimum program of money holdings is thus also unique.

Consider an intertemporal price system $p = (p_1, \ldots, p_n)$ in $P = \text{Int}$ $\mathbb{R}^{nl}_+$ (thus $p_t >> 0$ for all t). One can associate to p the unique optimum of (B.1.I), $(x_1, \ldots, x_n)$, where $x_t = (c_t, m_t)$ for all t, which is denoted:

$$\xi(p) = [\xi_1(p), \ldots, \xi_n(p)]$$

This defines a function $\xi: \text{Int } \mathbb{R}^{nl}_+ \to \mathbb{R}^{n(l+1)}_+$. The next results give more information about the properties of this function:

(B.1.1) *ξ is continuous.*

Proof. The problem leading to ξ is a particular case of (A.4.I), as we saw. One can thus apply (A.4.1).

Q. E. D.

(B.1.2) *Consider a sequence (p^k) of elements of Int $\mathbb{R}^{nl}_+$ that converges to $p^* \in$ $\mathbb{R}^{nl}_+ \backslash P$, with $p_1^* e_1 + \bar{m} > 0$ and $p_t^* e_t > 0$ for $t = 2, \ldots, n$. Then the sequence $(\xi(p^k))$ is unbounded.*

Proof. If the statement is false, there is a particular sequence (p^k) that satisfies the above conditions, such that the sequence $[x^k = \xi(p^k)]$ is bounded. Since every bounded sequence contains a convergent subsequence, as stated in (A.1.1), one can assume without loss of generality that (x^k) converges to $x^* \in \mathbb{R}^{n(l+1)}_+$. In view of (A.4.2), x^* is a solution of (B.1.I) for $p = p^*$. But one then gets a contradiction, since some component of p^* is equal to 0, in which case the household's consumption of the corresponding good, and thus the utility u, can be increased without violating the budget constraints. Therefore (B.1.2) must be true.

Q. E. D.

(B.1.3) *Consider a sequence (p^k) of elements of Int $\mathbb{R}^{nl}_+$ such that there exist two vectors ϵ and η in $\mathbb{R}^l$ satisfying $\eta \geq p_t^k \geq \epsilon >> 0$ for all k and $t = 2, \ldots, n$.*

If (p_1^k) converges to $p_1^* \in \mathbb{R}^l_+$ with $p_{1h}^* = 0$ for some h and $\bar{m} > 0$, or if the sequence (p_1^k) is unbounded and $n \geq 2$, then the sequence $(\xi_1(p^k))$ is unbounded.

Proof. Assume that the statement is false. This means that one can find a particular sequence (p^k) meeting the conditions of (B.1.3) such that the sequence $[x_1^k = \xi_1(p^k)]$ is bounded. Since any bounded sequence contains a convergent subsequence, one can assume without loss of generality that the sequences (x_1^k) and $(p_t)^k$ converge to $x_1^* \in \mathbb{R}_+^{l+1}$ and to $p_t^* \geqq \epsilon \gg 0$ for all $t = 2, \ldots, n$. It is easily checked by recurrence on t, that the sequences $[x_t^k = \xi_t(p^k)]$ are then themselves bounded, so that we can assume that they converge to $x_t^* \in \mathbb{R}_+^{l+1}$ for $t = 2, \ldots, n$.

If (p_1^k) converges to $p_1^* \in \mathbb{R}_+^l$ with $p_{1h}^* = 0$ for some h, and if $\bar{m} > 0$, one gets a contradiction to (B.1.2). In the other case, where the sequence (p_1^k) is unbounded, one can assume without loss of generality, by going to an appropriate subsequence, that the expression:

$$|p_1^k| = \sum_h p_{1h}^k$$

diverges to $+\infty$. The sequence of vectors $(p_1^k/|p_1^k|)$ is bounded and can be assumed to converge to $\bar{p}_1 \neq 0$, whereas the sequence $(1/|p_1^k|)$ tends to 0. If one divides the budget constraint for $t = 1$ by $|p_1^k|$ for each k, one can apply (A.4.2), with the sequence $[q_1^k = (p_1^k/|p_1^k|, 1/|p_1^k|)]$ which converges to $(\bar{p}_1, 0)$ and $[q_t^k = (p_t^k, 1)]$ tending to $(p_t^*, 1)$, and thus conclude that the program $x^* = (x_1^*, \ldots, x_n^*)$ maximizes u under the constraints:

$$\bar{p}_1 c_1 \leqq \bar{p}_1 e_1$$

$$p_t^* c_t + m_t \leqq p_t^* e_t + m_{t-1} \qquad (t = 2, \ldots, n)$$

But this is impossible when $n \geqq 2$, since the household can always increase m_1, and thus the consumption for $t \geqq 2$, without violating the constraints.

In all cases, one gets a contradiction. So (B.1.3) must be true.

Q. E. D.

B.2   Short-run Walrasian equilibrium

In this section we will prove the existence theorem stated in (1.4.1). We postulate accordingly all of the assumptions of this theorem.

Let Q_1 be the set of vectors q_1 in Int $\mathbb{R}_+^{l+1}$ such that $q_{1,l+1} = 1$. One can then write $q_1 = (p_1, 1)$. To such a q_1, one can associate, for each household a, the vector:

$$p_a(q_1) = [p_1, \psi_{a2}(p_1), \ldots, \psi_{an_a}(p_1)]$$

His behavior is then governed by (B.1.I), with $n = n_a$, $u = u_a$, $\bar{m} = \bar{m}_a$, $e_t = e_{at}$, and $p = p_a(q_1)$. The resulting current demand for goods and money is given by the corresponding value of $\xi_1(p)$, and is denoted $\xi_{a1}(q_1)$. Consumer a's vector of current excess demand for goods and for money is then defined as:

$$\zeta_a(q_1) = \xi_{a1}(q_1) - \bar{x}_a$$

where $\bar{x}_a$ is the initial endowment vector $(e_{a1}, \bar{m}_a)$. Summation over all households yields the aggregate current excess demand:

$$\zeta(q_1) = \sum_a \zeta_a(q_1)$$

With this notation, the system (1.4.C), (1.4.D) defining a short-run Walrasian equilibrium becomes $\zeta(q_1) = 0$.

In order to show the existence of a solution to this equation, we seek to apply the market equilibrium lemma of Section A.3 to the function $\zeta: Q_1 \rightarrow \mathbb{R}_+^{l+1}$. Q_1 is clearly a convex subset of the hyperplane H of $\mathbb{R}_+^{l+1}$ of equation $q_{1,l+1} = 1$, which is open in H. On the other hand, since the expectations functions ψ_{at} are continuous, ζ is continuous by (B.1.1). Since the current budget constraints are satisfied as equalities at every optimum of (B.1.I), ζ verifies $q_1\zeta(q_1) = 0$ for all q_1 in Q_1.

It remains to verify that ζ satisfies the boundary condition (A.3.B). In fact, we are going to show that (A.3.1) applies here, which implies trivially the boundary condition, since $q_1 \gg 0$ for every $q_1 \in Q_1$.

Clearly, $\zeta_a(q_1) \geq -\bar{x}_a$ for all a and all q_1 in Q_1, so that all correspondences are bounded below. Take a sequence (q_1^k) in Q_1 that either converges to $q_1 \in H \backslash Q_1$, or which is unbounded, and consider the particular agent a for whom $\bar{m}_a > 0$ and $n_a \geq 2$, whose price expectations are bounded. The associated sequence $p_a(q_1^k)$ satisfies the requirements of (B.1.3). The sequence $\zeta_a(q_1^k)$ is therefore unbounded. By (A.3.1), $\bar{q}_1 \zeta(q_1^k)$ diverges to $+\infty$ for all $\bar{q}_1$ in Q_1.

By the market equilibrium lemma, there is a $q_1^* \in Q_1$ such that $\zeta(q_1^*) = 0$. This completes the proof of (1.4.1).

Q. E. D.

B.3   Stationary states

This section is devoted to the proof of (1.6.1) and (1.6.2). We thus assume throughout (a) and (b) of Section 1.6.

The behavior of the consumers of type i along a stationary state where the price system is $p \in \mathbb{R}_+^l$ is governed by (1.6.IV), where we can replace without any loss of generality the equality signs by inequalities:

(B.3.IV) *Given* $p \in \mathbb{R}_+^l$, *maximize* $u_i(c_1, \ldots, c_{n_i})$ *with respect to* $(c_1, \ldots, c_{n_i}) \in \mathbb{R}_+^{l n_i}$ *and* $(m_1, \ldots, m_{n_i}) \in \mathbb{R}_+^{n_i}$, *subject to*

$$p c_\tau + m_\tau \leq p e_{i\tau} + m_{\tau-1} \qquad \tau = (1, \ldots, n_i), m_0 = 0$$

This decision problem is a particular case of (B.1.I), with $p_1 = p_2 = \ldots = p_{n_i}$. It has a unique solution whenever $p \in \text{Int } \mathbb{R}^l_+$. If $z_{i\tau}(p)$ and $m_{i\tau}(p)$ are the optimum values of $c_\tau - e_{i\tau}$ and of m_τ, one can define $z_i(p)$ and $m_i(p)$ as $\Sigma_\tau z_{i\tau}(p)$ and $\Sigma_\tau m_{i\tau}(p)$, respectively. If the functions $\zeta:\text{Int}\mathbb{R}^l_+ \rightarrow \mathbb{R}^l$ and $\mu:\text{Int}\mathbb{R}^l_+ \rightarrow \mathbb{R}_+$ are given by:

$$\zeta(p) = \sum_i z_i(p)$$

$$\mu(p) = \sum_i m_i(p)$$

the system (1.6.A), (1.6.B) defining a stationary equilibrium price system becomes:

(B.3.A) $\zeta(p) = 0$

(B.3.B) $\mu(p) = M$

Proof of (1.6.1). Since the function ζ is homogenous of degree 0 in prices, we can constrain the price system to lie in the set Q of all $p \in \text{Int } \mathbb{R}^l_+$ satisfying $\Sigma_h p_h = 1$. Q is then a convex subset of the hyperplane H of $\mathbb{R}^l$ of equation $\Sigma_h p_h = 1$, which is open in H. The problem is to find p^* in Q that satisfies (B.3.A).

In order to do so, we seek to apply the market equilibrium lemma of Section A.3 to the function $\zeta:Q \rightarrow \mathbb{R}^l_+$. Now, according to (B.1.1), ζ is continuous. We showed in Section 1.6 that it satisfies Say's Law, $p\zeta(p) = 0$ for all $p \in Q$. It thus remains to verify that it fulfills the boundary condition (A.3.B). To this effect, consider a sequence (p^k) in Q that converges to $p \in H\backslash Q$. Since $pe_{i\tau} > 0$ for every i and τ, (B.1.2) applies. The sequence $[z_i(p^k)]$ is therefore unbounded, for every i. For if it were bounded, the sequence $[z_{i\tau}(p^k), m_{i\tau}(p^k)]$ would also be bounded for each τ, according to the consumer's budget constraints, and one would get a contradiction to (B.1.2). Since the functions z_i are bounded below, this implies that $(\bar{p} \; \zeta(p^k))$ diverges to $+\infty$ for every $\bar{p}$ in Q, by (A.3.1).

Thus ζ satisfies the boundary condition (A.3.B). The equations have a solution in Q, which completes the proof of (1.6.1).

Q. E. D.

Proof of (1.6.2). We postulate, in addition to *(a)* and *(b)* of Section 1.6, the assumptions *(c)*, *(d)*, and *(e)* of the same section. There is accordingly a particular type i of consumers whose preferences depend on the "taste" parameter $\delta_i \in \Delta = (0,1)$. Their problem again fits in the framework described in (B.1.I), with the additional feature that the utility function u_i depends now on δ_i. Their aggregate excess demands for goods and their aggregate demand for money are then functions of δ_i, and are denoted

$z_i(p,\delta_i)$, $m_i(p,\delta_i)$. For the other types j of consumers, the notations are unchanged. We can define for every $p \in \text{Int } \mathbb{R}_+^l$:

$$\zeta(p,\delta_i) = z_i(p,\delta_i) + \sum_{j\neq i} z_j(p)$$

$$\mu(p,\delta_i) = m_i(p,\delta_i) + \sum_{j\neq i} m_j(p)$$

and the system (1.6.A), (1.6.B) reads, with this notation:

(B.3.A') $\zeta(p,\delta_i) = 0$

(B.3.B') $\mu(p,\delta_i) = M$

It is worth noticing at this stage that the properties (B.1.1), (B.1.2), and (B.1.3), which were derived for an unchanging taste parameter, are also valid when the household's taste parameter is varying. In particular, it is easily verified by a straightforward rewording of the proofs of (B.1.1) and (B.1.2) that:

The functions z_i *and* m_i *are continuous on Int* $\mathbb{R}_+^l \times \Delta$;
If one considers a sequence (p^k) *in Int* $\mathbb{R}_+^l$ *that converges to* $p^* \neq 0$ *with* $p_h^* = 0$ *for some* h, *and a sequence* (δ_i^k) *in* Δ *that converges to* $\delta_i^* \in \Delta$, *the sequence* $[z_i(p^k,\delta_i^k)]$ *is unbounded.*

By applying (1.6.1), (B.3.A') has a solution for every δ_i in Δ. In order to prove (1.6.2), we will show that there exists $\bar{\delta} < 1$ such that (B.3.A'), (B.3.B') has a solution p in Int $\mathbb{R}_+^l$ for every $\delta_i \in [\bar{\delta},1]$. Given the homogeneity properties of the functions z_i, z_j, and m_i, m_j, with respect to p, it suffices actually to prove that $m_i(p,\delta_i) > 0$ for all solutions $p \in Q$ of (B.3.A') when $\bar{\delta} \leq \delta_i \leq 1$, where Q is as before the set of all $p \in \text{Int } \mathbb{R}_+^l$ such that $\Sigma_h p_h = 1$.

Suppose that this last statement is false. This means that one can find a sequence (δ_i^k) in Δ that converges to 1, and a sequence (p^k) in Q that satisfies $\zeta(p^k,\delta_i^k) = 0$ for all k, such that $m_i(p^k, \delta_i^k) = 0$ for all k. The sequence (p^k) is bounded since it belongs to Q, and can therefore be assumed to converge to $p^* \in \mathbb{R}_+^l$. It is easily seen that p^* necessarily belongs to Q. For if p^* lay in $\mathbb{R}_+^l \backslash Q$, by the same argument used in the proof of (1.6.1), one would get that $[\bar{p}\,\zeta(p^k,\delta_i^k)]$ diverges to $+\infty$ for all $\bar{p} \in Q$, and it would be impossible that $\zeta(p^k,\delta_i^k) = 0$ for each k.

Thus $p^* \in Q$. Then, by continuity, $m_i(p^*,1) = 0$. But this leads to a contradiction, since we showed in Section 1.6 that, under assumptions (d) and (e) of that section, one had $m_i(p,1) > 0$ for every $p \in \text{Int } \mathbb{R}_+^l$. Hence, there must exist $\bar{\delta} < 1$ such that $m_i(p,\delta_i) > 0$ for all solutions $p \in Q$ of (B.3.A') when $\delta_i \in [\bar{\delta},1]$. This completes the proof of (1.6.2).

Q. E. D.

APPENDIX C

Money and credit in the short run

This appendix is devoted to the proofs of the existence theorems stated in Chapter 2. Assumptions *(a)* and *(b)* of Section 2.1 are thus postulated throughout. A few properties of an individual's demand and supplies are derived in Section C.1. The existence of a short-run Walrasian equilibrium when the interest rate is pegged is taken up in Section C.2. Finally, the case in which the Bank pegs its money supply is considered in Section C.3.

C.1   Demands and supplies

The decision problem of a typical consumer that was encountered in Chapter 2 specifies that he choose his current and future consumption (c_t), as well as his current and future net credit positions at the Bank (μ_t), by maximizing his utility function under the current and expected budget constraints, which involve the prices of goods and the rate of interest that are observed at the date of decision, and the consumer's expectations about these variables for the future – see (2.3.I).

We showed in Section 2.3 that the optimum consumption program could be derived by maximizing the household's utility function under a single intertemporal budget constraint, which stated that the present discounted value of consumption should not exceed the household's present discounted wealth.

If we write π_t for the current and expected prices of goods, discounted to the date of the decision $(t = 1)$ by using current and expected interest rates, we are led to consider the following program:

(C.1.I)   *Given $(\pi_1, \ldots , \pi_n)$, where $\pi_t \in \mathbb{R}^1_+$ for each* t, *subject to:*

170

$$\Sigma_t \pi_t c_t \leq \text{Max} \ (0, \ \bar{\mu} \ + \ \Sigma_t \pi_t e_t)$$

The problem is again a particular case of (A.4.I), with a single constraint. It therefore has a well-defined solution whenever $\pi = (\pi_1, \ldots, \pi_n) \in \text{Int} \ \mathbb{R}_+^{nl}$. In fact, the solution is unique since u is strictly quasi-concave, according to (A.2.4). For every $\pi \in \text{Int} \ \mathbb{R}_+^{nl}$, the optimum value of c_t is denoted $\chi_t(\pi)$, and we set:

$$\chi(\pi) = (\chi_1(\pi), \ldots, \chi_n(\pi))$$

The following results give some information about the properties of the function $\chi : \text{Int} \ \mathbb{R}_+^{nl} \rightarrow \mathbb{R}_+^{nl}$.

(C.1.1) χ *is continuous.*

Proof. Take a sequence (π_k) in Int $\mathbb{R}_+^{nl}$ that converges to $\pi^* \in \text{Int} \ \mathbb{R}_+^{nl}$. We wish to show that $[\chi(\pi^k)]$ converges to $\chi(\pi^*)$. If $\bar{\mu} + \Sigma_t \pi_t^* e_t > 0$, this results from (A.4.1). If $\bar{\mu} + \Sigma_t \pi_t^* e_t \leq 0$, $[\chi(\pi^k)]$ tends to 0. But then $\chi(\pi^*) = 0$ as well.

Q. E. D.

(C.1.2) *Consider a sequence* (π^k) *in Int* $\mathbb{R}_+^{nl}$, *which converges to* π^* *where some component of* π^* *is zero. Then, if* $\bar{\mu} + \Sigma_t \pi_t^* e_t > 0$, *the sequence* $[\chi(\pi^k)]$ *is unbounded.*

Proof. If the statement is not true, one can find a particular sequence (π^k) converging to π^*, where some component of π^* is equal to zero and $\bar{\mu} + \Sigma_t \pi_t^* e_t > 0$, such that $[\chi(\pi^k)]$ is bounded. Since every bounded sequence contains a convergent subsequence, one may assume that $[\chi(\pi^k)]$ converges to $c^* = (c_1^*, \ldots, c_n^*)$. By applying (A.4.2), c^* maximize u under the constraint:

$$\sum_{\tau} \pi_t^* c_t \leq \bar{\mu} + \sum_{\tau} \pi_t^* e_t$$

But this is impossible, since some component of π^* is equal to 0: the consumer could increase his consumption of the corresponding good, and thus his utility, without violating the constraint. Hence, (C.1.2) must be true.

Q. E. D.

Given $\pi = (\pi_1, \ldots, \pi_n)$ in Int $\mathbb{R}_+^{nl}$ and the corresponding outcome of (C.1.I), $\chi(\pi) = (\chi_1(\pi), \ldots, \chi_n(\pi))$, the consumer's desired net credit position at date 1 is given by his budget constraint at that date (see Section 2.3), that is:

$$\mu(\pi) = \pi_1[e_1 - \chi_1(\pi)] + \bar{m} - R_1(\pi)$$

where the reimbursement $R_1(\pi)$ to the Bank is the minimum of $\bar{b}$ and of $\bar{m} + \Sigma_t \pi_t e_t$. Since the intertemporal budget constraint is satisfied as an equality at the optimum of (C.1.I), $\mu(\pi)$ is equal to 0 when $n = 1$, and is given by the following expression otherwise:

$$\mu(\pi) = \sum_{t \geq 2} \pi_t [\chi_t(\pi) - e_t]$$

Let ξ_1 be the function which associates to every π in Int $\mathbb{R}_+^{nl}$ the vector $[\chi_1(\pi), \mu(\pi)]$ of $\mathbb{R}^{l+1}$. Of course, according to (C.1.1), ξ_1 is continuous. Moreover:

(C.1.3) *Consider a sequence (π^k) in Int $\mathbb{R}_+^{nl}$ such that there exist two vectors ϵ and η of $\mathbb{R}^l$ satisfying $\eta \geq \pi_t^k \geq \epsilon >> 0$ for all k and each $t = 2, \ldots, n$. If (π_1^k) converges to $\pi_1^* \in \mathbb{R}_+^l$ such that $\pi_{1h}^* = 0$ for some $h = 1, \ldots, l$, and $\bar{\mu} + \pi_1^* e_1 + \epsilon \sum_{t \geq 2} e_t > 0$, or if the sequence (π_1^k) is unbounded and $n \geq 2$, then the sequence $(\xi_1(\pi^k))$ is unbounded.*

Proof. Assume that the proposition is false. That means that one can find a particular sequence (π^k) in Int $\mathbb{R}_+^{nl}$ that satisfies the above requirements, such that the sequence $[\xi_1(\pi^k)]$ is bounded. Since every bounded sequence contains a convergent subsequence, one may assume without loss of generality that (π_t^k) converges to $\pi_t^* \geq \epsilon >> 0$ for each $t = 2, \ldots, n$, and that $[\xi_1(\pi^k)]$ converges to (c_1^*, μ^*).

For each k, one has, whenever $n \geq 2$:

$$\mu(\pi^k) = \sum_{t \geq 2} \pi_t^k [\chi_t(\pi^k) - e_t]$$

and $[\mu(\pi^k)]$ converges to μ^*. Each sequence $[\chi_t(\pi^k)]$ is thus bounded, and may be assumed to converge to $c_t^* \in \mathbb{R}_+^l$, for $t = 2, \ldots, n$.

If (π_1^k) converges to π_1^* such that $\pi_{1h}^* = 0$ for some h, and if $\bar{\mu} + \pi_1^* e_1 + \epsilon \sum_{t \geq 2} e_t > 0$, one gets a contradiction to (C.1.2). In the other case, where the sequence (π_1^k) is unbounded, we may assume by choosing an appropriate subsequence, that:

$$|\pi_1^k| = \Sigma_h \pi_{1h}^k$$

diverges to $+\infty$. Then the sequence of vectors $(\pi_1^k/|\pi_1^k|)$ is bounded and may be assumed to converge to $\bar{\pi}_1 \neq 0$. For each $t \geq 2$, the sequence $(\pi_t^k/|\pi_1^k|)$ tends to 0. If one divides the intertemporal budget constraint appearing in (C.1.I) by $|\pi_1^k|$ by eack k, the right-hand member tends to $\bar{\pi}_1 e_1$, which is positive. By another application of (A.4.2), the vector $c^* = (c_1^*, \ldots, c_n^*)$ maximizes the utility function under the constraint:

$$\bar{\pi}_1 c_1 \leq \bar{\pi}_1 e_1$$

But this is impossible when $n \geq 2$, since there are no restrictions on the consumptions $c_t \geq 2$.

One gets a contradiction in all cases. The proposition is thus correct.

Q. E. D.

(C.1.4) *Consider a sequence* (π^k) *in* Int $\mathbb{R}_+^{nl}$ *of the following form: for all k,*
$\pi_1^k \in$ *Int* $\mathbb{R}_+^l$ *and* $\pi_t^k = \psi_t^k/(1 + r_1^k)$ *for each* $t = 2, \ldots, n$, *where* $\psi_t^k \in$
Int $\mathbb{R}_+^l$, *and* r_1^k *is a real number in the open interval* $(-1, +\infty)$. *Assume
that there are two vectors* ϵ *and* η *in Int* $\mathbb{R}_+^l$ *such that* $\eta \geq \psi_t^k \geq \epsilon$ *for
all k and* $t = 2, \ldots, n$, *and that the sequence* (r_1^k) *converges to* -1.
If the sequence $[(1 + r_1^k) \pi_1^k]$ *converges to* $\pi_1^* \in \mathbb{R}_+^l$ *with* $\pi_{1h}^* = 0$ *for some
$h = 1, \ldots, l$, and* $\pi_1^* e_1 + \epsilon \sum_{t \geq 2} e_t > 0$, *or if the sequence* $[(1 + r_1^k)
\pi_1^k]$ *is unbounded and* $n \geq 2$, *then the sequence* $[\chi_1(\pi^k), (1 + r_1^k) \mu(\pi^k)]$
is unbounded.

Proof. Suppose that the statement is false. One can then find a sequence
(π^k) satisfying the assumptions of (C.1.4), such that $[\chi_1(\pi^k), (1 + r_1^k)
\mu(\pi^k)]$ is bounded. One may assume without loss of generality that the
sequences (ψ_t^k) converge to $\psi_t^* \geq \epsilon >> 0$ for each t, that $[\chi_1(\pi^k)]$ tends to
$c_1^* \in \mathbb{R}_+^l$ and that $[(1 + r_1^k) \mu(\pi^k)]$ converges to $\mu^* \in \mathbb{R}$. Now for each k,
when $n \geq 2$:

$$(1 + r_1^k) \mu(\pi^k) = \sum_{t \geq 2} \psi_t^k [\chi_t(\pi^k) - e_t]$$

The sequence $[\chi_t(\pi^k)]$ is thus bounded, and may be assumed to converge
to $c_t^* \in \mathbb{R}_+^l$, for each $t = 2, \ldots, n$.

Consider the case where $[(1 + r_1^k) \pi_1^k]$ converges to π_1^*, with $\pi_{1h}^* = 0$
for some h, and $\pi_1^* e_1 + \epsilon \sum_{t \geq 2} e_t > 0$. For each k, $\chi(\pi^k) =
[\chi_1(\pi^k), \ldots, \chi_n(\pi^k)]$ maximizes u under the budget constraint:

$$(1 + r_1^k)\pi_1^k c_1 + \sum_{t \geq 2} \psi_t^k c_t \leq \text{Max}[0, (1 + r_1^k)(\bar{\mu} + \pi_1^k e_1) + \sum_{t \geq 2} \psi_t^k e_t]$$

which is obtained by multiplying the constraint of (C.1.I) by $(1 + r_1^k)$.
By applying (A.4.2), $c^* = (c_1^*, \ldots, c_n^*)$ maximizes u under the constraint:

$$\pi_1^* c_1 + \sum_{t \geq 2} \psi_t^* c_t \leq \pi_1^* e_1 + \sum_{t \geq 2} \psi_t^* e_t$$

But this is impossible, as some component of π_1^* is equal to 0.

Consider now the alternative case where $[(1 + r_1^k) \pi_1^k]$ is unbounded.
Since (r_1^k) tends to -1, the sequence (π_1^k) must be unbounded, and one
can assume by going to a subsequence that the sequence $(|\pi_1^k| = \sum_h \pi_{1h}^k)$
diverges to $+\infty$. The sequence $(\pi_1^k/|\pi_1^k|)$ is bounded and may be assumed
to converge to $\bar{\pi}_1 \neq 0$. For each k, $\chi(\pi^k)$ maximizes u under the constraint
that is obtained by dividing the budget constraint of (C.1.I) by $|\pi_1^k|$. By
another application of (A.4.2), $c^* = (c_1^*, \ldots, c_n^*)$ maximizes u under
the constraint:

$$\bar{\pi}_1 c_1 \leq \bar{\pi}_1 e_1$$

This is impossible when $n \geq 2$, since there are no restrictions on c_t for $t = 2 , \ldots , n$.

In all cases, one gets a contradiction, and (C.1.4) cannot be falsified.

Q. E. D.

C.2   Pegging the interest rate

In this section we will prove (2.4.1). All assumptions of the theorem are thus postulated.

The interest rate r_1 is fixed in $(-1, +\infty)$. Consider the set Q_1 of all $q_1 \in \mathrm{Int}\ \mathbb{R}_+^{l+1}$, such that $q_{1,l+1} = 1$. A vector $q_1 \in Q_1$ can be written $q_1 = (p_1, 1)$ where $p_1 \in \mathrm{Int}\ \mathbb{R}_+^l$ stands for the prices of goods at date 1.

Given $q_1 = (p_1, 1) \in Q_1$ (and the interest rate r_1), we set for each household a:

$$\pi_{a1}(q_1) = p_1 \quad \text{and} \quad \pi_{at}(q_1) = \psi_{at}^*(p_1, r_1)/(1+r_1)$$

for $t = 2 , \ldots , n_a$. The household's behavior at date 1 is governed by (C.1.I), with $n = n_a$, $u = u_a$, $\bar{\mu} = \bar{\mu}_a$, $e_t = e_{at}$ for each t, and $\pi = (\pi_{a1}(q_1) , \ldots , \pi_{an_a}(q_1))$. The resulting demands for goods and the desired net credit position are then given by the corresponding values of $\chi_1(\pi)$ and of $\mu(\pi)$. They will be denoted $\chi_{a1}(q_1)$ and $\mu_a(q_1)$ respectively.

The household's demand for money and supply of bonds is then defined as:

$$m_a(q_1) = \mathrm{Max}\ (0,\ \mu_a(q_1))$$

$$b_a(q_1) = (1+r_1)\ \mathrm{Max}\ [0,\ -\ \mu_a(q_1)]$$

Lastly, the household's reimbursement to the Bank is:

$$R_a(q_1) = \mathrm{Min}\ [\bar{b}_a,\ \bar{m}_a + \Sigma_t\ \pi_{at}\ (q_1)\ e_{at}]$$

For each $q_1 \in Q_1$, let us set:

$$\zeta_a(q_1) = [\chi_{a1}(q_1) - e_{a1},\ \mu_a(q_1) - \bar{m}_a + R_a(q_1)]$$

for every a, and:

$$\zeta(q_1) = \Sigma_a\ \zeta_a(q_1)$$

The reader will easily check that the system (2.4.C), (2.4.D), which defines a short-run Walrasian equilibrium for the fixed interest rate r_1, becomes with this notation:

$$\zeta(q_1) = 0$$

In order to show (2.4.1), we seek to apply the market equilibrium lemma of Section A.3 to the function $\zeta : Q_1 \to \mathbb{R}^{l+1}$. First, Q_1 is a nonempty, convex subset of the hyperplane H of $\mathbb{R}^{l+1}$ defined by the equation $q_{1,l+1} = 1$, which is open in H. Next, since the functions ψ_{at}^* are continuous in prices, the functions ζ_a, and thus ζ, are continuous by (C.1.1). On the other hand, Walras's Law is equivalent here to $q_1 \, \zeta(q_1) = 0$ for all $q_1 \in Q_1$.

It remains to check that the boundary condition (A.3.B) is satisfied. To do so, we show that (A.3.1) applies. If $n_a = 1$, one has $\mu_a(q_1) = 0$, and the function ζ_a is bounded below. When $n_a \geq 2$, one has:

$$\mu_a(q_1) \geq - \sum_{t \geq 2} \pi_{at}(q_1) \, e_{at}$$

Since every consumer's price expectations $\psi_{at}^*(p_1, r_1)$ are by assumption bounded above by $\eta(r_1) >> 0$, one gets:

$$(1 + r_1) \, \mu_a(q_1) \geq - \eta(r_1) \sum_{t \geq 2} e_{at}$$

The function μ_a, and thus ζ_a, is bounded below.

Take next a sequence (q_1^k) in Q_1 that either tends to $q_1^* \in H \backslash Q_1$, or that is unbounded. Consider the particular consumer a for whom $n_a \geq 2$ and $\bar{\mu}_a \geq 0$, whose price expectations $\psi_{at}^*(p_1, r_1)$ are bounded away from zero, and look at the sequence of vectors:

$$\pi^k = (\pi_{a1}(q_1^k), \ldots, \pi_{ana}(q_1^k))$$

The sequence (π^k) meets all the requirements of (C.1.3). The sequence $[\chi_{a1}(q_1^k), \mu_a(q_1^k)]$, is unbounded. Since $R_a(q_1) = 0$ whenever $\bar{\mu}_a \geq 0$, the sequence $[\zeta_a(q_1^k)]$ is also unbounded. By (A.3.1), then, the sequence $[\bar{q}_1 \, \zeta(q_1^k)]$ diverges to $+\infty$ for all $\bar{q}_1 \in Q_1$.

The boundary condition (A.3.B) is thus satisfied. By the market equilibrium lemma of Section A.3, there exists $q_1^* \in Q_1$ such that $\zeta(q_1^*) = 0$, which completes the proof of (2.4.1).

Q. E. D.

C.3 Controlling the money supply

This section is devoted to the proof of (2.5.2). All conditions of this theorem are therefore assumed.

The Bank's money supply $\Delta M > 0$ is fixed. Consider the set Q of all $q \in \text{Int } \mathbb{R}_+^{l+2}$ such that $q_{l+1} = 1$. The first l components of q stand for the money prices of goods p_1 at date 1, $q_{l+1} = 1$ is the price of money, and q_{l+2} is the price of bonds and determines the interest rate $r_1 \in (-1, +\infty)$ by:

$$q_{l+2} = 1/(1 + r_1)$$

In the sequel we shall identify $q \in Q$ and the vector $(p_1, 1, 1/(1 + r_1))$.

Given $q \in Q$, one sets for each household a, $\pi_{a1}(q) = p_1$ and $\pi_{at}(q) = \psi_{at}^*(p_1, r_1)/(1 + r_1)$ for $t = 2, \ldots, n_a$. Here again, the household's behavior at date 1 is governed by (C.1.I), with $n = n_a$, $u = u_a$, $\bar{\mu} = \bar{\mu}_a$, $e_t = e_{at}$ for each t, and $\pi = (\pi_{a1}(q, \ldots, \pi_{an_a}(q))$. The resulting demands for goods and the desired net credit position are then given by the corresponding values of $\chi_1(\pi)$ and of $\mu(\pi)$. They will be denoted $\chi_{a1}(q)$, and $\mu_a(q)$, respectively.

The household's demand for money and supply of bonds are then:

$$m_a(q) = \text{Max}\,(0, \mu_a(q))$$

$$b_a(q) = (1 + r_1)\,\text{Max}\,(0, -\mu_a(q))$$

Lastly, the agent's reimbursement to the Bank is:

$$R_a(q) = \text{Min}\,(\bar{b}_a, \bar{m}_a + \Sigma_t\,\pi_{at}(q)\,e_{at})$$

For each $q \in Q$, and every a, let us set:

$$\zeta_a(q) = (\chi_{a1}(q) - e_{a1}, m_a(q) - \bar{m}_a + R_a(q), -b_a(q))$$

Next define the Bank's excess demand on all markets by:

$$\zeta_B(q) = (0, -\Delta M, (1 + r_1)\,\Delta M)$$

where $0 \in \mathbb{R}^l$. With this notation, the aggregate excess demand vector on all markets is:

$$\zeta(q) = \Sigma_a\,\zeta_a(q) + \zeta_B(q)$$

and the system (2.5.C), (2.5.D), (2.5.E), which defines a short-run Walrasian equilibrium corresponding to the fixed money supply $\Delta M > 0$, becomes:

$$\zeta(q) = 0$$

In order to show (2.5.2), we seek to apply the market equilibrium lemma of Section A.3 to the function $\zeta : Q \to \mathbb{R}^{l+2}$. Q is a nonempty, convex subset of the hyperplane H of $\mathbb{R}^{l+2}$ defined by the equation $q_{l+1} = 1$, which is open in H. Since the functions ψ_{at}^* are continuous in (p_1, r_1), the functions ζ_a, and thus ζ, are continuous, according to (C.1.1). On the other hand, Walras's Law is equivalent here to $q\zeta(q) = 0$ for all $q \in Q$.

We must check that the boundary condition (A.3.B) is fulfilled. Clearly, ζ_B is bounded below. If $n_a = 1$, one has $\mu_a(q) = 0$, and ζ_a is bounded below. If $n_a \geq 2$, one has:

$$\mu_a(q) \geq -\sum_{t \geq 2} \pi_{at}(q)\,e_{at}$$

By assumption, every consumer's price expectations $\psi_{at}^*(p_1, r_1)$ are uniformly bounded above by a vector $\eta >> 0$. Hence:

$$(1 + r_1)\,\mu_a(q) \geqq -\,b_a(q) \geqq -\eta \sum_{t \geqq 2} e_{at}$$

In this case too, the function $-b_a$, and thus ζ_a, is bounded below.

We seek to apply (A.3.1). To this effect, pick a sequence (q^k) in Q that either tends to $q^* \in H\backslash Q$ or that is unbounded. The associated sequences (p_1^k) and r_1^k) are given by definition by:

$$q^k = [p_1^k,\ 1,\ 1/(1 + r_1^k)]$$

If the sequence (r_1^k) is unbounded, then $(\zeta_B(q^k))$ is unbounded too, since $\Delta M > 0$. Let us suppose that, on the contrary, the sequence (r_1^k) is bounded, or equivalently, that there exists $\lambda > 0$ such that $q_{l+2}^k \geqq \lambda$ for all k. We have to distinguish two cases.

Case 1: The sequence (q_{l+2}^k) *is bounded.* In that case, there exist λ_1 and λ_2 such that:

$$-1 < \lambda_1 \leqq r_1^k \leqq \lambda_2$$

for all k. Then either the sequence (p_1^k) converges to $p_1^* \in \mathbb{R}_+^l$, and $p_{1h}^* = 0$ for some $h = 1, \ldots, l$, or it is unbounded. Now consider the particular consumer a for whom $n_a \geqq 2$, $\bar{\mu}_a \geqq 0$, whose price expectations $\psi_{at}^*(p_1, r_1)$ are uniformly bounded away from 0. For this consumer, the sequence (π^k) defined by:

$$\pi^k = [\pi_{a1}(q^k), \ldots, \pi_{an_a}(q^k)]$$

for all k satisfies the conditions of (C.1.3). Thus the sequence $(\chi_{a1}(q^k))$ is unbounded. But one has, for each k:

$$\mu_a(q^k) = m_a(q^k) - [b_a(q^k)/(1 + r_1^k)] \geqq -(\eta \sum_{t \geqq 2} e_{at})/(1 + r_1^k)$$

The sequence $(b_a(q^k))$ is bounded, whereas the sequence $[\chi_{a1}(q^k), m_a(q^k)]$ is unbounded. This implies that $[\zeta_a(q^k)]$ is also unbounded.

Case 2: The sequence (q_{l+2}^k) *is unbounded.* This means that there is a subsequence $(q^{k'})$ such that $(q_{l+2}^{k'})$ diverges to $+\infty$, or equivalently, such that $(r_1^{k'})$ converges to -1. There are now two subcases.

The sequence $(p_1^{k'})$ *is unbounded.* Then consider the particular consumer b for whom $n_b \geqq 2$, whose expected discounted prices $\psi_{bt}^*(p_1, r_1)/(1 + r_1)$ are uniformly bounded away from infinity and from zero when r_1 tends to -1. There are accordingly two vectors ϵ' and η' such that:

$$\eta' \geqq \psi_{bt}^*(p_1^{k'}, r_1^{k'})/(1 + r_1^{k'}) \geqq \epsilon' >> 0$$

for all $t = 2, \ldots, n_b$, and all k'. The sequence $(\pi^{k'})$ defined by:

$$\pi^{k'} = [\pi_{b1}(q^{k'}), \ldots, \pi_{bn_b}(q^{k'})]$$

satisfies the requirements of (C.1.3). Thus the sequence $[\chi_{b1}(q^{k'}), \mu_b(q^{k'})]$ is unbounded. But for each k':

$$\mu_b(q^k) = m_b(q^k) - [b_b(q^k)/(1+r_1^{k'})] \geqq - \eta' \sum_{t \geqq 2} e_{bt}$$

The sequence $[\chi_{b1}(q^{k'}), m_b(q^{k'})]$ is therefore unbounded, in which case the sequence $[\zeta_b(q^{k'})]$, and thus $[\zeta_b(q^k)]$, is also unbounded.

The sequence $(\mathrm{p}_1^{k'})$ *is bounded.* Then the sequence $[(1+r_1^{k'})\,p_1^{k'}]$ tends to $0 \in \mathbb{R}^l$. If we consider again the consumer a with $n_a \geqq 2$, $\bar{\mu}_a \geqq 0$, whose price expectations $\psi_{at}^*(p_1, r_1)$ are uniformly bounded away from zero, the sequence $(\pi^{k'})$ defined by:

$$\pi^{k'} = [\pi_{a1}(q^{k'}), \ldots, \pi_{an_a}(q^{k'})]$$

for each k' satisfies the requirements of (C.1.4). The sequence $[\chi_{a1}(q^{k'}), (1+r_1^{k'})\mu_a(q^{k'})]$ is unbounded.

But for each k':

$$(1+r_1^{k'})\,\mu_a(q^{k'}) = (1+r_1^{k'})\,m_a(q^{k'}) - b_a(q^{k'}) \geqq - \eta \sum_{t \geqq 2} e_{at}$$

The sequence $[\chi_{a1}(q^{k'}), (1+r_1)^{k'}\,m_a(q^{k'})]$ is accordingly unbounded. Since $(r_1^{k'})$ tends to -1, this implies that $[\chi_{a1}(q^{k'}), m_a(q^{k'})]$, and therefore $\zeta_a(q^k)$, is also unbounded.

We can therefore apply (A.3.1) to the sequence (q^k). Therefore $(\bar{q}\,\zeta(q^k))$ diverges to $+\infty$ for every $\bar{q} \in Q$.

The boundary condition (A.3.B) is verified. The market equilibrium lemma of Section A.3 implies that there exists $q^* \in Q$ such that $\zeta(q^*) = 0$. The proof of (2.5.2) is complete.

Q. E. D.

Classical stationary states with money and credit

In this Appendix we will prove the statements made in Chapter 3, namely, (3.4.1), (3.4.2), (3.4.3), and (3.5.1). Conditions *(a)* and *(b)* of Section 3.1 are assumed accordingly throughout.

We begin with a derivation of a few simple properties of the consumers' long-run demands and supplies. The existence and the properties of Golden Rule steady states are investigated in Section D.2. Section D.3 is devoted to Balanced steady states.

D.1   Long-run demands and supplies

If $r \in (-1, +\infty)$ is the nominal of interest, and $\pi \in (-1, +\infty)$ is the rate of inflation that prevail along a steady state, the real rate of interest $\rho \in (-1, +\infty)$ is defined by $1 + \rho = (1 + r)/(1 + \pi)$.

The excess demands for goods functions $z_i(p,\rho)$ that were used in Chapter 3 to write down the steady-state equilibrium equations were shown to be the result of the maximization, by the households of type i, of their utility function under an intertemporal budget constraint stating that the present discounted value of their consumption should not exceed the present discounted value of their lifetime real income – see (3.2.I) and the ensuing discussion. At some point, the impact of the traders' discount rate δ_i was taken into account (see Section 3.4). It is accordingly useful to include the influence of this "taste parameter δ_i" right at the outset of the present analysis. This leads us to consider the following program.

(D.1.I)   *Given $p \in \mathbb{R}_+^l$, $\rho \in (-1, +\infty)$ and $\delta_i \in \Delta = (0, 1]$, maximize $u_i(c_1, \ldots, c_{n_i}, \delta_i)$ with respect to $(c_1, \ldots, c_{n_i}) \in \mathbb{R}_+^{l n_i}$, subject to:*

179

$$\sum_{\tau} pc_{\tau}/(1 + \rho)^{\tau-1} \leq \sum_{\tau} pe_{i\tau}/(1 + \rho)^{\tau-1} \qquad where \; \tau \; runs \; from \; 1 \; to \; n_i$$

This problem is in fact a particular case of (C.1.I), the only difference being that the utility function now depends on the taste parameter δ_i. It has thus a well-defined (and unique) solution whenever $p \in \text{Int } \mathbb{R}_+^l$, and at the optimum, the intertemporal budget constraint is satisfied as an equality.

The optimum value of $c_{\tau} - e_{i\tau}$ is denoted $z_{i\tau}(p,\rho,\delta_i)$. The corresponding desired net credit positions $\mu_{i\tau}(p,\rho,\delta_i)$ are derived in turn from the budget constraints associated with each τ:

$$p \, z_{i\tau}(p,\rho,\delta_i) + \mu_{i\tau}(p,\rho,\delta_i) = (1 + \rho)\mu_{i,\tau-1}(p,\rho,\delta_i)$$

with the convention $\mu_{i0} = 0$. Summation over τ of the $z_{i\tau}$ (or $\mu_{i\tau}$) values yields $z_i(p,\rho,\delta_i)$ (or $\mu_i(p,\rho,\delta_i)$). These functions are defined on $\text{Int } \mathbb{R}_+^l \times (-1, +\infty) \times \Delta$.

The following two facts will be useful in the sequel.

(D.1.1) *The functions z_i and μ_i are continuous.*

Proof. Apply (A.4.1).

(D.1.2) *Consider a sequence (p^k) in $\text{Int } \mathbb{R}_+^l$, with $\sum_h p_h^k = 1$ for every k, a sequence (ρ^k) in $(-1, +\infty)$, and a sequence (δ_i^k) in Δ converging to $\delta_i^* \in \Delta$. If the sequence (p^k) is unbounded, or if (p^k,ρ^k) converges to (p^*,ρ^*) with $p_h^* = 0$ for some h, and/or with $\rho^* = -1$, then the sequence $[z_i(p^k,\rho^k,\delta^k)]$ is unbounded.*

Proof. Assume that the proposition is false. One can then find a sequence (p^k,ρ^k,δ^k) that satisfies the above conditions, such that $[z_i(p^k,\rho^k,\delta^k)]$ is bounded. If one sets of each k and τ:

$$c_{\tau}^k - e_{i\tau} = z_{i\tau}(p^k,\rho^k,\delta^k)$$

this implies that the sequence (c_{τ}^k) is bounded for every τ. It can thus be assumed to converge to $c_{\tau}^* \in \mathbb{R}_+^l$ for each τ. On the other hand, the sequence (p^k) is bounded, and may therefore be assumed to converge to some $p^* \in \mathbb{R}_+^l$ with $p^* \neq 0$.

Consider first the case in which the sequence (ρ^k) is unbounded. One may assume, by choosing an appropriate subsequence, that it diverges actually to $+\infty$. Then for each $\tau \geq 2$, the sequence $[p^k/(1 + \rho^k)^{\tau-1}]$ tends to 0. By applying (A.4.2), $c^* = (c_1^*, \ldots, c_{n_i}^*)$ maximizes the utility function u_i (with $\delta_i = \delta_i^*$) under the constraint $p^* c_1 \leq p^* e_{i1}$. This is, however, impossible, as there are no restrictions on the consumption vectors c_{τ} for $\tau \geq 2$.

Let us look at the other case where (p^k, ρ^k) converges to (p^*, ρ^*). If $\rho^* \neq -1$, it follows from another application of (A.4.2) that c^* maximizes u_i, with $\delta_i = \delta_i^*$, under the constraint:

$$\textstyle\sum_{\tau} p^* c_\tau / (1 + \rho^*)^{\tau - 1} \; \leqq \; \sum_{\tau} p^* e_{i\tau} / (1 + \rho^*)^{\tau - 1}$$

Again, we have a contradiction, since $p_h^* = 0$ for some h.

If $\rho^* = -1$, we multiply the budget constraint of (D.1.I) by $(1 + \rho^k)^{n_i}$ for each k. By applying (A.4.2) once again, c^* maximizes u_i, with $\delta_i = \delta_i^*$, under the constraint:

$$p^* c_{n_i} \; \leqq \; p^* e_{in_i}$$

We once again get a contradiction, since there are no restrictions on c_τ for $\tau < n_i$.

In all cases, one gets a contradiction, which shows that (D.1.2) is true.

Q. E. D.

D.2   Golden Rule steady states

In this section we will seek to prove (3.4.1), (3.4.2), and (3.4.3).

Proof of (3.4.1). Statement (3.4.1) asserts the existence of a price system $p^* \in$ Int $\mathbb{R}_+^l$, which brings the goods markets into equilibrium when $\rho = 0$.

Since at this stage no explicit consideration of the taste parameters δ_1 is made, we can assume them to be fixed. For each $p \in$ Int $\mathbb{R}_+^l$, we set:

$$\zeta(p) = \textstyle\sum_i z_i(p, 0, \delta_i)$$

The result that must be proved is that under *(a)* and *(b)* of Section 3.1, the equation $\zeta(p) = 0$ has a solution $p^* \in$ Int $\mathbb{R}_+^l$.

The proof is in fact a rewording of the proof of (1.6.1) given in Appendix B. Since ζ is homogenous of degree 0 in prices, one can restrict the attention to the set Q of all $p \in$ Int $\mathbb{R}_+^l$ satisfying $\sum_h p_h = 1$. Q is a nonempty, convex subset of the hyperplane H of $\mathbb{R}^l$, of equation $\sum_h p_h = 1$, which is open in H. From (D.1.1), ζ is continuous. We showed in Section 3.3 that it satisfies Say's Law, in which case $p\zeta(p) = 0$ for all $p \in Q$.

To show existence, we seek to apply the market equilibrium lemma of Section A.3. Now, for every i, the function z_i is bounded below. Consider next a sequence (p^k) in Q that converges to $p^* \in H \backslash Q$. According to (D.1.2), the sequence $[z_i(p^k, 0, \delta_i)]$ is unbounded, for every i. By applying (A.3.1), $[\bar{p}\zeta(p^k)]$ diverges to $+\infty$ for every $\bar{p} \in Q$. Hence the boundary condition (A.3.B) is satisfied.

By the market equilibrium lemma, there exists $p^* \in Q$ such that $\zeta(p^*) = 0$.

Q. E. D.

Proof of (3.4.2). Statement (3.4.2) concerns the desired aggregate net credit position of the households of a given type i, in relationship with their real income intertemporal profile and their discount rate δ_i.

We have seen in Section D.1 that the desired net credit position of a household of type i and of age τ along a steady state, $\mu_{i\tau}(p, \rho, \delta_i)$, is given by the budget constraint associated with every τ:

$$pz_{i\tau}(p, \rho, \delta_i) + \mu_{i\tau}(p, \rho, \delta_i) = (1 + \rho)\mu_{i,\tau-1}(p, \rho, \delta_i),$$

with $\mu_{i0}(p, \rho, \delta_i) = 0$.

Let us fix $p \in \text{Int } \mathbb{R}^l_+$, $\rho = 0$, and $\delta_i \in \Delta$, and set

$$c^*_{i\tau} - e_{i\tau} = z_{i\tau}(p, 0, \delta_i), \quad \mu^*_{i\tau} = \mu_{i\tau}(p, 0, \delta_i)$$

for each τ, and $\mu^*_i = \mu_i(p, 0, \delta_i) = \sum_\tau \mu^*_{i\tau}$.

We have to prove that under *(a')* of Section 3.4, $\mu^*_i = p\epsilon_i$ when $\delta_i = 1$, and $\mu^*_i \leqq p\epsilon_i$ when $\delta_i < 1$ (the definition of the vector ϵ_i was given in Section 3.4).

In order to evaluate μ^*_i for a given $\delta_i \leqq 1$, it is convenient to group the terms $\mu^*_{i\tau}$ and $\mu^*_{i,n_i-\tau}$. If one remarks that $\mu^*_{n_i} = 0$, this yields:

$$\mu^*_i = \sum_1^q(\mu^*_{i\tau} + \mu^*_{i,n_i-\tau})$$

when n_i is odd and equal to $2q + 1$, and:

$$\mu^*_i = \sum_1^{q-1}(\mu^*_{i\tau} + \mu^*_{i,n_i-\tau}) + \mu^*_{iq}$$

when n_i is even and equal to $2q$.

We can get $\mu^*_{i\tau}$ by adding the budget constraints corresponding to the τ first periods of the household's life:

$$\mu^*_{i\tau} = p\sum_1^\tau(e_{it} - c^*_{it})$$

The value of $\mu^*_{i,n_i-\tau}$ can be obtained by adding the budget constraints associated to the τ last periods of the consumer's life:

$$\mu^*_{i,n_i-\tau} = p \sum_{n_i-\tau+1}^{n_i} (c^*_{it} - e_{it})$$

Therefore:

(i) $$\mu^*_{i\tau} + \mu^*_{i,n_i-\tau} = p\epsilon_{i\tau} + p(\sum_{n_i-\tau+1}^{n_i} c^*_{it} - \sum_1^\tau c^*_{it})$$

where the vectors $\epsilon_{i\tau}$ are defined as in Section 3.4. This evaluation is valid independently of δ_i. Let us now distinguish two cases.

Case 1: $\delta_i = 1$. Then $c^*_{i\tau} = c^*_{i,\tau+1}$ for every τ. Indeed, assume that, on the contrary, $c^*_{i\tau} \neq c^*_{i,\tau+1}$ for some τ. If we set $c_{it} = c^*_{it}$ for $t \neq \tau$, $\tau+1$, and

$$c_{i\tau} = c_{i,\tau+1} = (c^*_{i\tau} + c^*_{i,\tau+1})/2$$

the program $(c_{i1}, \ldots, c_{in_i})$ satisfies the intertemporal budget constraint of (D.1.I) (with $\rho = 0$), and yields a higher utility level, since, by strict concavity of w_i:

$$w_i(c_{i\tau}^*) + w_i(c_{i,\tau+1}^*) < w_i(c_{i\tau}) + w_i(c_{i,\tau+1})$$

and we get a contradiction.

Therefore, the last term in (i) vanishes, and:

$$\mu_i^* = p\Sigma_1^q \epsilon_{i\tau} = p\epsilon_i$$

when n_i is odd and equal to $2q + 1$, whereas:

$$\mu_i^* = p[\Sigma_1^{q-1} \epsilon_{i\tau} + (\epsilon_{iq}/2)] = p\epsilon_i$$

when n_i is even and equal to $2q$. This completes the proof in that case.

Case 2: $\delta_i < 1$. We wish to show that $pc_{i\tau}^* \geq pc_{i,\tau+1}^*$ in such a case. Suppose that, on the contrary, there is a τ such that $pc_{i\tau}^* < pc_{i,\tau+1}^*$. Now, $c_{i\tau}^*$ clearly maximizes $w_i(c)$ under the constraint $pc \leq pc_{i\tau}^*$, and an analogue statement is true for $c_{i,\tau+1}^*$. Therefore, $w_i(c_{i\tau}^*) < w_i(c_{i,\tau+1}^*)$. Next define a new consumption program as in Case 1, by $c_{it} = c_{it}^*$ for $t \neq \tau, \tau+1$, and:

$$c_{i\tau} = c_{i,\tau+1} = (c_{i\tau}^* + c_{i,\tau+1}^*)/2$$

By strict concavity of w_i, one has

$$w_i(c_{i\tau}^*) + w_i(c_{i,\tau+1}^*) < w_i(c_{i\tau}) + w_i(c_{i,\tau+1})$$

and

$$w_i(c_{i\tau}^*) < w_i(c_{i\tau})$$

If one adds these two inequalities, the first one being multiplied by δ_i and the second one by $(1 - \delta_i)$, one gets:

$$w_i(c_{i\tau}^*) + \delta_i w_i(c_{i,\tau+1}^*) < w_i(c_{i\tau}) + \delta_i w_i(c_{i,\tau+1})$$

The program $(c_{i1}, \ldots, c_{in_i})$ satisfies the intertemporal budget constraint of (D.1.I), with $\rho = 0$, and yields a higher level of utility.

This contradiction shows that $pc_{i\tau}^* \geq pc_{i,\tau+1}^*$ for all τ. The last term in (i) is nonpositive, in which case:

$$\mu_i^* \leq p\epsilon_i$$

Q. E. D.

Remark. It was asserted in footnote 10 of Section 3.4 that $\mu_i^* < p\epsilon_i$ whenever $\delta_i < 1$, if one assumed *(b)* of Section 3.1 in addition to *(a')* of Section 3.4, if w_i was differentiable, and if the partial derivative of

w_i with respect to the hth good, $\partial w_i/\partial c_h$, was infinite whenever $c_h = 0$, for each h.

In view of the foregoing argument, it suffices to show that under these assumptions, $pc^*_{i\tau} > pc^*_{i,\tau+1}$ for every τ. Let us assume that, on the contrary, one has:

$$pc^*_{i\tau} = pc^*_{i,\tau+1}$$

for some τ. Now $c^*_{i\tau}$ necessarily maximizes $w_i(c)$ under the constraint:

$$pc \leqq pc^*_{i\tau}$$

and the same is true of $c^*_{i,\tau+1}$. The strict concavity of w_i implies $c^*_{i\tau} = c^*_{i,\tau+1}$.

It is easily checked that under the new assumptions, $c^*_{i\tau} >> 0$. Writing down the marginal conditions that must be satisfied at the optimum of (D.1.I) yields in this particular case:

$$Dw_i(c^*_{i\tau}) = \delta_i Dw_i(c^*_{i,\tau+1})$$

where $Dw_i(c)$ stands for the gradient vector of w_i at c, that is:

$$Dw_i(c) = [(\partial w_i/\partial c_1), \ldots , (\partial w_i/\partial c_h), \ldots , (\partial w_i/\partial c_l)]$$

The fact that $\delta_i < 1$ implies then $c^*_{i\tau} \neq c^*_{i,\tau+1}$.

We get a contradiction, which completes the proof of the statement.

Proof of (3.4.3). Let us set for each collection of $\delta_i \in \Delta$ and for every $p \in \text{Int } \mathbb{R}^l_+$:

$$\zeta[p,(\delta_i)] = \sum_i z_i(p,0,\delta_i)$$

$$\mu[p,(\delta_i)] = \sum_i \mu_i(p,0,\delta_i)$$

Statement (3.4.3) claims that under *(a')* of Section 3.4, *(b)* of Section 3.1, and if $\epsilon = \Sigma_i \epsilon_i > 0$, then there exists $\bar{\delta} < 1$ such that $\mu[p,(\delta_i)] > 0$ for every $p \in \text{Int } \mathbb{R}^l_+$ satisfying $\zeta[p,(\delta_i)] = 0$, whenever $\delta_i \geqq \bar{\delta}$ for all i.

Suppose that this proposition is false. Then there are sequences (δ^k_i) that converge to 1 for every i, and a sequence (p^k) in $\text{Int } \mathbb{R}^l_+$ such that:

$$\zeta[p^k,(\delta^k_i)] = 0$$

$$\mu[p^k,(\delta^k_i)] \leqq 0$$

for all k. Since ζ (or μ) is homogenous of degree 0 (or 1) in p, one can in fact constrain p^k to satisfy $\Sigma_h p^k_h = 1$ for every k. Then the sequence (p^k) is bounded, and may be assumed to converge to $p^* \neq 0$.

It is clear that $p^* >> 0$. For otherwise, the sequences $[z_i(p^k,0,\delta^k_i)]$ would be unbounded for every i by (D.1.2), contradicting the fact that $\zeta[p^k,(\delta^k_i)] = 0$ for all k. By continuity, the sequence $[\mu(p^k,(\delta^k_i))]$ converges to $\mu[p^*,(1)] \leq 0$. But for every i, the sequence $[\mu_i(p^k,0,\delta_i^k)]$ tends to $\mu_i(p^*,0,1)$, which is equal, by (3.4.2), to $p^*\epsilon_i$. Thus one should have $\mu[p^*,(1)] = p^*\epsilon > 0$.

This contradiction shows that the proposition is correct.

Q. E. D.

D.3 Balanced steady states

In this section we will prove (3.5.1). In this context, the "taste parameters" δ_i are not explicitly mentioned. We shall consider them as fixed. Our goal then is to prove that under (a), (b) of Section 3.1, there exists $p^* \in$ Int $\mathbb{R}_+^l$ and $\rho^* \in (-1, +\infty)$, which satisfies the system of equations:

(D.3.A) $\sum_i z_i(p,\rho,\delta_i) = 0$

(D.3.B) $\sum_i \mu_i(p,\rho,\delta_i) = 0$

Given the homogeneity properties of the functions z_i and μ_i, we can restrict the attention to those price systems $p \in$ Int $\mathbb{R}_+^l$ that satisfy $\sum_h p_h = 1$.

Let Q be the set of vectors $q \in \mathbb{R}^{l+1}$, of the form $q = (p, -\rho)$, where $p \in$ Int $\mathbb{R}_+^l$, $\sum_h p_h = 1$, and $\rho \in (-1, +\infty)$.

For each $q = (p, -\rho) \in Q$, let:

$$\zeta(q) = [\sum_i z_i(p,\rho,\delta_i), \sum_i \mu_i(p,\rho,\delta_i)] \in \mathbb{R}^{l+1}$$

With this notation, the system (D.3.A), (D.3.B) reads

$$\zeta(q) = 0$$

In order to show existence, we seek to apply the market equilibrium lemma of Section A.3 to the function $\zeta:Q \rightarrow \mathbb{R}^{l+1}$. Clearly, Q is a nonempty, convex subset of the hyperplane H of $\mathbb{R}^{l+1}$ of equation $\sum_1^l q_h = 1$, which is open in H. According to (D.1.1), ζ is continuous. The functions z_i and μ_i were shown in Section 3.2 to be linked by Say's Law, which means here $q\zeta(q) = 0$ for all $q \in Q$.

We will next show that ζ satisfies the boundary condition (A.3.B). Consider accordingly a sequence (q^k) in Q that either converges to $q^* \in H \backslash Q$, or that is unbounded. The associated sequence (p^k, ρ^k) meets the requirements of (D.1.2). Hence the sequence $[z_i(p^k, \rho^k, \delta_i)]$ is unbounded. As the functions z_i are clearly bounded below, we can again apply (A.3.1). Thus the sequence $[\bar{p}\sum_i z_i(p^k, \rho^k, \delta_i)]$ diverges to $+\infty$ for all $\bar{p} \in$ Int $\mathbb{R}_+^l$. This means that $[\bar{q}\zeta(q^k)]$ diverges to $+\infty$ for every $\bar{q} \in Q$ of the form $\bar{q} = (\bar{p}, 0)$. Therefore, ζ fulfills (A.3.B).

By the market equilibrium lemma, there exists $q^* \in Q$ such that $\zeta(q^*) = 0$.

Q. E. D.

APPENDIX E

Open-market policies and liquidity

We now prove the results of Chapter 4. We first give a few properties of an individual's demands (Section E.1). The case in which the interest rate is pegged is analyzed in Section E.2, and the case in which the Bank fixes its money supply in Section E.3. Section E.4 investigates the liquidity trap.

The conditions *(a)* and *(b)* of Section 4.2 are assumed throughout.

E.1   Short-run demand correspondences

The problem governing the short-run behavior of a typical consumer at date 1 was described in (4.3.I). As the equality signs appearing in the budget constraints of the problem may be replaced by inequality signs without altering the outcome, we have:

(E.1.I)   *Given* $p_t \in \mathbb{R}_+^1$, $s_t \in \mathbb{R}_+$ *for* $t = 1, \ldots, n$, *maximize* $u(c_1, \ldots, c_n)$ *with respect to* $(c_1, \ldots, c_n) \in \mathbb{R}_+^{n1}$, $(m_1, \ldots, m_n) \in \mathbb{R}_+^1$, $(b_1, \ldots, b_n) \in \mathbb{R}_+^n$, *subject to:*

$$p_1 c_1 + m_1 + s_1 b_1 \leqq p_1 e_1 + \bar{m} + s_1 \bar{b}$$

$$p_t c_t + m_t + s_t b_t \leqq p_t e_t + m_{t-1} + (s_t + 1) b_{t-1}$$

for $t = 2, \ldots, n$.

In the sequel, we shall speak indifferently, as in the text, of the price of perpetuities s_t at date t, or of the corresponding interest rate $r_t = 1/s_t$.

186

The above problem is a particular case of (A.4.I) – take $x_t = (c_t, m_t, b_t) \in \mathbb{R}_+^{l+2}$, $q_t = (p_t, 1, s_t)$ for all t. It thus has a well-defined solution whenever $p_t \in \text{Int } \mathbb{R}_+^l$ and $s_t > 0$ for every t.

It is easy to see that the optimum consumption program $(c_1, \ldots, c_n)$ that arises from (E.1.I) is in fact unique. For in order to find it, it is necessary and sufficient to maximize the household's utility function on the set of all $(c_1, \ldots, c_n)$'s for which there exists a choice of portfolios $(m_1, b_1, \ldots, m_n, b_n)$ that satisfy the constraints of (E.1.I). This set being convex, the optimum consumption program is unique by (A.2.4), since u is strictly quasi-concave. On the other hand, our discussion in Section 4.3 shows that the optimum portfolio (m_t, b_t) is not unique when the ratio $(s_{t+1} + 1)/s_t$ is equal to 1.

Let us write $\pi_t = (p_t, s_t) \in \mathbb{R}_+^{l+1}$ and $\pi = (\pi_1, \ldots, \pi_n) \in \mathbb{R}_+^{n(l+1)}$, and set $x_t = (c_t, m_t, b_t) \in \mathbb{R}_+^{l+2}$, $x = (x_1, \ldots, x_n) \in \mathbb{R}_+^{n(l+2)}$. For every $\pi >> 0$, $\xi(\pi)$ will denote the set of the corresponding solutions x of (E.1.I), whereas $\xi_1(\pi)$ will stand for the set of associated optimum values of x_1. This defines two correspondences ξ and ξ_1 from $\text{Int } \mathbb{R}_+^{n(l+1)}$ into $\mathbb{R}_+^{n(l+2)}$ and $\mathbb{R}_+^{l+2}$ respectively. The next two results will be useful.

(E.1.1) *The correspondences ξ and ξ_1 are convex-valued, compact-valued and UHC.*

Proof. By applying (A.4.1), one gets the result for ξ. Given that fact, one shows easily that ξ_1 is compact-valued and UHC by applying the characterization (A.2.3). The fact that ξ_1 is convex-valued is obvious.
Q. E. D.

(E.1.2) *Consider a sequence (π^k) in $\text{Int } \mathbb{R}_+^{n(l+1)}$ such that there exist two vectors ϵ and η of $\mathbb{R}^{l+1}$ satisfying $\eta \geqq \pi_t^k \geqq \epsilon >> 0$ for all $t \geqq 2$ and all k. Assume either that the sequence (π_1^k) converges to $\pi_1^* = (p_1^*, s_1^*)$, where some component of p_1^* is equal to 0, and $p_1^* e_1 + \bar{m} + s_1^* b > 0$. Or that the sequence $[\pi_1^k = (p_1^k, s_1^k)]$ is unbounded and $n \geqq 2$, with $\bar{b} > 0$ whenever (s_1^k) is itself unbounded. Then every sequence $[x_1^k \in \xi_1(\pi^k)]$ is unbounded.*

Proof. Assume that the proposition is false. Then one can find a particular sequence (π^k) that fulfills the foregoing conditions, and a sequence $[x_1^k \in \xi_1(\pi^k)]$ that is bounded. Since every bounded sequence contains a convergent subsequence, we may assume that (x_1^k) converges to x_1^*, and that (π_t^k) converges to $\pi_t^* = (p_t^*, s_t^*) \geqq \epsilon$ for each $t \geqq 2$.

For every k, and each $t \geqq 2$, one can choose a vector x_t^k such that $x^k = (x_1^k, x_2^k, \ldots, x_n^k) \in \xi(\pi^k)$. By recurrence on t, the budget constraints of (E.1.I) imply that the whole sequence (x^k) is bounded. One may again assume that it converges to x^*.

Consider first the case in which (π_1^k) converges to $\pi_1^* = (p_1^*, s_1^*)$. By applying (A.4.2), x^* is a solution of (E.1.I) for $\pi_1 = \pi_1^*$ and $\pi_t = \pi_t^*$ for $t \geq 2$. But this is impossible, since some component of p_1^* is equal to 0: there is accordingly no restriction on the consumption of the corresponding good.

Consider the alternative case in which (π_1^k) is unbounded. One may assume by choosing an appropriate subsequence that $|\pi_1^k| = \Sigma_l^{l+1}\pi_{1h}^k$ diverges to $+\infty$. Then, the sequence $(\pi_1^k/|\pi_1^k|)$ is bounded, and may be assumed to converge to $\bar{\pi}_1 = (\bar{p}_1, \bar{s}_1) \neq 0$. If the sequence (s_1^k) is bounded, this means that $\bar{s}_1 = 0$ and thus $\bar{p}_1 e_1 > 0$. If (s_1^k) is unbounded, one has $\bar{p}_1 e_1 + \bar{s}_1 \bar{b} > 0$ since $\bar{b} > 0$. One may divide for each k the budget constraint associated to $t = 1$ by $|\pi_1^k|$, and again apply (A.4.2). Hence x^* maximizes u under the constraints:

$$\bar{p}_1 c_1 + \bar{s}_1 b_1 \leq \bar{p}_1 e_1 + \bar{s}_1 \bar{b}$$

$$p_t^* c_t + m_t + s_t^* b_t \leq p_t^* e_t + m_{t-1} + (s_t^* + 1)b_{t-1}$$

for $t \geq 2$. But this is impossible when $n \geq 2$, since the household can increase m_1, and thus his consumption c_t for $t \geq 2$, without violating the constraints.

In all cases, we get a contradiction, which proves (E.1.2).

Q. E. D.

E.2   Pegging the interest rate

In this section we will prove (4.4.1). We postulate accordingly all of the assumptions of this theorem.

The interest rate r_1, or equivalently, the price of perpetuities at date 1, $s_1 = 1/r_1$, is fixed in (0, $+\infty$). Consider the set Q_1 of all $q_1 \in \text{Int } \mathbb{R}_+^{l+1}$, such that $q_{1,l+1} = 1$. A vector $q_1 \in Q_1$ can be written $q_1 = (p_1,1)$, where $p_1 \in \text{Int } \mathbb{R}_+^l$ stands for the prices of goods at date 1.

Given $q_1 = (p_1,1)$, and the price $s_1 = 1/r_1$, we set for each household a:

$$\pi_{a1}(q_1) = (p_1,s_1), \text{ and } \pi_{at}(q_1) = [\psi_{at}(p_1,r_1), \rho_{at}(p_1,r_1)]$$

for $t = 2, \ldots, n_a$. The household's behavior at date 1 is governed by (E.1.I), with $n = n_a$, $u = u_a$, $\bar{m} = \bar{m}_a$, $\bar{b} = \bar{b}_a$, $e_t = e_{at}$ for each t and $\pi = [\pi_{a1}(q_1), \ldots, \pi_{an_a}(q_1)]$. The resulting set of demands for goods, money, and bonds is then given by $\xi_1(\pi)$. It will be denoted $\xi_{a1}(q_1)$.

For each $q_1 \in Q_1$, let $\zeta_a(q_1)$ be the set of all vectors of $\mathbb{R}^{l+1}$ of the form:

$$(c_{a1} - e_{a1}, m_{a1} + s_1 b_{a1} - \bar{m}_a - s_1 \bar{b}_a)$$

where $(c_{a1}, m_{a1}, b_{a1}) \in \xi_{a1}(q_1)$. This defines a correspondence $\zeta_a : Q_1 \to \mathbb{R}^{l+1}$ for each a.[1]

Let us finally consider the correspondence $\zeta : Q_1 \to \mathbb{R}^{l+1}$, which is the sum of all ζ_a:

$$\zeta = \sum_a \zeta_a$$

That is, $\zeta(q_1)$ is the set of all vectors z that are of the form $z = \sum_a z_a$, where $z_a \in \zeta_a(q_1)$ for every a. With this notation, the system (4.4.C), (4.4.D$_1$), which defines a short-run Walrasian equilibrium for the fixed interest rate r_1, reads:

$$0 \in \zeta(q_1)$$

In order to show (4.4.1) we seek to apply the market equilibrium lemma of Section A.3 to the correspondence ζ. First, Q_1 is a nonempty, convex subset of the hyperplane H of $\mathbb{R}^{l+1}$ defined by the equation $q_{1,l+1} = 1$, which is open in H. Second, since the functions $\psi_{at}(p_1, r_1)$ and $\rho_{at}(p_1, r_1)$ are continuous in p_1, and according to (E.1.1) the correspondences ζ_a and ζ are convex-valued, compact-valued, and UHC. Finally, since the budget constraints are satisfied as equalities at the optima of (E.1.I), one has $q_1 z = 0$ for all $z \in \zeta(q_1)$ and all q_1.

We will now show that the boundary condition (A.3.B) is satisfied. First note that each correspondence ζ_a is bounded below. Next take a sequence (q_1^k) in Q_1 that either tends to $q_1^* \in H \backslash Q_1$, or that is unbounded. Consider the particular consumer a for whom $n_a \geqq 2$ and $\bar{m}_a + s_1 \bar{b}_a > 0$, whose expectations are bounded with respect to current prices. The sequence of vectors:

$$\pi^k = [\pi_{a1}(q_1^k), \ldots, \pi_{an_a}(q_1^k)]$$

meets the conditions of (E.1.2). Then every sequence $[(c_{a1}^k, m_{a1}^k, b_{a1}^k) \in \xi_{a1}(q_1^k)]$ is unbounded, which implies that every sequence $[z_a^k \in \zeta_a(q_1^k)]$ is also unbounded. Thus we can apply (A.3.1) and conclude that every sequence $(\bar{q}_1 z^k)$, where $\bar{q}_1 \in Q_1$ and $z^k \in \zeta(q_1^k)$ for each k, diverges to $+\infty$.

Thus, the boundary condition (A.3.B) is fulfilled. By the market equilibrium lemma, there exists $q_1^* \in Q_1$ such that $0 \in \zeta(q_1^*)$.

Q. E. D.

---

[1] We remarked in Section 4.3 that $m_{a1} + s_1 b_{a1}$ was uniquely defined since u_a is strictly quasi-concave. Hence ζ_a is actually a function. But that really does not matter for the ensuing argument.

E.3   Controlling the money supply

In this section we will prove (4.5.1), and therefore assume all of the conditions of this theorem.

The Bank's money supply $\Delta M > -M$ is fixed. Consider the set Q of all $q \in \text{Int } \mathbb{R}^{l+2}_+$ such that $q_{l+1} = 1$. We shall write $q = (p_1, 1, s_1)$, where $p_1 \in \mathbb{R}^l_+$ is the price vector of goods, and $s_1 = 1/r_1$ is the price of perpetuities at date 1. For every $q \in Q$, define for every household a:

$$\pi_{a1}(q) = (p_1, s_1) \quad \text{and} \quad \pi_{at}(q) = [\psi_{at}(p_1, r_1), \rho_{at}(p_1, r_1)]$$

for $t = 2, \ldots, n_a$. The household's behavior is again governed by (E.1.I), with $n = n_a$, $u = u_a$, $\bar{m} = \bar{m}_a$, $\bar{b} = \bar{b}_a$, and $e_t = e_{at}$ for all t, and $\pi = [\pi_{a1}(q), \ldots, \pi_{an_a}(q)]$. The resulting set of demands for goods, money, and perpetuities is then $\xi_1(\pi)$. It will be denoted $\xi_{a1}(q)$.

For each $q \in Q$, let $\zeta_a(q)$ be the set of vectors of $\mathbb{R}^{l+2}$ of the form:

$$(c_{a1} - e_{a1}, m_{a1} - \bar{m}_a, b_{a1} - \bar{b}_a)$$

where $(c_{a1}, m_{a1}, b_{a1}) \in \xi_{a1}(q)$. This defines a correspondence $\zeta_a: Q \to \mathbb{R}^{l+2}$ for each a. Consider next the correspondence ζ_B that associates to every $q \in Q$ the element of $\mathbb{R}^{l+2}$:

$$(0, -\Delta M, r_1 \Delta M)$$

where $0 \in \mathbb{R}^l$. Define the aggregate excess demand correspondence $\zeta: Q \to \mathbb{R}^{l+2}$ by:

$$\zeta = \sum_a \zeta_a + \zeta_B$$

Then, with this notation, the system (4.5.C), (4.5.D), (4.5.E) reads:

$$0 \in \zeta(q)$$

Since the expectations functions ψ_{at} and ρ_{at} are continuous, and by (E.1.1), the correspondences ζ_a, and thus ζ, are convex-valued, compact-valued, and UHC. Moreover, the households' budget constraints imply $qz = 0$ for all $z \in \zeta(q)$ and all $q \in Q$.

It was shown in the text that if $q = (p_1, 1, s_1) \in Q$ was such that $s_1 \leq 1$, or equivalently, $r_1 \geq 1$, then every household's demand for money would be equal to zero. Thus there cannot exist $q \in Q$ with $r_1 \geq 1$ such that $0 \in \zeta(q)$, since then there would be an aggregate excess supply of money equal to $M + \Delta M$, which is positive by assumption.

In order to show (4.5.1), we therefore have to restrict our attention to the set $\bar{Q}$ of all $q = (p_1, 1, s_1) \in Q$ such that $s_1 \in (1, +\infty)$, and to prove that there exists $q^* \in \bar{Q}$ such that $0 \in \zeta(q^*)$. To do so, we seek to apply once again the market equilibrium lemma of Section A.3 to the correspondence $\zeta : \tilde{Q} \to \mathbb{R}^{l+2}$.

$\tilde{Q}$ is clearly a nonempty, convex subset of the hyperplane H of $\mathbb{R}^{l+2}$ of equation $q_{l+1} = 1$, which is open in H. It remains accordingly only to verify the boundary condition of Section A.3.

Consider first a sequence (q^k) in $\tilde{Q}$ that converges to $q^* = (p_1^*, 1, s_1^*)$, with $p_1^* \in \text{Int } \mathbb{R}_+^l$ and $s_1^* = 1$ (hence $q^* \in H\backslash\tilde{Q}$ and $q^* \in Q$), and take an arbitrary sequence $[z^k \in \zeta(q^k)]$. Since ζ is compact-valued and UHC at q^*, there is a subsequence $(z^{k'})$ that converges to $z^* \in \zeta(q^*)$, by (A.2.3). Since $s_1^* = 1$, the households' aggregate demand for money is equal to 0, and therefore:

$$z_{l+1}^* = -M - \Delta M < 0$$

By Walras's Law:

$$\Sigma_1^l p_{1h}^* z_h^* + s_1^* z_{l+2}^* = -z_{l+1}^* > 0$$

Define now $q^\lambda \in \tilde{Q}$ by $q^\lambda = (\lambda p_1^*, 1, \lambda s_1^*)$, with $\lambda > 1$. Then:

$$q^\lambda z^* = \lambda(\Sigma_1^l p_{1h}^* z_h^* + s_1^* z_{l+2}^*) + z_{l+1}^*$$

is surely positive. Since $(q^\lambda z^{k'})$ tends to $q^\lambda z^*$, we have $q^\lambda z^k > 0$ for infinitely many k.

The boundary condition is accordingly satisfied for this particular sequence (q^k). Now take a sequence (q^k) in $\tilde{Q}$ that either converges to $q^* = (p_1^*, 1, s_1^*) \in H\backslash\tilde{Q}$, with $p_{1h}^* = 0$ for some h, or that is unbounded. Consider the particular consumer a for whom $n_a \geqq 2$ and $\bar{b}_a > 0$, whose expectations are bounded. Then the sequence of vectors:

$$\pi^k = [\pi_{a1}(q^k), \ldots, \pi_{an_a}(q^k)]$$

meets the requirements of (E.1.2). Hence every sequence $[z_a^k \in \zeta_a(\pi^k)]$ is unbounded. Now, the correspondences ζ_a are clearly bounded below, and ζ_B is also bounded below, since $r_1 < 1$ for all $q \in \tilde{Q}$. Therefore (A.3.1) applies. Every sequence of the form $(\bar{q}z^k)$, where $\bar{q} \in \tilde{Q}$ and $z^k \in \zeta(q^k)$ for each k, diverges to $+\infty$.

The boundary condition of Section A.3 is therefore verified in all cases. By the market equilibrium lemma, there exists $q^* \in \tilde{Q}$ such that $0 \in \zeta(q^*)$.

Q. E. D.

E.4   The liquidity trap

Our goal in this section is to prove (4.6.1). The assumptions of (4.5.1) are accordingly postulated.

We consider as in Section E.3, the set Q of all $q \in$ Int $\mathbb{R}_+^{l+2}$ such that $q_{l+1} = 1$, and write $q = (p_1, 1, s_1)$. For each such q, we define as in the preceding section, $\pi_{a1}(q) = (p_1, s_1)$ and $\pi_{at}(q) = [\psi_{at}(p_1, r_1), \rho_{at}(p_1, r_1)]$, for each $t = 2, \ldots, n_a$, and denote by $\xi_{a1}(q)$ the resulting set of demands (c_{a1}, m_{a1}, b_{a1}) for goods, money, and perpetuities, for every a.

Take a sequence $q^k = (p_1^k, 1, s_1^k)$ in Q such that (s_1^k) tends to $+\infty$ (or equivalently such that (r_1^k) tends to 0). Assume that for each k there exist:

$$(c_{a1}^k, m_{a1}^k, b_{a1}^k) \in \xi_{a1}(q^k)$$

for all a, which bring the goods markets into equilibrium, i.e., which satisfy:

$$\sum_a (c_{a1}^k - e_{a1}) = 0$$

With this notation, (4.6.1) claims that $(\sum_a m_{a1}^k)$ diverges to $+\infty$ for all such sequences.

Suppose that this proposition is false. That means that one can find particular sequences (q^k) and $(c_{a1}^k, m_{a1}^k, b_{a1}^k)$ that verify the foregoing conditions, and such that $(\sum_a m_{a1}^k)$ is bounded. This implies that the sequence (m_{a1}^k) is bounded for each a. The sequence (c_{a1}^k) is also bounded for every a, since the goods markets are in equilibrium for all k.

Now note that the budget constraints are satisfied as equalities at the optimum of (E.1.I), for every household. This implies for each k:

$$\sum_a [p_1^k(c_{a1}^k - e_{a1}) + (m_{a1}^k - \bar{m}_a) + s_1^k(b_{a1}^k - \bar{b}_a)] = 0$$

If one takes into account the fact that the goods markets are in equilibrium, one gets for every k:

$$\sum_a m_{a1}^k = M + s_1^k(B - \sum_a b_{a1}^k)$$

Since $(\sum_a m_{a1}^k)$ is bounded, the sequence $(\sum_a b_{a1}^k)$ is also bounded (indeed, it must tend to B since (s_1^k) diverges to $+\infty$). Thus each sequence (b_{a1}^k) is itself bounded.

One finds therefore that for each a, the sequence $(c_{a1}^k, m_{a1}^k, b_{a1}^k)$ should be bounded. But this leads to a contradiction if we consider the particular consumer a for whom $n_a \geqq 2$ and $\bar{b}_a > 0$, whose expectations are bounded. For this household, the sequence of vectors:

$$\pi^k = [\pi_{a1}(q^k), \ldots, \pi_{an_a}(q^k)]$$

indeed satisfies the requirements of (E.1.2), which implies that for that a, the sequence $(c_{a1}^k, m_{a1}^k, b_{a1}^k)$ is unbounded.

This contradiction proves (4.6.1).

Q. E. D.

References

Akashi, S. "Market Equilibrium, Optimality and Expectations in Credit Economies," Disc. Paper (1981), Hitotsubashi University, Tokyo.

Archibald, G. C. and R. G. Lipsey, "Monetary and Value Theory: A Critique of Lange and Patinkin," *Review of Economic Studies 26* (1958), 1–22.

Arrow, K. J., *Essays in the Theory of Risk Bearing*, North-Holland, London, 1970.

Arrow, K. J. and F. H. Hahn, *General Competitive Analysis*, Holden-Day, San Francisco, 1970.

Barro, R. J., "Are Government Bonds Net Wealth?", *Journal of Political Economy 82* (1974), 1095–1117.

"Rational Expectations and the Role of Monetary Policy," *Journal of Monetary Economics 2* (1976), 1–32.

Bartle, R. G., *The Elements of Real Analysis*, Wiley, New York, 1964.

Branson, W. H., *Macroeconomic Theory and Policy*, Harper & Row, New York, 1972.

Cass, D. and M. Yaari, "A Re-examination of the Pure Consumption Loans Model," *Journal of Political Economy 74* (1966), 353–67.

Crouch, R. L., *Macroeconomics*, Harcourt Brace Jovanovich, New York, 1972.

Debreu, G., *Theory of Value*, Wiley, New York, 1959.

Fisher, I., *The Purchasing Power of Money*, rev. ed., Kelley, New York, 1963.

Fisher, S., "Anticipations and the Non-Neutrality of Money," *Journal of Political Economy 87* (1979), 225–52.

Friedman, M., "The Quantity Theory of Money: A Restatement," in M. Friedman (ed.), *Studies in the Quantity Theory of Money*, University of Chicago Press, Chicago, 1956.

The Optimum Quantity of Money, Aldine, Chicago, 1969.

Gale, D., "Pure Exchange Equilibrium of Dynamic Economic Models," *Journal of Economic Theory 6* (1973), 12–36.

Gordon, R. J. (ed.), *Milton Friedman's Monetary Framework*, University of Chicago Press, Chicago, 1974.

193

Grandmont, J. M., "On the Short Run Equilibrium in a Monetary Economy," in J. Dreze (ed.), *Allocation Under Uncertainty, Equilibrium and Optimality.* Macmillan, New York, 1974.

"Temporary General Equilibrium Theory," *Econometrica 45* (1977), 535–72.

Grandmont, J. M. and W. Hildenbrand, "Stochastic Processes of Temporary Equilibria," *Journal of Mathematical Economics 1* (1974), 247–77.

Grandmont, J. M. and G. Laroque, "Money in the Pure Consumption Loan Model," *Journal of Economic Theory 6* (1973), 382–95.

"On Money and Banking," *The Review of Economic Studies 42* (1975), 207–36.

"The Liquidity Trap," *Econometrica 44* (1976a), 129–135.

"Temporary Keynesian Equilibria," *The Review of Economic Studies 43* (1976b), 53–67.

Grandmont, J. M. and Y. Younès, "On the Role of Money and the Existence of a Monetary Equilibrium," *Review of Economic Studies 39* (1972), 355–72.

"On the Efficiency of a Monetary Equilibrium," *Review of Economic Studies 40* (1973), 149–65.

Gurley, J. G. and E. S. Shaw, *Money in a Theory of Finance*, The Brookings Institution, Washington, 1960.

Hahn, F. H., "On Some Problems of Proving the Existence of an Equilibrium in a Monetary Economy," in F. H. Hahn and F. P. R. Brechling (eds.), *The Theory of Interest Rates*, Macmillan Press, London, 1965.

Money and Inflation, Blackwell Publisher, Oxford, 1982.

Hicks, J. R., *Value and Capital*, 2nd ed., Oxford University Press, London, 1946.

Hildenbrand, W., *Core and Equilibria of a Large Economy*, Princeton University Press, Princeton, 1974.

Hool, B., "Money, Expectations and the Existence of a Temporary Equilibrium," *Review of Economic Studies 43* (1976), 439–45.

"Liquidity, Speculation, and the Demand for Money," *Journal of Economic Theory 21* (1979), 73–87.

Johnson, H. G., *Essays in Monetary Economics*, Allen & Unwin, London, 1967.

Kareken, J. H. and N. Wallace (eds.), *Models of Monetary Economies*, Federal Reserve Bank of Minneapolis, Minneapolis, 1980.

Keynes, J. M., *The General Theory of Employment, Interest, and Money*, Harcourt Brace Jovanovich, New York, 1936.

Lange, O., "Say's Law: A Restatement and Criticism," in Lange (ed.), *Studies in Mathematical Economics and Econometrics*, University of Chicago Press, Chicago, 1942, 49–68.

Price Flexibility and Employment, Cowles Commission, 1945.

Lucas, R. E., Jr., "Expectations and the Neutrality of Money," *Journal of Economic Theory 4* (1972), 103–24.

"An Equilibrium Model of the Business Cycle," *Journal of Political Economy 83* (1975), 1113–14.

"Equilibrium in a Pure Currency Economy," in Kareken and Wallace (eds.), op. cit.

"Tobin and Monetarism: A Review Article," *Journal of Economic Literature 19* (1981), 558–67.

Niehans, J., *The Theory of Money*, Johns Hopkins University Press, London, 1978.

Patinkin, D., *Money, Interest, and Prices*, 2nd ed., Harper & Row, New York, 1965.

Studies in Monetary Economics, Harper & Row, New York, 1972.

Pesek, B. P., and T. R. Saving, *Money, Wealth and Economic Theory*, Macmillan, New York, 1967.

Pigou, A. C., "The Classical Stationary State," *Economic Journal 53* (1943), 343–51.

Samuelson, P. A., "An Exact Consumption-Loan Model of Interest with or without the Social Contrivance of Money," *Journal of Political Economy 66* (1958), 467–82.

"What Classical and Neoclassical Monetary Theory Really Was," *Canadian Journal of Economics 1* (1968), 1–15.

Sargent, T. J., *Macroeconomic Theory*, Academic Press, New York, 1979.

Sargent, T. J. and N. Wallace, "Rational Expectations, the Optimal Monetary Instrument and the Optimal Money Supply Rule," *Journal of Political Economy 83* (1975), 241–54.

Sondermann, D., "Temporary Competitive Equilibrium under Uncertainty," in J. Dreze (ed.), *Allocation under Uncertainty, Equilibrium and Optimality*, Macmillan, London, 1974.

Tobin, J., "Liquidity Preference as Behavior Towards Risk," *Review of Economic Studies 67* (1958), 65–86.

Asset Accumulation and Economic Activity, Yrjö Jahnsson Lectures, Blackwell Publisher, Oxford, 1980.

Index